Dick,

Hope you enjoy and
thanks for your support!

Fred T.

2014

American Sky

by Fred Tribuzzo

www.fredtribuzzo.com

© Copyright 2014 by Fred Tribuzzo

ISBN 978-1-938467-91-2

Published by

◄ köehlerbooks ™

210 60th Street
Virginia Beach, VA 23451
212-574-7939
www.koehlerbooks.com

Publisher
John Köehler

Executive Editor
Joe Coccaro

AMERICAN SKY

GOOD LANDINGS AND OTHER FLYING ADVENTURES

Fred Tribuzzo

VIRGINIA BEACH
CAPE CHARLES

This book is dedicated to my father,

Fred Joseph Tribuzzo

A GOOD LANDING

MY FIRST FLIGHT emergency happened shortly after takeoff in a Cessna 152, a small two-seat trainer. There was no warning, no seat-of-the-pants magic alerting me to engine failure.

"Nail the airspeed—we're hardly climbing," I said without urgency, seeing my student in a shallow climb. "We need altitude." A moment later the engine rolled back to idle.

It was summer, late afternoon, the cockpit full of sunshine and very quiet, except for the wind rushing by. I barked, "I've got it" and grabbed the control wheel and knocked his hand off the throttle, making sure it was shoved all the way forward. My heart pounded as I lowered the nose, transitioning to my best glide speed.

We were about five hundred feet off the ground and had enough time and distance for two turns, but not enough altitude to make it back to the runway. The carb heat and mixture controls were both in and the engine was still idling, developing barely enough power to overcome inertia and to taxi, had we been on the ground.

My student—normally cocksure—now stared straight ahead. Nothing promising to my right, I looked past him and found a clearing alongside a cornfield. My first turn put me on a modified base leg with a short final to go. I lowered flaps twenty degrees and trimmed to relieve pressure on the control wheel. The sun would be at my back on final approach.

I turned final and lowered the remainder of the flaps. My student asked if we should get on the radio, talk to somebody. "Not now—make sure I don't hit anything." It appeared the clearing offered about two thousand feet for landing with another cornfield bordering the far end.

Full flaps allowed for a steeper descent without increasing the airspeed needed to clear obstacles and to land as slow as possible near the beginning of the field. We flew over a stand of trees and a barn. When my touchdown point advanced farther down the field, I lowered the nose and steepened the descent. The airspeed slightly increased, but I didn't make another adjustment. The speed would decrease rapidly when I raised the nose to slow the rate of descent, and the wheels rolling through heavy grass would further help to decelerate the small trainer.

At touchdown, from the corner of my eye, I saw my student reach for the controls and stop, wanting to grab something as the sixteen-hundred-pound trainer shook heartily across the uneven ground. With the nosewheel held off and still traveling near sixty miles per hour, I feared hitting an unseen hole or a steep ditch burying the nose gear and flipping us on our backs.

Slowing, the wing lost more lift and the plane's weight was transferred to the main wheels. Gravity started the nose toward the ground, and I saw the cornfield rapidly approaching. I kept pressure on the brakes and pulled the mixture out, starving the engine of fuel. It died with a shudder and the prop parked at the two o'clock position. Had a tailwind surprised us, increasing our landing distance, we would have crashed through rows of corn before stopping. We halted just as the white spinner of the Cessna nosed into the first row of cornstalks at barely walking speed.

Both of us exhaled, smiled and started to climb out. I almost forgot the battery switch and leaned back inside, turned it off and grabbed the keys. Shifting my weight to exit, I missed the step, scraped my shin and banged my knee—"Dammit!"

My lower leg burned and I limped, making my way around the plane. There was no damage or dents along the skin and looking into the front of the engine cowling, no obvious signs why we had lost power. At first neither my student nor I said a word. It was quiet in the "back forty" and humid on this August afternoon. Before long, a car appeared. It was Frank Corbi, my boss and owner of Miller Field.

"Frank, I finally learned something from you," I said loudly, soon as he got out of the car.

"What's that?" He smiled, dressed in his dark-blue jumpsuit, six feet tall, short-cropped gray hair, walking in his slow, thoughtful manner, arms swinging gently, timed to the internal rhythm of problem solving.

"I had one clear thought after another: Fly the airplane. Make a decision. Don't over control!" I said, hyperventilating.

I looked over at my student to make sure he was absorbing this great lesson in flying. I added with bravado, "I nailed the pitch and airspeed." I took a deep breath and shook my head, lowering my voice, saying, "And then I lost it—getting out, I skinned my leg."

Everyone laughed and we followed Frank, who started his inspection at the elevator, moving the control surface up and down. I stepped higher, fearful of stumbling or driving my foot into a groundhog hole.

My student trailed me. He kept saying how glad he was to be back on terra firma in one piece, and that from now on he would always nail the best climb speed—straight to altitude with his hand on the throttle. Although this guy could really get under my skin, he had temporarily shed the cool-dude persona. I saw a decent guy, a guy not hiding behind the dark mustache and smug, playboy exterior. He caught up with me and thanked me with his eyes, and I acknowledged him with a nod.

"You and your student are safe, and this little bird is pretty as ever," Frank said, standing in front of the spinner, the cornstalks touching his back. "I watched you take off and heard that engine get real quiet. I knew where you were headed. Good choice. You were too low anyway to make it back to the runway," he said with relief. "You both get on the struts. I'll push on the prop."

We moved the Cessna back about ten feet. Clear of the field, Frank continued his inspection. Walking past the left wing strut, fingers gliding over the plane's skin, he touched it like you do a horse, informing the animal of your presence as you move alongside it.

Feeling lightheaded, I said, "Frank, I know it's been only a couple hours ago since lunch, but I'm starving."

"Well, you just burned up a bunch of calories making this landing. Once that old farmer gets here, we'll go back and have a piece of pie, maybe some ice cream."

"Pie and ice cream for everyone," I announced as Frank pulled a screwdriver from his back pocket and started unbuttoning the cowling for a look at the engine.

"I hope they have vanilla," my student added.

That night my mind kept playing out a number of ugly scenarios: a wing striking a tree, driving through the corn which would have really ripped the plane apart, or flipping on our backs. And, as always, there was fire. My heart was a balled fist being squeezed by one much larger.

Near midnight, a long walk through my neighborhood helped me to relax and calm my shaky legs. On the street I thought about the other side of the ledger: I had grown up that day, exercising emotional discipline and receiving a lesson in the unexpected for both student and instructor.

The following day I had a trip, so I missed Frank replace the air filter and make the two-minute flight back to Runway 27 at Miller's. He had discovered that the paper air filter had rotted and was sucked into the carburetor, drastically reducing power. According to Frank's son, his dad eyeballed the takeoff distance and watched the wind, noting changes in its direction and velocity for several minutes before climbing into the Cessna. Frank taxied to the east end of the field, ran the power up, checked the magnetos and, holding the brakes, added full throttle and let it roar. He brought the nosewheel out of the grass almost immediately at the start of the takeoff roll and freed the Cessna, climbing at a steep angle of attack to a comfortable altitude.

In the moments following the engine failure, I had picked up a smidgen of Frank's "aristocratic cool" and now remembered where my basic training had begun.

1

FAIR PLAY IN ACTION

IN MY EARLY twenties I started checking IDs at a popular bar in Kent, Ohio. There, I came to respect and admire the two owners, both hardworking men who really enjoyed their business and the thrill of making money, providing a good life for themselves and their families.

I witnessed fair play in action when the one owner would politely ask a college kid to refrain from some objectionable behavior. If the troublemaker continued, the next warning, issued in a soft voice, asked for manners to be observed, common sense to prevail, respecting the establishment they had worked long hours to make successful. However, after a third warning, the culprit got the bum's rush, courtesy of the owner himself dragging the loser past me and crashing through swinging doors onto the street.

These same businessmen had to defend their operation in the mid-sixties from bikers terrorizing their business. For at least a year, one of them sat checking IDs with a shotgun at his side. Learning that, I felt ashamed, having been part of the Vietnam antiwar riots in downtown Kent.

My generation had stormed the old world with calls for *justice* and *truth*, with the beauty of youth. Our professors and the press hailed us as saviors who would eradicate evil itself. We knew life to be so much grander than anything our parents' generation had ever offered. So we took to the streets smashing windows, fighting with cops, producing silly underground newspapers, disrupting classes on campus, and passing out leaflets calling for a noon rally that ultimately became the Kent shootings of May 4th, 1970.

I don't know what my bosses knew of my recent past, but they showed me only kindness. At the end of the night, my buddies and I would sit around the bar swapping stories about oddball conversations overheard, or, the sad, quiet talk from older regulars. We laughed at the pissing contests between patrons and often the biggest bartenders and, as always, we recounted the impossibly beautiful young women all of us had fallen in love with. Thirsty and famished, we enjoyed pizza and beer—on the house.

When I started flight lessons in the mid-seventies, I held fast to the good lives of those two businessmen and their lessons on kindness and decisiveness. I stumbled upon a host of new teachers: Jimmy Stewart playing Lindbergh, or a grouchy cab driver's pithy remarks before a long flight home. Like the sun coming out after a heavy rain, the past opened and I heard once again a friend's father on a summer evening speculate with passion on the journey that follows this one. From one mechanic I learned not only the basics of cleaning spark plugs or repacking wheel bearings, but the rhythm of work itself and the guts to handle an aircraft in a strong crosswind. Early on, I learned that a teacher could often be a place, a stranger, a storm, the sky itself. The red-and-orange sunset regularly seen at the higher altitudes showed me the constancy of the natural world and the promise of eternity right around the block.

My parents were heartbroken after my shenanigans at Kent State, especially my dad, yet my entry into aviation pleased him. Over time others would speak to me of that father-son universe, clarifying the sacrifices of both my parents and pointing to the direction for becoming a man.

Frank Corbi would become a good friend and mentor, especially after the emergency landing had put real meat on my bones. Frank had survived the Bataan Death March, over three years of imprisonment, and the Hell Ships that carried him to Japan to work as slave labor. After the war he found his way into the testing division at Wright-Patterson Air Force Base. Later on, Frank and his son would take over Miller Field outside of Alliance, Ohio, where I started working for them as a flight instructor in the early 1980s. The Corbis changed the airport name several times while they had it, but I simply refer to it here as Miller Field, in deference to Russ Miller, who built the airport prior to World War II.

Often I had to wait for the fog to lift on an early morning flight out of Miller's. I'd call flight service for weather, file my flight plan, preflight the plane, and run the takeoff data. At the plane I'd check the cockpit for the navigation charts, pens and plotter, update the altimeter and review the initial radio frequencies for communication, handwritten on a piece of paper clipped at the top of the control wheel. As the fog thinned, unevenly up and down the three-thousand-foot runway, a faint blueness slid into view. As the powdery blueness spread, my spirits lifted. Above was an American sky, spanning blue space and time. Once airborne with the power set, the plane trimmed, pilot and machine balanced in three dimensions, I accomplished practical tasks for every phase of flight, yet never forgetting that every mile of the journey commanded the same respect given to navigating the great oceans of the earth.

2

FLYING AND HUNTING

IN EARLY SUMMER of 1976, Joe Z and I sped north on the freeway east of Cleveland, a line of thunderstorms paralleling our route. Inspired by the spectacle, Joe sang at the top of his lungs, an American Pavarotti belting out pop tunes.

Something of the storm's energy struck my chest. It felt like a home run—I could learn to fly. I guarded the revelation and waited until after our performance that night to say anything. After four sets of dance music, we started home at three in the morning. With the cool air rushing through the car, I blurted out my news.

"My father will have something to say about this," Joe said. "He learned to fly before the war started."

On the nights we played out, I usually got to Joe's house a bit early so I could talk with his father. Recently, hunting—and our unsuccessful attempts at it—had been the focus. We asked his dad to go with us, but he declined, saying he no longer had the stomach for deer hunting. But he was pleased with our excitement and proud that his son could navigate the woods for hours and shoot with precision. Joe utilized these skills for his first kill.

Separated from his father and the other men, Joe was leaning against a tree when the hair on the back of his neck rose. Instinctively, he turned toward the bottom of a hill and spotted a deer twenty-five yards away. His gunshot pounded across the valley. He told me that his hands trembled as he made the cuts and gutted the animal.

His dad's last kill had been a female black bear in Canada. It was a mother with cubs. He listened to their cries, unable to claim the bear or leave. After several hours, and thoughts of silencing the cubs, he left as night approached. This incident ended his big game hunting and made him more homebound, yet he never discouraged Joe's appetite for adventure.

We put the hunting stories aside and began to discuss flying. Although Joe's dad washed out in World War II because of a vision problem, he climbed into any aircraft that came his way. But when the war ended, so did his flying. He had a family to think about, he said, and commercial aviation was an uncertain field. His spirits were finally dampened when he witnessed a young soldier absentmindedly walk into the turning prop of a large transport.

One evening, after finishing a story about his first flight in a P-47 Thunderbolt, Joe's dad glanced out the window and quietly studied the sky and a few passing clouds. He turned to me, saying that I might get checked-out someday in a seaplane, making it possible to combine both interests. "Just think, a few hours north of here would put you and Joey in the middle of some of the most isolated, beautiful woods in the world."

"Just soloing for the first time is all I can think about, Mr. Z. I might even try gliders."

Usually, his advice was gentle, but the mention of sailplane instruction made him lean forward from his chair and speak up.

"Sure, it's beautiful to float around the sky, no engine turning out in front of you. But it's powered flight you need to experience. You don't want to be helplessly towed by some other guy, get a little altitude, and then figure how you're going to stay aloft. You need that horsepower, the feel of driving straight up into the clouds."

3

UNCLE GUS

THAT SUMMER, A massive heart attack nailed my Uncle Gus
exactly two months before his forty-sixth birthday. My aunt said
a mirror cracked and a clock stopped at the moment of his death.
Perhaps the leap from his body startled the world on his departure.

On the day he was buried, a cool wind haunted a cloudless
blue sky. My father and I were at the far end of the yard, next to
the garden. Closer to the house, my relatives stood and talked,
holding their drinks, while the wind rippled their dresses and
suits and blew their hair out of place.

I asked my father if my uncle had known of my flying lessons.
He wasn't sure. He couldn't remember. I had meant to call Uncle
Gus, let him know that I was flying an airplane just like the one
he had owned and given me my first ride in when I was fifteen, a
Cessna 150, a two-seat trainer.

On the afternoon of my first flight, my uncle leveled the plane
at altitude and set the power. He pointed to the horizon and the
nose of the plane—the basic cues for maintaining an aircraft in
level flight—and told me to keep it there. Briefly, I sensed the
balance, the suspension of the plane between land and sky. However, when I banked the Cessna, everything went to hell. The

speed picked up and I lost altitude. My uncle laughed, taking the controls, leveling the wings as he adjusted the power.

I mentioned that first ride to my dad as my aunt approached us. She wore sunglasses, and her movements were deliberate and graceful. Her first order of business was the insurance policy. She and my dad talked for several minutes before she asked about my flying. I didn't say much. Instead, I asked about my uncle's years as a private pilot and the radio-controlled models he built in the 1950s.

She shrugged and glanced about the yard, then at the sky. "Summer's over today. You can feel it in the wind." She looked at me. "Will you take me flying someday?"

"Sure," I replied.

She reminisced about their flights to the islands in Lake Erie, and trips with another couple in a twin-engine Beech. "Gus's friend would take off in all kinds of weather. But Gus never cared for that kind of flying. He hated flying blind."

My uncle avoided instrument flight, driving through the clouds, relying strictly on the gauges. His training was for good weather days, seat-of-the-pants flying. And the larger, more sophisticated aircraft, like his friend's, never held his interest, either, which was unusual in a field where most pilots dream of bigger and faster aircraft.

"He was a good pilot," she said.

"He was," I agreed and thought how attuned to the present he had been, the skimming of things, the ocean at his feet. He could sense the future as a distant wave before it took form.

"Your uncle knew you loved flying. He said you were suited for it—maybe to even do it for a living. That impressed him," my aunt said.

Her dark hair blew across her face as she spoke. Instead of fussing with it, she turned slightly, letting the wind sweep her hair back.

"Maybe we have to believe that when someone goes so quickly, they see their children grown up in an instant. I think God must give this. Before I walked over here, that's what I was thinking."

My dad said nothing. When she reached over to smooth down his lapel, he took her hand in his.

"This morning, I finally thought about his last couple of

days," she said. "When I lost him, all I could see was Gus and I as newlyweds, or the kids being very young. But when I got up this morning, I remembered how he raced around, visiting everyone he loved just a few days ago. He saw his mother twice. And he kept calling his friends, setting up dates for all of us to get together. But at night, he was anxious. He told me he didn't want to sleep, that he felt fine in the morning with practically no sleep at all. Late at night, he'd walk or sit in the backyard. He liked how the garden looked when it was dark and the neighborhood quiet." Another gust of wind surprised my aunt, and she turned her face away from us. "And his last morning, he picked a bunch of things—tomatoes, zucchini, beans, peppers. When I got home, they were laid out on the counter."

That evening, after most of the people were gone, I made a sandwich from the leftovers. After my snack I sat alone in the kitchen. When I got up to get a glass of water, I noticed the unwashed vegetables my uncle had picked only days ago. No one had cleaned them, and they looked beautiful and warm, resting on the white tile counter.

Two months after my uncle's death, I soloed. It was a warm day, high overcast, and the fall color-flamed woods had peaked. That day, October 20, became a second birthday, a personal All Saints Day. Before I climbed into the Cessna, I heard my uncle's voice, a deep voice with fractures in it, a hint of cruelty: "You've got to have guts. I don't care what it is you do—sales, landscape or fly a plane." I remembered him in his lounge chair on a summer night, salting a tomato or slicing a cucumber. "If you've got guts," he'd say, "you can look at someone's yard and tell them exactly what tree or bush they need. You take the trees and you plant them, and you know exactly what you're doing, even if it's the first time."

4

SOLO

I HEARD TINA'S laughter before I ever saw her, a rolling laugh that made the chief pilot cringe as he signed my logbook. At the Chagrin Falls Airport, my instructor had been king of the hill before Tina's arrival. Now everything shifted toward her: students, loyalty, the number of hours flown on any given day. She was a big woman, an opera star who transformed an aria into the thunder of laughter.

The chief and I hated each other. He warned me during my first few hours of flight instruction that if I were ever so stupid as to stall an airplane—the curse of a high angle of attack, separation of air from the wing, and the airplane falling like a hawk shot through the heart—I would spin, crash and burn. He knew I had been touched by Tina's charisma.

Before I changed instructors, my fire-and-brimstone teacher tried to soften his contempt for me. He introduced me to his young friend, the cucumber salesman. This boy lived not far from the airport. He grew hundreds of cucumbers and sold them at the end of summer before grade school started. The airport was one of his daily stops.

One morning the three of us met outside the office. Standing next to one of the monstrous shrubs that hid the building, the grade-school kid asked me how many cucumbers I wanted. When I said I didn't want any, he forged ahead with other enterprises: grass cutting, shoveling snow, selling magazines and chocolate bars. The chief pilot smiled with affection at the forthright sales-man. I listened patiently and answered "no" to every offer. The chief's face darkened. He glared at me as if I were an anarchist, a schmo for all seasons, which given my history, was an honest appraisal.

Tina rescued me that day from the cucumber salesman and his publicist. Several flight hours later, I would solo a Cessna 150.

During my pre-solo hours, Tina took the controls on occasion, nudging the nose down or giving a shot of power if I moved too slowly. Often, she delivered a quick sermon on an aspect of flight followed by a burst of laughter. I never received from any teacher such a complete offering of spirit, intellect and instruction: a con-tagious experience where disappointments could be hammered into success.

Tina's own foibles in flying were just as amusing to her as those of her students. We were discussing spins once, and she related how early in her training she read the chapter on stalls and spins and decided to go out and teach herself the maneuver.

Spins were no longer required for the private pilot license but still practiced at the discretion of the flight instructor. Without her instructor's knowledge, she flew out over our practice area, LaDue Reservoir, and began to stall and spin the aircraft over the lake. Within several hundred feet of the water, she recovered after using opposite rudder and smoothly pulling out of the sub-sequent dive. She told me the sensation of standing still, then falling off into space with a rapid twisting motion, was a power-ful attraction. She had no clear understanding of the maneuver and no fear during her tight recovery each time above the spar-kling reservoir. She admitted to timing it just moments before she would have hit the lake. A pilot who lived close by spotted the daredevil performing and recognized the single-engine trainer as belonging to the flight school. Later on, when she landed, she was reprimanded and given the appropriate instruction for her new-found maneuver.

Near the time of my first solo, Tina asked me what spurred me to start flying. I mentioned my uncle and the time I tried jumping off my grandparents' garage with an umbrella. There was even an application to the Air Force Academy and a brief stint in high school with the Civil Air Patrol.

Tina prepared me for my first solo. "Don't forget, without me on board you'll get airborne quicker and have more of a tendency to float during landing." She insisted I not attempt to salvage a bad landing and stressed the sooner-rather-than-later decision of executing a go-around. The last couple hours of instruction dealt entirely with takeoffs and landings and possible emergencies. Frequently, I practiced go-arounds only a few feet above the runway. The go-around or missed approach required decisive action: full throttle, positive change in the angle of attack and raising the flaps up a notch.

One simulated emergency she had me perform was the unexpected loss of power abeam the approach end of the runway with only eight hundred feet of air between the plane and terra firma. The Cessna 150 became a glider and the wind a secondary indicator for airspeed control. Tina covered the airspeed indicator, making me aware that changes in the wind meant changes in aircraft speed. Without power I learned when to turn toward the runway, when to add flaps, confident that I wouldn't overshoot or undershoot the runway. There was both an analytical function and seat-of-the-pants feel in any landing situation, making the final moments before touchdown a brief marriage between Newton and the last line of a poem.

I soloed on October 20, 1976. For years I've remembered that, not just in October, but the twentieth of any month.

After Tina left the airplane, smiled and closed the door, she retreated to the tall grass alongside the runway and sat. She had told me in a matter-of-fact voice that she'd fill the cabin with her presence, a moment of active metaphysics entwined with Newtonian physics. The takeoff and climb were busy, athletic, with the adrenaline flowing through my limbs. I applied pressure on the control yoke and the Cessna lifted toward the sky, making me forget Tina wasn't in the aircraft. I leveled off downwind, parallel to the runway, and set the power. At a mere eight hundred feet above the ground, I was alone under a blue-gray overcast sky.

With the carburetor heat on to prevent icing, I throttled back for the approach. On final, the runway seemed narrower, a bit elusive, perhaps a runway for more experienced pilots. I adjusted the power, modified the pitch and, unceremoniously, glided toward the earth.

Several feet above the ground I applied enough back pressure to resist the plane's downward movement in the last few seconds of flight. I made a good landing, off the nose, on the main wheels, straight down the center. I taxied up to Tina, and she opened the door and gave me a hug. Her big, warm smile added to what I felt soloing: the extra light in the cockpit dissipating my anxiety, and the physical sensation that radiated from the earth moments before touchdown—pressure against the seat of my pants, the alternating currents of gravity and buoyancy.

The next couple of takeoffs and landings were thrilling and uneventful. Finally, Tina jumped in and we taxied back to the hangar. A pilot getting his plane ready at the grass tie-down area waved as the news spread via radio of my first solo flight. My spirit felt visible like the outline of a Christmas tree.

On the drive home, the smooth black asphalt road cut the gold and red leaves of fall. The solo flight had flung me into the present, on the verge of the unknown. I returned home sensing that I was still above the trees as a new dream flooded me that night and I fell into a deep sleep.

* * *

After I passed my private pilot check ride, I continued to build time and started working on my instrument ticket that'd allow me to bury myself in the clouds in IFR (instrument flight rules) conditions. When I came out to fly one morning, the airplane I had scheduled was not in sight. Tina was talking to Ray, one of the lineboys that serviced the aircraft. Ray was nineteen. He walked away red-faced.

"I've asked him three times to pull out two-three-Victor." Tina was annoyed rather than angry.

We went inside the office and reviewed the day's lesson.

Tina had been teaching students back to back, sometimes twelve hours a day for the past three years. She had witnessed all the degrees of talent in her students and realized that Ray handled an airplane like the early heroes of flying. The pressure of his touch and perfect eye-hand coordination connected him intimately to the ship. But it was his affection that made it all work so beautifully.

When we walked outside, our airplane still hadn't been pulled out. Tina went alone into the dark hangar. I sat on the warm bench and watched a parade of Cessna 150s execute takeoff and landings. Three decades had created a flight school with discipline and tradition. Invisible lines of communication passed between instructors and pilots aloft.

Tina and Ray emerged from the hangar, pushing a different airplane than the one I had scheduled. They quickly positioned it in front of the fuel pump. Ray ran the fuel hose out to the right wing, and Tina brought him a ladder to reach the fuel cap on top of the wing. She approached me; her eyes were on fire with amusement.

"You're not going to believe this. I dreamed last night that Ray pulled two-three-Victor out of the hangar for me to fly. The wind was from the southwest, like it is today. We'd be on Runway 24. Somewhere on final, a ferocious gust hit us causing structural failure. That's why I was so adamant about taking two-three-Victor. I had to beat the dream. Stop that awful feeling I had after I woke up this morning." A laugh rumbled through Tina's body. "Until I discovered that Ray dreamed the same dream."

5

TOO FAST

TOM COLE PRODUCED art from the raw material of flying. By his sixties he developed his own body language for flight. He utilized his height and long limbs to comically imitate pilots at the controls in a crosswind or getting slow on final. His wit was playful and dark. He could zing a person with a single remark. Blind in one eye, the other a bit filmy, Tom somehow had full perception.

Tom and I worked together at the Congress airport south of Canton, Ohio. A long table in the pilot's lounge gave us a place for lunch and a perfect view of aircraft landing on Runway 28. I planned my flight instruction so that at noon I could sit down with Tom and George, the other mechanic. Seated for lunch, Tom would push his chair away from the table and start pumping his long legs and arms, mimicking the likely moves of the student pilot shooting past the window. By Tom's own admission, his thin, pockmarked face was one of the ugliest mugs on the planet, yet it nimbly mimicked expressions of befuddlement and terror. If Tom wasn't entertaining us with his pantomime, I could pester him with questions about flying or mechanics. No one I had ever met showed such native genius in aviation. Tom flew like a champ and worked on planes with a subtle touch and thorough knowledge.

Sometimes we'd go to a restaurant in town. Once on our return, we passed a guy running down the road dressed like a jogger. He pointed out that this fellow was running on instinct, pushed and pulled by a thousand demons. The desperate, focused eyes confirmed it and made the case for a heartbreaking divorce or the loss of a close friend.

While working on one of our training ships, Tom demonstrated the art of *seeing by touch*. With an inspection plate removed, he leaned against the tail, faced me and talked with his hands stuffed inside the cavity, working blind. His deftness reminded me of someone cracking a safe. Tom laughed as he fished around.

"No sense straining to see anything, so much is out of view anyway. Some knucklehead will talk another knucklehead into holding a flashlight and then things just get all cross-threaded. Often you don't have the luxury to see what you happen to be fixing. Give your fingers eyes. Imagine the area where your hands are working. No such thing as working in the dark. Braille is the key."

I repacked bearings, opened and closed inspection plates and stood around asking questions. I was water boy and young Igor, handing the two mechanics tools or scrambling for parts. On occasion I was chosen to crawl into the tail cone or jump into the big Piper twin and watch the mechanics troubleshoot.

Tom added rhythm to his secret of fine mechanics. Unashamedly, he danced next to the aircraft he was working on. Instead of stretching, Tom would moonwalk.

"You know, I take my wife out dancing every weekend. If the drummer and bass player have what it takes, we glide around for hours. The guitar player can be a fool, but it doesn't matter if the rhythm section is locked in." I knew drummers that would smile at that statement, especially when the guitar player packed more ego into a long guitar solo instead of taste.

The hangar faced the approach end of Runway 28. Standing with Tom on a sunny, warm morning, I watched him mirror the fright of a student pilot leveling off too high above the runway. When the plane hit on all three gears, Tom raised his shoulders, shoved a long leg forward, and moved his foot spastically. "Someone cut the string," he said. "We better check that nose gear."

I had taken the job at Congress shortly after completing my

flight instructor rating with Tina at Chagrin Falls. Chagrin lacked the runway length for the larger twin-engine planes and the seductive promise of flying them. Although the pay for instructing was mediocre at Congress, I loved the smooth, five-thousand-foot airstrip, long enough for the occasional Learjet. The ominous Lear 35, with its bomb-looking fuel tanks and fighter-jet appearance, would enter the traffic pattern overhead like a bird of prey.

Sal, an Italian immigrant and owner of the FBO, had made the temptation tangible with a ride in a Piper Navaho. He knew I was hungry and ambitious. The ride sealed the agreement in blood and oil. In my carelessness, I cut my hand on the doorframe after checking the oil. Sal smiled, saying in his heavy accent: "I hope you are no baby."

A couple thousand feet above the ground, I banked smoothly into a steep turn and kept it there for three hundred and sixty degrees. Proudly I pointed to the altimeter, showing Sal that I hadn't lost a foot of altitude. For a mere ten minutes, I flew underneath an overcast that faced the gold and green fields.

While dreaming of future opportunities, I fell into a loose coalition with the two mechanics. Sal wanted me to work in the shop with Tom and George when I had time between students. George disliked Sal and often tormented him. I too realized that I drew a certain amount of pleasure from torturing the boss. George confronted Sal on a daily basis with increased downtime because of a serious mechanical problem, progressive inspection or deadline. When Sal complained, pointing to his own balance sheet dipping into the red, he lived George's adage: "Figures never lie; liars figure."

Leaving Italy at age ten with his parents, Sal started flying in the early sixties on Long Island, aggressively climbing into any plane that came his way. When he convinced a general contractor from Youngstown to buy his own aircraft, Sal moved to Ohio and became the owner's personal pilot. For the next decade, Sal built his hours in the tough Eastern U.S. before taking over the Congress operation.

Tom was hardly ever confrontational with Sal, enjoying a nimble sidestep while the fight rolled past. George, however, went head to head with the boss, admonishing him for his lack of fiscal sense and basic decency.

"What's this crap about Freddy flying around a seventy-year-old man who is almost totally deaf?" George asked Sal one morning.

"Man has money. Wants to fly."

"Sal, you and I know he'll never solo. He had a gift certificate for a few hours of dual, that's fine. But Freddy isn't going to egg him on after that."

"He does it if he wants job."

Ivan came to me with a coupon bought by his family. An old desire surfaced and Ivan found himself flying over Ohio farmland in a Cessna 150, an extravagant joyride that widened his smile each time we went up. It was apparent that Ivan had no intention of seeking his private license. The little bit of informal instruction enabled him to handle the aircraft by himself with the instructor on board. I demonstrated straight and level flight, banking left and right. Yet at some point in the lesson, it was always necessary for me to take over the controls since Ivan never heard my instructions.

"Ivan, let's make a turn back to the airport." He was all smiles, looking toward the horizon. "Ivan, we need to turn back to the airport," I said directly into his right ear. "Ivan, how about that left turn."

For Ivan it was straight ahead and no turning back. What I communicated to Ivan on the ground he soon forgot once we were airborne.

Sal insisted that I give him dual forever, and I refused. Taking Ivan aside after a lesson, I explained that if he occasionally wanted to fly for the pure enjoyment, I'd be happy to accompany him, but that soloing or a private pilot license was not possible. Ivan shrugged and let me know that he had gotten what he had been dreaming about for so many years.

It was shortly after Ivan that I flew with a young woman who came from a family of flyers. However, she lacked the passion of her parents and brother. Her father, a successful doctor, insisted that she continue the family tradition and work for her license. On our first flight one of the maneuvers so frightened her that she went for the door handle. Terror in a student usually translated into locking up on the controls, not attempting to exit the plane. Sal was furious when he heard that I had told yet another student to forget aviation. The young lady thanked me for telling her father the truth. The dad later said, "I thought she'd make a good pilot. Oh, well, maybe she'd be more interested in skydiving."

* * *

From the long table in the flight lounge, the mechanics and I had a chance to meet the pilots and passengers arriving and keep an eye on Sal as he ran the front desk. On quiet days one of us would launch a couple of fiery salvos in Sal's direction and wait for a response.

Sal would shake his head and say, "Freddy, you watch yourself. I talk with your girlfriend. She no dummy."

George taunted him on occasion to come over to the table and join us. Looking wounded, Sal said, "You guys are killing me," a litany he recited throughout the day. He kept a mental notebook on what was said and by whom, remembering the idiosyncrasies of not only his employees but of the pilots who flew in on a regular basis. The only time his situational awareness went to hell was when a hot-looking woman showed up at the airport. Then he cranked into hormonal high gear—setting up an airport tour and plane ride, yelling orders for us to get back to work, anything to impress the woman and make the next move to a local bar and a few drinks. The three of us sat spellbound and amused. Nothing on TV compared.

"His gyros tumble whenever a broad shows up," Tom said. "He's got the look of a man who would do anything for a skirt. Myself, I'm not interested in women anymore, unless the gal set the stage."

* * *

Time spent in the shop lessened my resistance toward most things mechanical. With Tom and George as teachers, I developed patience and a bit of success with tools. These teachers also kept an eye on my extended adolescence.

"For God's sake, Fred, he's your boss!" A reminder from George who never hesitated to spar with Sal but saw through my game of breaking the boss's back. My scraps with Sal covered not just his hustling of students but my own pay scale and the draconian tactics he used for building my flight experience.

Sal crewed a single-engine, two-hundred-and-fifty horsepower Piper Comanche. Larry, another Congress flight instructor and charter pilot, flew the plane mostly, as did Sal. When the owner of the Comanche had a pop-up flight the next day, Larry was out on a trip and Sal had a court date. It was up to me.

"I'd like a few hours in the plane. Maybe Tom should go with?"

Sal said, "Cole stays here. You go out now; preflight before I go home and eat, getting late."

This was to be my checkout, a dash around the traffic pattern and Sal pointing out the aircraft's peculiarities.

The panel was a random gaggle of switches, engine instruments and ancient radios. The flight instruments occupied their traditional "T" directly in front of the pilot but the rest of the panel was clearly in rebellion.

"You fly this airplane, Freddy. Okay, you got fuel switches, off when you shut down. Don't be dumb like Larry. He leak gas over ramp. Run tips airborne. Start with mains. Don't forget, no toe brakes, this, your brake handle."

The brake handle was a short lever that poked down below the panel. Since my first flying lesson, the brakes had always been at the top of the rudder pedals, toe brakes. Now, I needed to remember to reach for this black handle, which would evenly apply pressure to both brake discs.

The next morning I talked with Sal over the phone about the weather conditions and the altitude I was going to fly. The minimum en route altitude over the Allegheny Mountains was six thousand feet. Nine thousand feet was the altitude I selected to keep my ship out of the ice and the forecasted turbulence in the lower altitudes. I was headed for Gaithersburg, Maryland, to pick up three passengers and bring them back to Cuyahoga County Airport, located on the east side of Cleveland. Tom and George reassured me that everything on the airplane was up to snuff. It was fueled and ready to go. Tom reminded me it was slicker, more streamlined than the other planes I had been flying, and it would be easy to build up speed in a descent. Other than the heated pitot tube to insure accurate functioning of the airspeed indicator in icing conditions, the airplane had no deice equipment. I didn't consider this a problem since my altitude would keep me above the clouds and I would be descending into warmer air at my destination.

I picked up my clearance over the phone and headed for the plane. Tom shuffled backward through the doorway facing the ramp, rhythmically moving his shoulders to an imaginary beat. He took off his baseball cap, bowed and began laughing.

As I taxied past the pilot lounge, I never looked to see if Tom and George were watching. I faced another solo, kicked from the nest into smoke-gray skies. The engine matched the pace of my heart when I increased the power to check the magnetos. Quickly, I reviewed the initial heading and altitude, and then scanned the traffic pattern for other planes before taxiing onto the runway.

Adrenaline and speed created a new chemical that jumped through my limbs as I climbed and banked the Comanche. Reaching the clouds a few minutes later, I felt a stab of claustrophobia—the cockpit darkened and moisture clung to the windshield. When I glanced down a slice of farmland, railroad track or a small town popped into view, a dizzy montage of life below that made me return to my flight instruments for assurance of proper airspeed and aircraft attitude.

Radar coverage and the handoff from one air traffic controller to the next lent me security as I passed through seven thousand feet and remained in the clouds. With no ice forming, I asked for my assigned altitude. Nine thousand feet would keep the Comanche clear of the ice, above the clouds with a smoother ride than the climb.

Still climbing, I saw that a thin film of ice had formed in the right corner of my windshield. It appeared in the last few hundred feet near the cloud tops. The tops of clouds are notorious for a bumpy ride and a quick hit of ice.

Leveling off and just above the cloud deck in blue sky, I gave the controller a pilot report: light ice in the climb, no turbulence at altitude and an estimate of the base of the next cloud layer.

With the power and trim set, I took a closer look at the panel, attempting to mentally organize the odd placement of switches and gauges, and reviewed the approach plates for the Gaithersburg airport. The landing strip was a four-thousand-foot, hard-surfaced runway configured on a northwest-southeast line.

The latest weather report for the area showed basic VFR (visual flight rules) conditions. Without a control tower at the airport, the approach chart called for right turns in the traffic pattern and a frequency for automatic weather information.

As I dialed in the next frequency on the navigation radio, the petty fights with Sal burned away as I drove the aircraft through autumn skies. I picked up the microphone, answered the controller and computed again my ETA. A bit more relaxed, I thought of a Sunday evening when Sal and I were surprised by a royal visit.

It was already dark when we had heard the call over Unicom of a Lear 35 landing at Congress. The two of us had been exchanging verbal blows when Sal challenged me to a stand-up arm wrestling match. We placed our feet side by side, hands clasped, and proceeded to throw each other off balance.

Sal won the first bout, and on the second round I realized he was attempting to break my wrist. I crouched lower and lower, giving him less leverage. We were behind the desk and beneath the countertop when the doors flew open and several armed men in suits came rushing in. Sal and I instantly raised our heads above the counter and stood up with our hands still clasped in combat and began shaking hands, mumbling pleasantries to each other. Arab bodyguards stared at us, weapons at the ready, shouting that the Prince had arrived. We hoped this normal gesture would ease the security guards' suspicion and allow their royal passenger to deplane. We stopped the hand pumping, and Sal made an official greeting that was ignored. A few minutes passed before the Prince and his entourage swept through the lobby to a caravan of limos. They acknowledged no one, not even their pilots. Later, the crew told us that they had shot a missed approach trying to get into Cleveland Hopkins and immediately came to Congress, their alternate. The next day the local newspaper revealed that the Prince's father was being treated at the Cleveland Clinic.

* * *

At first I was challenged, not alarmed when the cloud tops rose and swallowed my aircraft. I notified the controller, and he asked if I wanted a change in altitude. "Negative," I responded.

There was a mere twenty minutes before I began my descent into Gaithersburg.

The wings were still clear of ice when the gray clouds darkened and turbulence shook the plane. When a film of ice formed on the windscreen, I checked the engine instruments for any changes in power and the top of the engine cowling for ice buildup. In a fuel-injected aircraft, ice blocking the inlet meant an engine failure if the alternate air source failed.

In a matter of seconds the film of ice became milky white and grew quickly along the leading edges of the wing. I called the controller but only heard static and something unintelligible. On an IFR flight plan, I was committed to this altitude unless changed by air traffic control or I declared an emergency. I needed the warm air of a lower altitude.

I tried the radio several times, squirmed and grew hot in the face, feeling the abyss that separated me from the warmth and fickleness of life below. Approaching the time for my descent, I again tried the radio. Normally, without radio contact, one flew the highest altitude given or expected until reaching the initial approach fix for the destination airport.

When I heard the call sign of my plane over the speaker, I hit the transmit switch. Another pilot nearby had heard my calls to ATC (air traffic control) and the controller's inability to raise me on the radio. ATC relayed through the other plane that I was cleared down to six thousand feet. Descending, I saw the ice on the windshield begin to get syrupy and patches break off in fragments from the cowling and prop, slapping the side of the fuselage. As the antennas lost their ice, ATC spoke directly to me.

With clean, ice-free wings, I requested five thousand feet. The controller confirmed my transmissions were loud and clear and said to expect the visual approach into Gaithersburg.

Finally out of the clouds, I caught sight of the airport and its single runway. A runway can be on the other side of the planet or resting on top of a mountain and look better than home, especially in bad weather. All I needed was an hour's rest, breakfast, and I'd be ready for the return flight. Hunched over my plate of eggs and toast, I ate slowly and reviewed my first IFR cross-country flight for pay. What did I miss in my preflight planning that could have alerted me to the potential of ice and the winter clouds rising above my altitude? I ignored the lower altitudes because of the turbulence. But the air was warmer and my aircraft not outfitted for ice.

The airport restaurant was busy. I watched the arrivals and departures of single- and twin-engine aircraft, giving my fuel order to a young woman behind the operations desk. I had the names of the passengers but had never met them. They'd find me through the girl at the desk. Butterflies accompanied my breakfast. I felt satisfied with my flight planning for the return leg, but my passengers were the new variable.

When they arrived, my spirits fell. Awkwardly, I greeted them. Each man weighed in excess of two hundred pounds. I had already computed the average weight of one hundred and eighty pounds and had fueled accordingly. No wonder Sal had smiled when he asked me how much fuel I would return with.

They were stuck with me for the next couple of hours in a light single-engine aircraft that was starting to look underpowered. I spun a few flying tales to relieve their anxiety and mine, but it didn't work. Mentioning Sal or Tom's name never got a laugh or a word.

With all eyes on me, I went to start the engine. When nothing happened after a couple of tries, I remembered that I had the fuel selector in the off position to keep the fuel from dumping overboard. Clumsily, I reached down and turned it on.

The silent vote of no confidence continued as I became airborne with a momentary blast of the stall-warning horn. I should have eased the aircraft off the runway with the extra weight and maintained a shallow angle of attack for better airspeed and solid climb-out. When I hauled the Comanche off the runway, I heard the passengers groan as we struggled to stay airborne.

I sighed as the aircraft firmly gripped the sky.

There was less turbulence at six thousand feet than I had expected. But two and a half hours later as I descended through sickly yellow skies just east of Cleveland, a bout of low-level turbulence jarred everyone.

At the Cuyahoga County Airport, the tower reported a strong crosswind out of the west and possible windshear. Calling for seat belts fastened, I heard a collective moan and remembered Sal flying dead bodies around the U.S. The hair stood on the back of his neck when the body in the backseat belched then sat up.

Final approach was an airborne rodeo. I needed to keep the plane crabbed, that is turned into the wind in order to stay lined up with Runway 23 and not blown into the next county. Each blast of turbulence twisted the aircraft away from its heading. The next gust knocked my hand off the throttle as I controlled the rate of descent with power. I struggled the last two miles to keep my body square in the center of the aerodynamic forces while the turbulence pummeled the Comanche. Maintaining the crab angle, I flared, stopped the rate of descent and leveled the plane above the runway. Then I straightened the nose with rudder and lowered the right wing into the wind. The wind didn't let up, yet I landed smoothly on the right wheel first, then the left main and nosewheel without a thud or swerve. I fought with the turbulent air through the landing rollout then taxied slowly and confidently to the ramp.

I called Sal from the FBO in Cleveland, announcing that the mission was accomplished and that I was coming home. I expected fanfare for these early flying pursuits—yelling at one another, obscene gestures, Hollywood posturing of courage and skill. But I was left with my passengers running for their cars.

It was after five, quitting time at Congress, so I missed both Tom and George. Sal, a few pilots and their wives were "hangar flying," a term for hanging around the airport, talking, watching the planes come and go.

"Freddy, you scare my people," Sal said.

"They'll be scared for months, but I gave them a good flight."

"They better come back more business."

"They better lose some weight."

The people near the front desk watched in silence. An off-duty United Airlines captain leaned against the wall, enjoying the show.

"I got a lot of ice going over, Sal, and lost communications."

"I know at altitude you ice up."

Sal laughed, demonstrating his superiority.

"Why didn't you give me that bit of precious information? I thought we were a team."

"You learn hard way like everyone else. Nothing easy. You have to tink. I tink all the time."

All of a sudden George walked in and Sal looked upward, beseeching a higher power.

"I got home, Sal, and started looking at this paperwork on the Comanche and found out that it's all screwed up. This airplane's going to be down for the next week."

"You guys are killing me," Sal complained.

Sal lowered his head toward the cash register, shifting through a series of glum facial expressions.

"You guys screwing up. This one scares my people with bad flight. You and Cole keep my planes grounded."

Most of the audience had left except the tall captain from United. He ignored us, quietly watching the low dirty clouds and field of dead cornstalks across the runway brighten steadily before fading.

Out of this leaden atmosphere came Tom. I yelled his name and Sal headed for the office. The Fred Astaire of general aviation, Tom tipped his baseball cap and tapped a beat with a fluid one-two of his shoulders. He glided to a stop before us and asked if we had spooked the boss. He was not only impervious to Sal, but evil sunsets and airport gossip as well.

Tom questioned, grinning as I elaborated. As he listened, he pantomimed my passengers and me with grimaces, looks of terror and the thousand-yard stare.

Sal watched through the office window, shaking his head, mumbling a litany to save himself from the gang of three. He could mess with my pay, chase me around the ramp with the tug or argue with George for days, but Tom just passed him by in a long-legged stride of stellar grace. Sal launched attacks on nearly every pilot that walked through the door except Tom. He lost steam when confronted by him.

"Cole, you know I do nothing with you," Sal said, walking out of the office. "At least talk to George. Make him settle down. Freddy too."

Sal turned to me. "Tom flies like bird. One eye, sixty-five years old, he handle plane better than anybody. Go with him in Cub. You maybe learn something. Rare man. No better," he said.

The next morning a charter flight dropped off its passenger just before a heavy downpour. We were seated at the big table drinking coffee, enjoying the rain, when the stranger walked over and joined us. He questioned us about our work, how many years we had under our belts. Finally, Tom asked him about his line of work. The man smiled and lowered his head as if embarrassed to speak. "Well, I don't like to tell people what I do. It makes them jealous."

George shook his head, and Tom started laughing.

"You see, I write books. I'm also an English professor on sabbatical. You can do that in my profession."

"Well, Mr. Writer, I'm not jealous of what you do," Tom said. "But I'm curious, is that fat ass of yours one of the perks of the profession?"

The professor shot Tom a dirty look and left the table. Tom shrugged it off and went back to work. Later on, the writer's mother showed up and the two started an intimate discussion. Often the man leaned close to his mom, looked to see if anyone was watching, and then whispered something that made them both laugh.

By afternoon the weather improved and Tom, at Sal's suggestion, agreed to take the Piper Cub for a quick flight. Sal allowed only Tom to fly his beloved J-3 Cub. Tom put me in the front seat and said that I could make the first takeoff and landing. "Don't worry. I won't let you ground loop this bird." With limited taildragger experience, I was prone to let the heading wander as the ship slowed up on landing. This was a common mistake since my training was in nosewheel aircraft that had positive directional steering at all speeds. With the plane's back end sitting on its tiny wheel, the taildragger's center of gravity was behind the main gear, which gave it a tendency to weather-vane, notably at slower speeds when the controls became less effective.

I danced lightly on the rudder pedals, as Tom suggested, keeping the plane straight down the runway centerline. On my first approach he said to go around if I didn't like how things looked. Even a little boost of power would make the controls more effective if I decided to land. I didn't go around, but my bounce and awkward recovery got Sal on the radio yelling at us.

Tom laughed. He took the controls and the bright yellow Cub behaved itself, even during taxiing. His smooth takeoff and steep turn barely a hundred feet off the ground confirmed that a master was at the controls.

"All I do is drive," Tom said, while making a perfect three-point landing. "I'm a lazy bastard. Always looking for the easiest way to make the bird do what I want it to."

After shutdown and oil check, we pushed the Cub back into the hangar. Tom mentioned the Twin Beech that he once flew for a Cleveland charter company.

"Now that big taildragger could really bite you—especially in a crosswind. That was enough airplane for me. Think you'll know when some plane is enough?"

"You could fly anything, even a jet as well as this Cub," I said, avoiding his last question.

"You think so? I tried jets but didn't care for them. Everything happens too fast. Remember, I'm lazy."

"Good skills—"

"Too fast," Tom said as a gust whipped through the hangar, kicking up dust from the floor, rocking the Cub's wings.

6

MILLER FIELD

I ARRIVED AT Miller Field in 1981 with a few hundred hours and all my ratings, looking to build my cross-country time flying the gas pipeline. Just a few miles south of the Berlin Reservoir, the airport was outside of Alliance in the rural town of North Benton.

Frank Corbi met me that day, and I followed him as he hunted for the keys to the plane, stopping in the restaurant to tell his beautiful young daughter that he was going flying. When Frank introduced me and mentioned my credentials, she just shrugged and told us to go fly. In defiance of his daughter's command, he started toward his office, stopped, and spun around, muttering that he'd better avoid it since it was too easy to get lost among the papers and lists of things he needed to do. He looked at me brimming with things to say, slowing before we walked outside, startled from a "message on high." He dug into his left pants pocket, finding the keys.

We stepped into the sunlight, and Frank commented on the pretty day. He said he didn't get a chance to fly as often as he liked and wished his son Alan were here to join us. We flew together for thirty minutes in a Cessna 172. At two thousand feet, north of the east-west runway, Frank banked steeply to the right, saying that the empty field and woods below could support a dozen cottages around a lake that still needed to be dug. His dream would be alive at the end of the eighties, though unfulfilled, and I'd be in the seat of a corporate jet thanks to Frank and Alan Corbi.

7

CRUELEST MONTH

GROWING UP IN a time when the father's role was in doubt, I instinctively sought out the mentor who delineated the world in blacks and whites. The so-called grays in life never held much meaning for Frank Corbi or me.

Through the eighties my friendship with Frank and his son grew. On a quiet evening I'd get a lesson in engine starting depending on its make, temperature and the correct position of throttle and mixture controls. And in the midst of the technical stuff, Frank would inform me of the difficulties people faced with the arrival of spring, not necessarily a lovely time according to him, but a dangerous time when people died easily, unexpectedly, from high winds, lightning and floods.

Shortly after I started at Miller's, a terrible crash took the lives of five area pilots. I had known two of them. I asked Frank about it, and what he had heard, as we preflighted the Cessna Skyhawk for a short hop to Youngstown Executive Airport to drop off a radio that needed repair.

"Just what's in the papers," he said. "I heard of the one fellow from Middlefield."

"That's Dave Lindsay," I said. "He just gave me my multi-engine ride in January. And the young guy, Ray, from Chagrin Falls, was a real natural. He worked at the airport fueling and doing a thousand other things for the boss. He loved flying. He was one of Tina's students."

"It's hard to figure out, say much right now. I'll make some calls this week. It takes time to sort through all the second guessing."

Before starting at Miller's, I had been teaching part-time at

Geauga County Airport, where Dave, in his thirties, ran the operation. Once after a lesson, my female student had smiled at him,
saying, "No one should have eyes that green." I remembered his
wife standing in the doorway, watching, frowning. He was a pilot's pilot. Everyone became enamored of him—men because of
his skills and women because of his skills and those green eyes.
Ray became so attached to Dave he declared that he'd follow him
into fiery places. Sadly, this was realized.

Frank and I took off after lunch. From the air the earth looked
raw, unsettled. It was late April. I had filed an IFR flight plan
to keep current on my instrument procedures. Frank fiddled
with one of the navigation receivers, listening to the Morse code,
turning the dial until the needle centered. I felt nervous when
he started playing with the mixture control that metered fuel to
the engine. He slowly moved the red knob until the engine began
to sputter before pushing it back into the normal flight position.
Frank hardly ever looked outside an airplane. He examined the
panel, gently tapped the glass face of each instrument and talked
continuously, saying that, "Flying along nicely is the perfect time
to take a nap." If he looked out he was looking down, and then
usually at his property at Miller's.

Without a tower and no one answering the Unicom at the
Youngstown airport, I made position reports, making the last one
on short final. One reason for having Frank along was to help me
find the right building amid the torn-up taxiways and decrepit-
looking hangars and deserted buildings. By the time we landed,
the sky had become overcast.

After securing the plane with the wheel chocks, Frank pointed
to a scarred old door and we walked in with the sick radio. With
the sun erased, the gloomy airport became gloomier as we stepped
into the workshop. I wondered where the light switch was.

His friend Carl greeted us. A small man with a stoop and a
grin notched permanently across his face, he nodded when Frank
said hello. The entire office was littered with hundreds of radios
and parts spread across tables or sitting on shelves waiting for the
Wright Brothers to claim them.

"No hurry on this one, Carl," Frank said, patting the radio as
Carl tagged it and Frank explained its problem.

"You know, I've tried to talk Carl into coming over to our

place," Frank said to me. "But he likes this quiet little shop. Now we'd keep things quiet for him at our place too, but busy."

"Frank," Carl said, placing the radio on a shelf near the only window that admitted some daylight, "I live ten minutes from here. Why would I work at your place?"

He said no more. Frank talked about the recent plane accident, business opportunities at Miller's and the restaurant.

"Carl, who do you go out to lunch with?" Frank asked.

"Nobody. I eat here."

"Well, Fred and I will fly up in the Skyhawk some afternoon and take you back to our place for a good meal."

Carl nodded his head and a real smile brought light to his face before the frozen expression returned.

On the ramp it looked like a rain shower wasn't that far off. I was able to contact air traffic control on the ground and receive my clearance. Frank was impressed.

"Now, Mario would never bother with a clearance for a short flight like this," Frank said. "He's an old scud runner. But you're using the system well. Let them watch out for traffic, get you on radar. That makes sense."

Frank was still messing with the mixture control as I took the runway, not looking out as I lined up for takeoff.

"Frank, let's put the mixture back in."

"It's running too rich but that's all right. I'll take a look at it later," he said, pushing the red knob forward.

On the flight back I glanced out more often, noticing that the brown fields were puddled with temporary lakes from the recent spring rains. Northwest of us, on the upwind leg at Miller's, a large rain shaft hung from the belly of a dark cloud mass, frozen in time and space.

On final approach Frank continued to talk to himself about the sound of the engine, with the carburetor heat on and the throttle back to seventeen hundred rpm. I was configured for landing—full flaps, on airspeed and glide path, when Frank asked me to reduce the power then increase it so he could check the rpm. The extra power increased the airspeed, and I floated during my flare, increasing the landing distance. Normally, I would have made another takeoff and landing, end the day with a good landing, but I just taxied in.

Before shutting down, Frank had me turn into the wind as he

ran the engine up to various rpm settings. A little engine rough-ness on one magneto was cured when he leaned the mixture with the red knob, changing the fuel/air ratio, burning the carbon off the spark plugs. I asked Frank if he talked to his brother about the accident.

"Mario has seen this all before. He once watched a man in a T-6 crash on takeoff. The pilot wasn't ready for all that torque from that six-hundred-horse engine and went in on his back. When Mario got to him he was bone-white, nearly cut in half. It happens. But you sound a little shaken up by this plane going down," Frank said, finally pulling out the mixture control, killing the engine.

"I sure am. Frank, I was just with the man in January for my check ride."

I climbed out first, hands on the strut, leaning, stretching my back. Frank didn't move from his seat. He was thinking, tapping the red mixture knob with his finger. He turned the battery off and handed me the keys.

Frank said, "I know you're upset. A lot of people will be thinking about this. And they should be. There was a screwup somewhere. I'm not saying your man did anything wrong. But accidents just don't happen out of the thin blue air. It could have been a mechani-cal problem, but that falls on somebody's head too. That flight I had years ago with General Boyd, at Wright-Patterson, when ev-erything went wrong with that damn airplane, and he landed off the runway and saved our lives—that wasn't the pilot's fault but engineering. Some mechanic had to answer for it."

"I always heard real good things about this fellow from Mid-dlefield," Frank said. "He was an exceptional pilot and people really liked him. That's rare. Usually, a guy like that has a lot of jealous people chasing him down. Although I heard the women liked chasing him down too. Maybe his wife got a little upset, but I heard he was a good family man."

A sudden gust of cool air reminded us that a storm wasn't far off and that we needed to get the plane in the hangar. Above the trees, lightning flashed.

With the Skyhawk tucked inside and the hangar door closed, we walked to the picnic table and sat down.

"This wind feels good," I said. "Do you want me to go get us some coffee?"

"Not now. This is fine."

"That young pilot that died, I gave him some training when I was a brand-new flight instructor at Chagrin. He enjoyed climbing in a plane and flying with anybody. But when he met Dave, he met his idol."

"A whole bunch of lousy pilots, reckless guys, will die as old men, in their beds." Frank threw his hands down as if saying, "Life's never fair."

"The trouble for me is, this isn't the first time this has happened."

"It won't be the last."

"I don't mean just knowing someone who dies in a crash. This is the second time that I've taken a check ride and the examiner died soon afterward."

"Who died first?" Frank asked.

"An examiner at Hopkins, two years ago. He gave me my check ride for instrument instructor before I started here. A few months later he's giving two guys in a Lear their check when they get into a high-speed dive, and they don't recover. They vaporized—just a crater."

"I remember that one," Frank said, slowly scratching the back of his head. "Now those guys may have been hot-dogging, showing the instructor a dive that wasn't necessary. I'm not sure."

"That's what my old boss from Congress had said. He knew both of them, called them cowboys. When I flew with the examiner I remembered him acting nervous, scanning for traffic. He said he had a close call recently and was frightened about running into someone. A few months later he gets killed just hours before I show up for my check ride. Everyone's walking around with long faces when I walked in. So they just scheduled me the next week with someone else."

"He didn't know when to sit it out," Frank said, annoyed, "or take charge with those two Learjet pilots. He should have told them to go to hell when they started doing maneuvers not required. You see, he had warnings."

"But that doesn't explain why I'm around right before something bad happens."

Frank looked at me with a puzzled expression. "There were lots of people around right before these men were killed. It doesn't matter who's around. Look at all the men I was around who were beaten to death or had a bayonet slid through them. You know, I had been selected for flight training when I was in the Philippines. I was waiting to be called up. Instead of being a prisoner, I could have died as a pilot in that war."

Frank examined my face like I might be suffering from an illness. "You're not going to stop flying because of this?"

"No way," I said, regaining a bit of strength.

Frank said, "You're lucky—none of these men were close friends. Now that'd be hard to live with."

A large crack of thunder made us head for the airport restaurant. Inside we watched the trees in the distance wave as mighty gusts hit the ground and spread out across the field, striking the windsock, turning it a hundred and eighty degrees from its last position. With my hands safely wrapped around a hot cup of coffee, I listened as Frank continued to talk about dreams vanishing.

"Maybe you're feeling all that potential lost when those fellows died," he said.

I answered with a nod. Other than Ray and Dave, I didn't know the other men, except one fella I had seen in passing. He was a high-energy, successful businessman who loved to fly and happened to be driving by when he saw Dave getting the plane ready. On a whim he turned in and joined the doomed group of flyers.

"Whatever the government says about these fellows in their report, they were good men," Frank insisted. "That's what's important. They made mistakes that became terrible mistakes. We all make them, but this time they added up to a bad crash. I just know that in those last moments, they were working hard to keep that ship under control."

The accident occurred on Sunday, April 18, 1982. Years later I looked up the crash on the Internet. Dave was simulating a single-engine approach, getting Ray prepared for his check ride with the feds. The NTSB listed the probable cause as pilot error. The brief report stated that the approach was poorly planned and minimum airspeed for safe flight had not been maintained.

Of the five men who died, I only knew Dave and Ray. The third man was a flash of energy, a go-getter I had never even talked with. The remaining two were strangers. The old line that "The world goes on" is only partly true. Of course the world goes on, but with a heavy heart, having lost five unique souls that can never be replaced.

8

BUDDING EMPIRES

ON AN EARLY morning flight out of Miller Field, I pre-flighted the Cessna Skyhawk just as the sun rose. Often the sun looked bloody when it first appeared, making me wonder what it had been up to all night. Its sudden lunge from a sleepy horizon brought to mind the ancient practice of calling the sun through prayer, throwing a fit or offering sacrifice. This daily miracle sent an amber glow across the treetops.

With the sun at my back, I made a decent landing at Cuyahoga County Airport twenty minutes later and met Jack Mellon. He swaggered across the tarmac and let off a "Hey, guy!" followed by a few chuckles. Jack was short, thirty years old and nearly bald. He had a big, phony smile that was also handsome and trusting and a pained, puppy-dog expression for moments of anguish.

Jack owned a music club on Euclid Avenue near Cleveland's Little Italy. Nearly an hour drive from Miller Field, he rented from the Corbis, saying he needed to get away from all the craziness of rock and roll bands and drunks underfoot. He almost always flew with another instructor or seasoned pilot, a fact that everyone appreciated.

Jack was always pushing some new scheme that usually involved the future purchase of an expensive aircraft with someone else's money, if not an entire fleet. Often he tagged along with me on pipeline patrol, talking constantly, tempting me with the co-pilot seat of his rich buddy's Learjet, an unwelcome distraction when flying so close to terra firma sprouting tall manmade towers. Nonetheless, I still enjoyed his company.

We leaned inside the plane from either side and went over our route, clearance and initial radio frequencies. I folded the chart to show our first fix, and Jack mentioned our flying itinerary once we arrived at his hometown of Atlantic City, New Jersey. With his relatives on board, he planned to handle the takeoff and some low flying over the beach while I'd execute the landing.

* * *

The circular storm of fire and light moved well above the horizon. I was flying and working the radio, grabbing the mike before Jack could pick it up and say something odd to the air traffic controller.

At seven thousand feet, with the sun boring into the cockpit, we crossed north of Pittsburgh. Jack dialed in a music station on the ADF radio. The voices and guitars stabbed at us from the overhead speaker that was made to carry flight transmissions, not country music. Saying nothing, I reached over and flipped the speaker mode off. Jack laughed. "Don't sweat the small stuff. C'mon, we're not flying the pipeline. You need to relax."

On pipeline patrol, Jack was a good spotter. When the gas company radioed us with some ugly encroachment—junkyard men building a fire or some guy building a catfish pond in his backyard over buried lines—another pair of eyes really helped. Jack came to my rescue one morning when I had a terrible need to relieve myself and we were thirty minutes from landing. Using his Swiss Army knife, he cut off the lid from an empty pop can. Thankfully there was no turbulence for a few minutes as I maneuvered awkwardly above my seat and negotiated the jagged opening, ending my misery.

* * *

Close to noon, we landed at a grass airfield outside of Atlantic City and greeted Jack's aunt and uncle, who lived close by.

"We follow everything Jack has been doing back in Ohio; we're so proud of him," said his aunt, a tall, clear-eyed woman in her early fifties. "You know, most small businesses fail within a few years, and Jack's been going strong since he got out of college."

"Are you Jack's partner?" his uncle asked.

Before I could answer, Jack said I was his partner in his budding aviation empire. When I mentioned an imaginary West Coast operation, Jack began to improvise, building on the fantasy, finishing with a winning smile.

After tucking the aunt and uncle in the backseat, Jack took the left seat. He asked for the takeoff and landing checklist before he even started the engine.

On a short, grass runway, a soft-field takeoff was necessary. Unlike a normal takeoff, the nosewheel needed to come off the grass right away and stay there, which allowed the plane to become airborne sooner. After starting the engine, more checklists and a short taxi, we lined up for takeoff and Jack gave it power. As the seconds passed, Jack grimaced and stared straight ahead before I placed a few fingers behind the yoke and increased the back pressure, freeing the nosewheel from the thick grass.

Jack lost his fear as the Cessna lifted off. I lowered the nose in order to build speed within a wingspan distance of the ground. With climb airspeed and a couple hundred feet of altitude, Jack turned to his aunt and uncle to explain the common practice of two guys trading off the different phases of the takeoff. Then I handed the plane over to him and began to look for traffic.

We leveled off at eight hundred feet above the ground, and Jack talked nonstop about the "beautiful day beneath our wings," pointing at the boardwalk and hotels along the ocean. After circling the home of his cousin a few miles inland, he decided it was time to return and began the education of his aunt and uncle on the "complexities" of landing a single-engine aircraft. He explained the necessity of two pilots sharing the approach and landing, each watching the actions of the other. Turning in my seat, I saw that the relatives were duly impressed. The gray-haired man observed his nephew with admiration. Jack leaned over the seat, talking about adjustments of power and why they would see us trading the flying duties back and forth. I asked Jack if he was ready for the approach.

"I'm all set. Let's have that landing checklist again. Got the strip. I'll just cross about midfield and check out the traffic situation. You can't be too careful. Let's have twenty degrees of flaps."

I gave him ten.

The strip was twenty-five hundred feet long, skinny, with tele-phone lines a few hundred feet from the landing threshold. Jack overcontrolled with the rudder, and everyone lazily swung back and forth. I locked the pedals on my side to stop all the extra mo-tion, and Jack just chuckled.

"Keeping me honest," he said. "Hey, when I turn final why don't you take over, and I'll handle the flaps."

I stayed quiet as Jack bobbed and weaved the Skyhawk onto final approach. He kept glancing my way, a bit more desperate each time. He wasn't accustomed to such a short landing strip.

"You got it?" he asked,

"You're doing fine, Jack, just back off on the power a little." He quickly throttled back and jerked the nose up. I asked him to add a little power and keep the nose down. Jack's nervousness added turbulence to the smooth air. The greater his uncertainty, the bigger the movements he took with the controls.

"You've got it?" Jack asked, affecting his puppy-dog look that probably got him out of most scraps in life. Staring at the airspeed indicator that showed us ten knots too fast, he whispered his de-mand, "You make the landing."

"You're fine, Jack," I said brightly for the relatives to hear. "Now, slowly, come back on the power. Watch your speed."

Jack mumbled something, and I folded my arms. He stopped grinning and started sweating. As the ground came up, I added a little pressure on the yoke to prevent landing on the nosewheel. He made a nice touchdown, and the Cessna slowed quickly.

"Each landing is a learning experience for Fred and me," Jack blurted, relieved when I took over the controls to taxi. "Now when we leave here, we'll switch seats."

Soon he was smiling, cocky again. "Fred will handle the land-ing back in Cleveland." Lying outright, he added, "Then, I'll taxi back to our corporate hangar. Beautiful, spacious, a hangar floor so clean you could eat your dinner off it."

* * *

The breeze was steady with occasional gusts. The airplane, parked in the shade, was the backdrop for a picture that Jack took of his aunt and uncle before they said goodbye.

Jack and I sat on an old picnic table in an open grassy area next to the runway, waiting for a newspaper reporter. It was necessary to keep the hometown abreast of one of their local boys who had "made good." Overhead, a large military transport flew several thousand feet above us. Jack looked with pleasure at the gray machine and asked how I'd like to fly something that size.

"Don't have much interest. Too big."

"You've got to be kidding. That's a freedom machine, moving troops and supplies all around the world, protecting lives."

"True, but today, in this life, I'm flying a Skyhawk."

Mellon started to chuckle, shaking his head. "I don't believe this guy."

The remainder of the afternoon was tranquil. The altocumulus clouds recreated the sky. The configuration of a new continent came into view then was torn apart by upper-level winds. The universe boiled over with preternatural strength: a realm of emerald deities, cosmic oceans, bloody suns and Jack Mellon near the center telling a lovely string of lies to a young woman from the town's paper.

He touted his achievements, pointing to a seagull overhead as a metaphor of his own destiny, saying that the bird was a loner, driven to succeed by its own standards and not a birdbrain like the rest of the avian community. Jack drove home his big vision and looked to me for confirmation even though I said nothing throughout the interview. He reiterated his earlier sentiment, saying that what was really important was the beauty of the day laid out before us. Silently, I agreed.

The woman flew through pages of note-taking as Jack fantasized out loud about charter operations and jet aircraft in the near future. He mentioned a possible FBO partnership and a franchise deal with a Southern fast-food chain. And he talked about how wonderful it was that we decided to show up in Atlantic City and give our time to her two-bit, but fine little newspaper.

From the picnic table, I noticed a calendar hanging upside down in the cluttered airport office. Everything visible in the window was off the mark in some fashion: words spelled wrong, a trophy on its side, a desk ornament of a fat person with its head missing.

From the picnic table I watched the Cessna rock slightly, marked by wind, shadow and sunlight.

9

PAPER WINGS

I SAT WITH Frank's son in Miller's restaurant, drinking coffee. Also named Frank, he went by Frankie, Frank Jr., Corbi or simply Alan, his middle name. His big rolling laugh often startled people from their quiet lunch or private conversation. Its magnitude crushed decorum. Alan was my age and taller than his dad, with a full beard, short dark hair with plenty of wave and a broad, dimpled face. His light-filled eyes took in the world by the bushelful, ready for the unexpected moments of charm and absurdity.

We both stared at the runway and woods. I spotted a single tree, its upper branches changing color in late August though the day promised to stay loyal to summer, hot and humid. I had a student in about an hour.

"You remember when you first wanted to fly?" Alan asked, still watching the humble universe outside our window with the intensity of someone peering into the Grand Canyon.

"Sure, right after I started to walk and noticed the sky. When I was twelve, I called the Chagrin Falls Airport and asked about lessons."

"What'd they tell you?"

"They said my feet had to reach the rudder pedals."

Alan's laugh stunned a young boy at the next table who, after reeling from the shotgun burst of laughter, pointed at him and giggled, shaking a toy airplane at us.

"I looked down at them, wiggled my toes, and said that I'd come out some time and get measured. Of course, I never did. I didn't make it to the Chagrin Falls Airport until I was twenty-six."

"If you had started in high school, you might have all your ratings by now. Whatever, you made it here and decided not to blow up the country."

"Thank God," I said, amazed to be fulfilling a boyhood dream and not wandering the world as a professional protester. Alan knew about Kent State but was decent enough not to go into the gory details with his dad or anyone else at the airport. My mom had recently told me that the FBI had visited the house a couple of times after the May 4th shootings, asked about me, but never appeared at my door in Kent. She took it in stride, only remarking how good looking the two men were.

The young boy kept laughing and shook the toy plane like he was forcing it to fly. Besides us, he and his mom were the only customers at ten in the morning. My student, a middle-age woman named Martha, would show early in order to quietly listen to Alan or his dad's stories, preferring black tea to coffee to accompany the morning's entertainment. She was my expert on local flora, able to identify any tree, bush or plant. One of the more worthwhile practices of my hippie youth was learning about the edible plants that grew in abundance throughout Ohio. A college friend and I still spent a good deal of time hunting them, just like Euell Gibbons of *Stalking the Wild Asparagus* fame. Later, as "healthy eating" infected the nation, my friend and I remembered Euell's demonic grin on the book's cover, and inside, his liberal use of butter, bacon and salt in his recipes. When I told Martha, after a lesson, that I occasionally cooked and ate cattails and milkweed flowers, she laughed loudly—unusual for her.

The young boy stopped waving the toy plane around and grew quiet after his mom told him to settle down. He stared at us in wonder.

"After I called Chagrin for lessons—I'll never forget this—my dad and I are in the car on a Saturday morning running errands and he asks me what I want to do when I grow up."

"Be a pilot?" Alan guessed, giving a wink to the young boy.

"I was even more specific. I told him I was going to fly in South America and write books."

"Well, you're getting close," he replied. "You fly and play in a great band and write your own music. Your dad had to be proud—you, just a kid, and all that ambition."

"Not really. He thought I was daydreaming. He told me to be realistic."

Alan shrugged at my remark and looked at the child. "He's ready for his first flight lesson."

The child yelled in our direction, and Alan stood up and walked over and introduced himself to the boy and his mom. "We're pilots," I heard him tell the kid, pointing at me as I smiled and waved.

* * *

At six years old, I made my first pair of wings while spending the weekend with my grandparents in Cleveland. Jumping off a tree limb or the garage roof seemed dangerous, so I put my younger brother in charge of gathering old newspapers. Together, we cut strips of paper and glued them to a long piece of cardboard. Using kite string, my brother attached the wings at my shoulders and wrists. I flapped about the house like a wounded bird.

The couch was my first runway. When I took off too close to my grandmother, who sat watching TV, a flurry of tiny fists appeared in my flight path, and I crashed to the floor, laughing.

I wore those wings from the moment I awoke. I ate with them on, played, and wondered how I would climb the pear tree in the backyard without damaging my creation.

One Saturday, my aunt promised to take my brother and me to the Avalon Theater on the condition that I remove my wings. Nobody flew at the movie house, she warned. But I told her the aisles were actually runways that shot you into the story. My aunt countered that the screen was flat. Shouting from the kitchen, my grandmother added that I looked like some bird with a disease. But I didn't abandon my wings for the Avalon because of insults. The prospect of a horror movie made me quietly turn them over to my grandfather, a man indifferent to make-believe.

I didn't ask about the wings when I returned from the mati-
nee. I was too busy reenacting scenes from the movie. Months
passed. My brother said we could make the wings again, but I
reminded him they were hanging in Grandpa's closet, next to his
winter coat.

On a weekend visit, my aunt told me that the paper wings
were burned one morning with the trash. I smugly replied, "Next
time I'll make gold ones—ten feet long!" As I crashed through the
screen door, headed for the pear tree, I yelled back that I had my
wings forever.

* * *

The mother and child had left, and Frank and Martha had
joined us. Short, elegant pear shape and neatly dressed in white
jeans and a green long-sleeved blouse, Martha sat up straight,
holding a second cup of tea. On her face a nascent smile was ready
to blossom depending on Frank's next remark. Frank had been
drawn into "getting the bug to fly" conversation. He was trying
to figure out when everything clicked and I had made the com-
mitment.

"Now, I bet money was an issue," Frank said, seriously. "It
always is, unless you're rich like Martha here."

Martha's eyes widened, the smile disappeared.

"Frank, I've had to save like everyone else. I'm on a budget."

In the wake of Alan's laughter and Martha's reprimand, Frank
settled deeper into the chair, surprised at the hole he had just dug
for himself. He stammered through his recovery.

"Well, that's good ... most people like to have a strategy ...
maybe a financial planner, so they don't get stuck halfway to their
private license and have to stop...."

Frank's sentence trailed off, a worried look that he had
crossed some line, perhaps jeopardizing business with a loyal,
pay-up-front customer. His son rocked in his chair, the back of
his fist pressed to his mouth, inhibiting the next explosion. Martha remained aloof, waiting for a better answer, and I jumped in
before Frank made things worse.

"It takes more than money. It did for me anyway. It takes a
jolt. And I finally got it on the way to a club one night. A big storm

got my attention. Electricity everywhere—right behind the breast-
bone too," I said, striking my chest with an open hand, making
Martha jump, my chest thumping now part of her instructor's
arsenal.

"You heard voices?" Frank asked, and his son's next explosion
melted into a smile.

Martha sipped her tea, waiting for my answer. A twinkle in
her eye told me she'd keep me as her instructor no matter how
flaky my past, even if it involved messages from a storm or pulling
off the freeway because I spotted one of Euell's edible roadside
plants.

"No voices. I just knew."

10

EARTH, SKY AND MUSIC

"I GREW UP with flying—Dad, Uncle Mario, someone always around to jump into a plane with and go." Alan stared at his coffee cup, cocked his head, and then shattered his thoughtfulness with laughter. I had put cream in, forgetting for the thousandth time that he drank it black.

"Sorry."

"Don't worry," he said, amused.

It was early evening, hot, humid, the air still. That morning I had signed off Martha for her long cross-country flight and had checked the forecast for the next several days against her schedule. It appeared the weather would cooperate, putting her only a few flight hours away from the private pilot check ride. After a full day of students, Alan and I left the restaurant and headed outside as a twin Cessna zoomed past on takeoff. Halfway to the open hangar, where his dad was working alone on the Skyhawk, we sat atop a wooden picnic table and faced the sun, visible through the trees. The table was still warm.

"You didn't have my opportunities, so it made you hungry," Alan said, his voice deeper, his expression serious. "I could have gone into a commercial job right out of high school. I had my license at sixteen. But that's all right. I like sales, talking, meeting new people. To fly all day, every day, doesn't sound like a lot of fun to me—but you're different, and you have other interests— your music. Now you got to choose. I'm not trying to talk you into anything. We lose you too when you start flying full time."

"I plan to keep a few students."

"We'll see," Alan said.

Only a break from my current band would allow the move into bigger, more complex aircraft. All the band guys had daytime gigs, keeping them free for rehearsal and club dates, whereas much commercial flying operated twenty-four/seven and often required you to be ready to launch on short notice and be gone overnight, living out of a suitcase.

"I better get over to Kent and see you guys play," Alan said.

We both turned, hearing the electrically operated hangar door start to close. Just inside the hangar, Frank shielded his eyes and made a slow wave. He was drenched in the rich light of sunset.

"A lot of talent in that band," Alan mused. "That one time I brought up friends from Alliance and they just shook their heads—I mean, they liked the music, they just never heard anything like it."

The Numbers Band of Northeastern Ohio began playing the Kove in downtown Kent in the summer of 1970. The Numbers took blues classics and made them their own, a stunning alchemy of breakneck poetry and rocket-ship rhythm-and-blues. The lead singer, Bob Kidney, restructured bass parts, taking out the thumping, loping figures in a lot of bass lines. He tightened the sound, more of a martial arts punch than a roundhouse, and gave space at unusual points in a bass riff. He broke down a drummer's set—kick drum, snare, high-hat—and rewrote the rhythm's DNA, creating a music that made other white guys playing the blues sound like college professors on music sabbatical. Even Eric Clapton, whose genius resides in guitar playing and writing beautiful pop songs, sounds like the Dean of the School of Blues when doing "Sweet Home Chicago" compared to the Numbers Band's version.

I told Alan that not only riots brought us into the street in the seventies, but music, played by a host of bands in nearly a dozen bars throughout Kent. Fans crowded the sidewalks; college and working class kids spilled into the streets in front of clubs like The

Kove, JB's and Pirate's Alley.

"Alan, in the sixties there were big rooms, converted car dealerships, a few blocks from the center of town that brought thousands through their doors on a Friday and Saturday night."

"Wasn't that going on all around the country? I mean, kids picking up guitars."

"Sure. But there was something in the air, the water, maybe the drugs that gave us more of it, more originality and experimentation. And from what I know, the big clubs popping up in a small town like ours wasn't typical. Besides, music was a lot more exciting than any day job. And for me, it was a lot more fun than finishing college and going into the classroom and brainwashing the next generation with a bunch of lousy leftist ideas."

Alan's laugh flew out, unrestrained, and was answered by the airport dog and a pickup truck rumbling fast down the road. I almost pointed to the musical composition in the making but refrained. I was more focused on the sun's departure and the electric-blue sky in its wake.

"You had a lifetime of experience in a few years of music," Alan said, tapping his pipe on the side of the picnic table, reaching in his pants pocket for a small pouch of tobacco.

"I remember watching the James Gang with Joe Walsh in '69. We sat in awe, no dancing. Outside, the sidewalks full, some of the kids stalled out, talking to friends, or just staring up at the sky. Along the north end of Water Street there were a-half-dozen bars, and they all had bands playing."

"You remember the first time you got up and played with Bob and the boys?" Alan's first puff rose above his head, a cloud for the twilight sky.

"I never hopped a train, but I came close sitting-in the first time. The guitar player leaned down from the stage and lent me a hand like he was reaching out from a moving boxcar. I slung my bass on, plugged in, nervous as hell. When the song kicked in I was dragged along, answered back with a half-baked riff. I was playing catch-up. Alan, the music still takes a lot of physical energy. You hang on. It's exhausting. But I've never been bored. A few of their originals are such a force of nature, I'm tempted to stay in the band just so I can keep playing them several nights a week."

"You're gonna miss the band," he said matter of fact, nodding his head. "That's okay. You should. It's important to you."

"It's like having to wake up from a great dream," I said. "But it does nothing for another part of me. And if anything, the emotions run so high when you make music, especially someone else's, it eats up the energy in the rest of your life. There's a lawless feeling too, and a seriousness that's more deadly than anything I've ever seen among pilots."

"Boy, if Dad heard you talk like that, he'd say it's a good thing you're leaving."

"Yeah, I know. It's Ulysses getting hung up in some pleasure garden and forgetting who he is, rooting around with a beautiful woman nearby."

Pipe in his mouth, Alan choked, burying the next laugh.

"Believe me, I'm tempted to stay."

Alan cleared his throat. "Look it, you need to build your time. You're all primed for experiences the band could never give you. You're a good musician. You could always get back into music someday, but it'll be on your terms."

"That's true. The ego takes a beating now ... regrets later on."

"Maybe. Just don't forget, it's also about what you love. You've been falling in love with aviation for a long time."

We sat in silence for a few minutes—Alan smoked peacefully, and I ran a few bars of a favorite blues tune through my head, memory now its home. Right then I decided to leave the band. I still loved it. What better time to walk away?

A bittersweet knock to the chest was answered by a sudden rise in the late summer chorus of insects.

* * *

Like my uncle, who knew what gave him the most pleasure in aviation and stuck with it, I was driven by the lore of a new plane, quiet study, classes and the prospect of flying jets. Music alone left me lopsided, another part of me untapped.

As a kid I read all about the test pilots of the 1950s. Pictures of handsome, confident men climbing into the cockpit of the early jet fighters, helmet in hand, smiling one of those big American smiles of opportunity. They were heirs to Davy Crockett, Daniel

Boone, Lewis and Clark.

The early test pilots had the Mercury and Apollo astronauts beat. Space travel was empty to me, like the vacuum it operated in. My imagination could follow only something as big and beautiful as the *Starship Enterprise*, because there I could work out and have lots of elbow room and not worry about muscles atrophying after skidding round the planet for a few weeks in a tin can or taking months just to get to Mars. I loved the earth and sky too much to trade it for the bleakness of outer space, a place better explored in storytelling, especially in the movies with their gorgeous musical scores.

11

AZTEC SACRIFICE

THE EIGHTIES WAS a difficult period to acquire multi-engine time. After a flurry of phone calls I had arranged to fly as co-pilot on a Twin Beech moving freight out of the Youngstown Executive Airport. After the plane taxied in and shut down, I watched the pilot drag himself out of the cockpit with his foot in a cast, handing me his crutches as he slid down the wing. A few months later the Corbis paired me with a local aviator in a King Air, a twin-engine propjet. I flew with a consummate professional, observing his techniques and working the radios. That day, January 28, 1986, was memorable since the Space Shuttle Challenger had fallen from the sky minutes after we returned from our early morning trip.

In February I left the Numbers Band when a Cleveland-based company hired me to fly bank checks along the Great Lakes. Until electronic checking arose, all checks needed to be processed by the home bank or a Federal Reserve facility. The original document needed to be in the bank's possession before payment could be made. Cash flow needs, the avoidance of penalties and the accruing of interest demanded that the pilots fly with all the power levers forward.

I flew a twin-engine Piper Aztec that demanded sacrifice.

From the cockpit of my dimly lit cave, I cruised in the larger cave of snow squalls, turbulence and thunderstorms. I got thrown in with poor radios, no autopilot, no radar and a gas heater that failed on the coldest of nights. Flying the shoreline of Lake Erie in early February, I watched the engine and navigation instruments for possible failure. And when the heater died, I drummed the floor of the plane with my feet and struck my shoulders with my hands until I needed to make a correction in altitude or heading.

I flew the coast from Cleveland to Buffalo several times over my twelve-hour night. Starting in Pittsburgh at eight in the evening, I sat quietly on the ramp, waiting for the courier. With the bulky David Clark headset tight across my temples, I checked a few switches for their proper position. I sat empty of desire and complaints. When the courier drove onto the tarmac, I started the left engine. He opened the door on the right side of the plane and heaved a large bag of checks into the baggage space behind my seat. I signed for the delivery and taxied to the runway. After my drop-off and pick-up in Cleveland, I headed to Buffalo.

Buffalo was the hapless recipient of some of the worst weather the Great Lakes snow machine produced. Where Cleveland usually missed the brunt of lake-effect snow showers, Buffalo stood directly in line. Often I left the cold clear skies over Cleveland only to find Buffalo digging out of the ice age.

I arrived in Buffalo near midnight. My next run wouldn't start until three in the morning. I shut down the engines, and the courier grabbed my freight. During the day I slept no more than three or four hours. The lack of sleep, the indulgence in cigarettes and coffee, robbed my natural vitality. Each night my bad habits won out, and I walked to a nearby restaurant, punctual, without thought.

After eating I returned to the pilot's lounge to rest. A few other check pilots wandered about. We hardly ever spoke to one another. Energy had to be conserved for hours of flying yet to come. I didn't sleep. I just attempted to lie still with my eyes closed. The cleaning man was my alarm. Near two-thirty he entered the small lounge, turned on the light, and fired up his vacuum cleaner. Even if I anticipated the rude wake-up call, I still jumped—a violent reentry into my tired body.

I left Buffalo only to return after my drop-off at Cleveland.

The sun rose near the time of takeoff, a signal that I was returning to the Pittsburgh airport, empty of checks, without the rush of a deadline. The sun's arrival was as mean and abrupt as the cleaning man's appearance. Cigarette butts overflowed from the ashtray, and my windshield was a dirty smear of sunblock. Every sunrise was a nuclear explosion that cruelly spared me and the plane.

I returned to the hotel by nine in the morning. Four consecutive days I would spend raising myself from the dead and flying throughout the night. Gone was that feeling of peace and accomplishment I had won with both music and my first solo. Once I locked the door to my hotel room, I'd light another cigarette and a rapid series of regrets brought out the tears. Sometimes I'd call Alan Corbi—a gratuitous call from the nether world. After I hung up, I closed the curtain and turned on the TV, my true companion. Normally entertaining, commercials and sitcoms were heart-wrenching dramas that convulsed my body with sadness.

By two in the afternoon I was finished with sleep. My routine was to work out. I struggled through the warm-up then began a series of isometrics. The workout never countered the abuses of bad food, little sleep, and chain-smoking, but it connected me to a thin line of vitality. This realm of strength existed a few feet from my body—a pocket of light, a corner of wilderness. I was waiting for room service one afternoon when an unknown peace flooded me, like the vision of a summer lake. In that instant I knew I was immune to any disease, any threat and perhaps to death itself.

12

TOO MUCH HEART

SIX MONTHS LATER I quit the check-flying job and returned to Miller Field, working again for the Corbis.

It was late spring of '87, and Frank and I sat behind Alan and Mario in a Cessna 310, a rakish, fast twin with streamlined tip tanks. Mario loved the 310. The four of us were taxiing out to Akron-Canton's Runway 19. Mario, a few years younger than Frank, had spent his aviation career buying and selling used aircraft. Even though the two brothers briefly teamed up early on, they worked separate businesses over the years.

"My brother could talk to someone all day long and never make a sale," Mario had once said, preferring to hunt alone. His smooth approach with customers belied his strong sense of who was a buyer and who was not. Unlike Mario, Frank would get distracted by someone's work, travels or the people they knew in common. I once watched Mario climb out of an airplane and greet the man waiting for us as if they were old friends. Later I found out that this was the first time the two had met. As far as Mario was concerned, Frank could wind up talking to the wrong person for hours and never make a sale, wasting everyone's time.

Attempting to relax, Alan sighed as we entered a long taxiway. The reduced activity, except for a commuter ahead of us, helped him to settle in, anticipating the challenge of returning to Miller's short, poorly lit runway. We had left while it was still daylight.

On the takeoff roll, everything went smooth except Alan never looked back inside to check on the engine instruments when the plane started to move.

"Nice job," Mario said as they broke ground. "Just don't forget to glance over at those engine gauges."

Once we leveled off at thirty-five hundred feet, Mario told me I could move up between the seats. "Just don't say anything. Alan's busy enough. I might throw in a few distractions, though. But I need you buckled in on final. Okay?"

I stayed in my seat, obeying Mario until approach control placed us on a long ten-mile final, allowing me to move closer again. I blurted out a few questions in a row.

"I'll answer that on the ground," Mario said more than once.

At fifty feet above the pavement on his first approach, Mario had Alan go around. He intervened when Alan forgot to first set the prop controls before increasing the power. Alan swore and fumbled with the gear handle then flew the twin Cessna almost to his assigned altitude before remembering to bring the flaps up.

"Alan's doing all right," Mario said, laughing, patting Alan's shoulder. "But you see he was expecting to land the first time. Why should he or anyone think it's going to be that easy? I've landed then taken off on icy runways when I knew I couldn't stop."

Alan shook his head, mumbling what a shitty job he had done. Frank and I remained quiet in the backseat.

On the next approach, Mario said nothing and let him land. It was a good landing and Frank broke his silence, saying that Alan was "back in the saddle." After a few more approaches, we headed back to Miller Field. The night takeoff and landing practice in the Cessna 310 was Mario's idea to get Alan practical training before making trips for him. Since Alan showed interest in sales, Mario thought it wise for him to start getting acquainted with a variety of aircraft besides the single-engine Pipers and Cessnas he knew so well.

The lights that riddled the landscape in the Akron area grew sparse as the Cessna sailed smoothly along at three thousand feet. Tonight the earth looked like a dark fabric someone had blasted with a shotgun, making the lights of cities and towns visible. Tonight, the shotgun was a symbol of progress.

As a student pilot, Tina had made me close my eyes while she drove around the night sky, making turns, climbing and descending. When she said "look up," I saw only blackness and a few dim lights on the ground that I couldn't place with a road or a town. Without dialing in the VOR (ground-based system for short-range navigation), she wanted me to find my way back to the Chagrin Falls Airport. I took control of the plane, made a few turns and let the gravity of home pull me in the right direction. A few minutes later, the runway lights came into sight. I felt fortunate to live in a country where even the lights of Akron, Ohio, were dazzling.

"I don't see a thing," Alan said, looking for the runway. According to the DME (distance measuring equipment) we were flying within three miles of the runway. Mario keyed the microphone five times to operate the automatic system that brought the lights on for the next fifteen minutes. When the single row of lights appeared, Alan banked the plane and crossed over the field to enter downwind. He was still a bit fast and Mario pointed to the throttles. Passing abeam the approach end of Runway 27, Alan attempted to lower the speed by raising the nose and pulling off more power.

"Don't reduce the power too much. I want the engines warm. If you want, extend downwind," Mario said.

Alan did just that. He kept looking over his shoulder, attempting to keep the airport in sight with its weak lighting. When he finally reached the flap speed he lowered them fifteen degrees, followed by the gear. On base he couldn't see the runway lights and thought to hold his north heading for a few more seconds. Mario suggested that he start his turn to final. Rolling out on a west heading, Alan gripped the control yoke and strained to see the rotating beacon and lights.

"Watch your descent," Mario snapped. "Scan the instruments—you're getting low."

Alan spotted the airport and instinctively dove toward the runway. Mario instructed with one- and two-word commands. Just as the plane got on speed and altitude, the single row of lights appeared off the nose of the plane. Unable to remember what side of the lights he should land on, Alan smoothly pushed the props up, increased the power and started to climb, raising the gear and flaps.

Mario chuckled.

"Nice job. You should have gone around sooner. But, hey, you got it under control until those goofy lights screwed you up. Maybe your dad will replace the burned-out ones on the north side someday." Mario glanced back at his brother, who said nothing, only smiled.

Alan leaned forward to stretch and loosen up, helping him stay alert.

"Let's try this again," he said, banking the aircraft, placing it at the proper distance downwind from the runway and maintaining an airspeed of one hundred and forty knots, the ballpark speed before turning final. He found the rails again, the plane balanced by its two engines, riding invisible tracks. He rolled out onto final and placed the lights on his left, the south side of the runway. He checked his heading, airspeed and altitude and asked Mario to call one hundred feet above the ground.

"Your son has it nailed," Mario said, signaling us that our response wasn't needed as we flew down short final, and Mario called a hundred feet.

After the call-out and clearing the last stand of trees, Alan smoothly brought the power back to idle as he looked down the midpoint of the dark runway. He let out another long sigh, relaxing from his gut to his legs, the proverbial seat-of-the-pants sensation. The smooth landing elicited a war cry from me, but Mario remained silent during the rollout on the narrow runway.

Mario's shutdown was from memory, and he pointed to the pitot heat switch on the panel. Electrical power heated the pitot tube mounted on the side of the fuselage that used ram air for the airspeed indicator. The metal tube was heated to prevent icing and erroneous airspeed readings. Since pitot heat was a large draw on the electrical system, Alan turned it off before killing the engines with the two mixture controls.

"If your ego isn't too big, you get a hundred different lessons when you take a short flight like this," Mario said, turning to face me. "Anyone can navigate for hours, but you got to be ready for anything when you take off or enter that traffic pattern, especially when you're a lot faster than some student in a Skyhawk. You guys know that when you go into some strange airport, you're dodging traffic all the way to the ground."

We were silent as the four of us walked around the parked aircraft with Mario. The security light on the upper corner of the restaurant aided Alan's post flight.

The next morning the four of us met for breakfast, sitting at the table that gave us a good view of the runway. Mario sat closest to the window, adding a few remarks on Alan's night flight when a Cessna 182 made a hard landing on all three gears. The plane bounced off the ground like a stunned deer and smacked again on all three wheels. Both Frank and Mario winced, and Alan started to swear but caught himself when the waitress returned to take our orders.

"That's why I sold him his own airplane," Mario said matter of fact. "Years ago I knew after five minutes with McCormick that he was a yank-and-smash guy—yank it off the runway, then smash it on."

Frank started to say something, but let his brother continue.

"I thought he was going to pull the controls out of the firewall," Mario said with the aplomb of a seasoned hunter describing the destructive capacity of a rogue bear. "You can't believe the way he battles with an airplane. Alan, you ever see him work on his truck?" Ron McCormick was a cross-country truck driver who worked on his own rig in a large pole building behind his house.

"I'd rather have him in the garage than in the air," Alan said.

"He's a butcher in the garage too," Mario replied.

"Well, he keeps the plane on the runway," Frank said, entering the conversation. "That nose gear may need some attention, but he's going to bring the airplane back without too many problems. McCormick can't be trained, but he won't crash and burn."

"That's true, Frank," Mario said, turning toward me. "My brother knows. McCormick always struggles, but finds his limit before he really screws up. And he can take his punishment. If any one of us chews him out, he nods that big head of his, gets red-faced and says 'I'm sorry' a million times."

Even though he was in his mid-sixties, Mario still drew the gaze of younger women. He used his hands when he talked with the strong, confident motions of a CEO. He pointed with his thumb at McCormick standing by the window, smiling sheepishly at the four of us having breakfast.

"Look at him," Frank said. "The gorilla knows he did something wrong. I better check that nose gear." He stood up and grabbed the check, adding, "He needs to lose weight. And I've got the diet for him—fish heads and rice."

A man from the next table said, "I know what those bastards did to you in the war, Frank. We should've dropped A-bombs for a year on 'em after we got you guys outta there."

"Now, it's true, they didn't give us the fish heads and rice out of the kindness of their hearts. But that food had nutrients. We got our protein."

"I know, Frank, but I'm still mad as hell how they treated you."

"Well, they all weren't sadistic," Frank replied. "Some were even ashamed of what they did. You could see it on their faces."

The man returned to his breakfast, shaking his head at Frank's answer.

"Dieting won't help with his landings," Mario opined, visibly relieved that the war discussion was over for now. "He should be on steel skids. That guy doesn't understand the wheel."

Once Frank headed toward the door, McCormick, dressed in his work bibs and greasy short-sleeve T-shirt, turned and walked back to his plane.

"What's that you're eating?" Mario asked, staring at the bowl in front of his nephew.

"Just oatmeal," Alan said.

"See, you young guys, getting all this information now; doesn't help an old man like me. If I knew this stuff when I was thirty, I'd be a superman today. Live to a hundred and twenty. But who knew? We were old at thirty. But today everybody can be young. I guess I never really wanted to be young forever, just strong and live a long time."

"You're in great shape," Alan told his uncle. "And you love what you do."

"That's true. I don't know how it all adds up for a long life. But I always knew that if a guy believes in what he's doing, like selling, he could sell pickles, put all his energy and time into selling pickles and do great."

Mario was the consummate salesman. Whether on the phone

or meeting someone for the first time, he exuded confidence. He wasn't bubbly nor a bad actor reading his lines, hungry for a sale, but someone so comfortable in his own skin you wanted to walk with him for a while, maybe buy a plane, and see if that male smoothness and certitude were transferable with the aircraft title.

"Today, these doctors talk like we can live to a hundred and fifty," Mario said. "I bet they'll figure it out after I'm gone. Now some guys are lucky and have those good genes."

"You have great genes," I said.

"We'll see. Now look at McCormick."

Frank and McCormick were examining the nosewheel.

"I don't know how I know this," Mario said, "but I don't think he'll make seventy."

"With that gut I don't think he'll make sixty," Alan said.

"There's something else, something you can see in some people, a sadness in their eyes. Like they're not going to be around long and somehow they know that."

"Hopefully, you're wrong," I said.

"Yeah, I know, I'd like to be wrong."

"There're other things that can keep you going," Alan countered, "good friends, family."

"You ever look at McCormick's family, Alan?" Mario shot back. "The man would have been dead years ago if they were all he had. They're all standing around with shovels, waiting to throw dirt. They like his money, and he hands it over. But the day he misses a payment, they'll bury him."

Frank had taxied for a few minutes with McCormick and returned for another cup of coffee. He joined the conversation, saying the shimmy damper needed servicing and that McCormick's biggest asset was his friends.

"Let's make it just you, Frank," Mario stated flatly. "You're true-blue. Everyone else wants something from him. Like me. But his wife and those kids are first in line."

"I like Twyla," Frank said.

"She's still good to look at, but the woman's a running headache," Mario mused, "hardly a bargain. You're lucky we still have that public phone on the side of the building."

Alan tried to hold back an explosion of laughter, but it flew out in two sonic bursts.

"Hell, he knows he can't use my office phone anymore. He broke the base," Frank said. Alan stifled another burst.

"What?" I said.

"You ever watch him on the phone?" Mario asked. "You've taken him up for checkouts. What's the first thing he does after he lands?"

I thought about it for a moment, with all the Corbis smiling at me. It felt like a test. Did he hit the restroom? I had only a few flights with the guy during my first few years at Miller's. And I usually had to find McCormick for the post-flight briefing.

"The phone!" I yelled.

"You ever watch him?" Mario asked.

"Sure, but I can't remember what he says. I'm not that close."

"You don't have to be close," Frank said.

"He talks loud," I said.

"He always talks loud," Mario replied. "He's deaf."

"But when he talks to Twyla," Frank said, "if it's not a whisper, which is hard for him anyway, he's screaming because she's gone off and done something pretty bad and then he doesn't hang up, he slams it down. That's why we only let him use the public phone. I don't care if it's a blizzard. He stays outside."

"That phone is built like his plane," Mario said. "He can beat on either one all day long, and they'll both survive."

"Well, that's what he gets for marrying a hooker from Vegas," Frank said loudly, ending with a sigh. "I warned him. But he's a good old boy, too much heart."

13

BRICKS AND FOREST

I PULLED INTO the Miller parking lot, and Frank approached, smacking the car roof to get my attention.

"Old man Miller died this morning," Frank said. "I need to go and comfort his wife." He stared at the windsock. "You have any flights in that pretty twin?" He smiled, referring to the Cessna 402.

"Nothing until next week. I came down to do some paperwork. Did Russ die at home?"

"He sure did," Frank said. "He was walking out to work on the Silver Thing. Every day I told him to wait until I came by. He was always doing too much. Oh well, he loved that stupid homebuilt. I'm surprised he didn't die in it." Frank shook his head. "He was a better mechanic than inventor anyway."

I followed Frank to his car. Lost in thought, he tapped the key on the ignition. "You know, in high school I pedaled out here whenever I could, and old Russ would let me work on whatever he had in the shop. I crawled all over an airplane. Couldn't get enough of it." The Cadillac started smoothly. "He was my manual arts teacher. A hard-nosed guy, but you learned."

Frank drove off, and I ambled alongside the runway with my coffee.

There was frost on the ground. That day the east-west runway reminded me of a straight country road with some cracks and a few hardy weeds making their way toward the sky. Everything was quiet except for the birds and a dog barking in the distance.

Russ had owned Miller Field long before Frank and his son. On the north side of the runway, Russ had planted a pine forest decades ago. The uneven rows of full-grown pines were a Christmas tree farm, never harvested. Beyond the evergreens, the fall colors enveloped the crowns of tall hardwoods.

One of Russ's creations after his retirement was a homebuilt called the Silver Thing. This plane, powered by a Chevy Corvair engine, flew only a few feet off the ground before it crashed alongside the grass runway at his farm. From the Corbis I learned Russ experimented with other types of homebuilts, including a large, flat-bottom boat for the twenty-two-mile-long Berlin Reservoir just north of the airport. It wouldn't steer properly, so Russ had to dock and turn it with ropes before he could set off in another direction. Frank mentioned that the dispirited boat maker went out in a canoe one night, punched holes in the bottom of his creation and let it sink.

Russ operated Miller field for over thirty years, getting scores of people their private pilot's license. He built the brick buildings in the fifties. The main one, near the center of the runway, had offices with a restaurant, a clubroom and bedrooms upstairs. Even the runway was originally brick and sand before it was paved over with asphalt.

A Cessna 152 was parked on the ramp next to the fuel pump. I thought of my training, patrolling the gas line, and the many students I had taught in this aluminum kite with its one hundred-and-twelve-horsepower engine. Now, I rarely flew it. I opened the small door and marveled at the unadorned, cramped interior. It had been an incubator, the small cave of the philosopher, a bucket for a child in a fairytale to travel the ocean. I closed the door and walked around the Cessna. Standing in front of the propeller, I examined the elegant tapering of the fuselage and the proportioned tail and wings. This was a stick airplane, barely fleshed out.

Sipping my coffee, I remembered the engine failure and Russ later congratulating me on the emergency landing. Even though he lived close by and was an airport regular, this was the first time we ever talked.

On the drive home, I saw Russ sitting on the edge of the desk, smiling at my story. Yet I still wondered why he had ignored me over the years I had worked at the airport. When the driver ahead of me stopped suddenly for a deer running across the freeway, I hit the brakes and the surge of adrenaline erased my thoughts. Once we were all safe, including the deer, I realized I had never stepped into Russ Miller's world with much pressure. That emergency landing gave me the extra poundage that allowed me to press into Russ's field of vision. I became visible, like the solid red brick buildings and the Christmas tree forest north of the runway.

14

LAKE EFFECT

ONE WINTER MORNING, Forrest Barber flew into Miller Field and found Frank and me finishing breakfast. He had business in Columbus and wondered if I'd like to tag along. He said the short trip gave him an excuse to visit his friend who owned a large flight operation for maintenance and charter at the Columbus airport. Forrest gently blew across the surface of his coffee and teased Frank, asking him to fly down with us and actually meet someone older than himself.

Forrest Barber grew up with his hands and feet on the controls of an airplane. His father owned a small airport several miles west of Miller Field, and every year on Christmas morning, father and son flew over the grandparents' house before dinner. One holiday, after takeoff, seven-year-old Forrest banked the aircraft toward the lake north of the airfield. From their position, he saw a snow shower in the approximate vicinity of his grandparents' home. As the snow began racing past the wing, Forrest instinctively lowered the nose for better forward visibility. When he could no longer see straight ahead, he asked his father to take the controls. The father refused. "You're flying, make a decision. What would you do if I wasn't here?"

"I'd go home," his son replied.

Unassisted, Forrest turned the plane one hundred and eighty degrees, pivoting above a large, red barn and headed back to the airstrip.

At his dad's airport, Forrest honed his flying and mechanic

skills and later became a test pilot for the Taylorcraft Aviation company during the seventies. Over time he earned the respect of the Ohio aviation community as a top-notch aerobatic pilot and instructor. It was stick and rudder, seat of the pants flying—never far from the treetops or the shouts of children.

Once the Columbus tower cleared us to land, Forrest gingerly turned the plane into the wind and kept it tracking straight down the runway centerline. The crosswind evaporated near the surface, and he took out the rudder and aileron correction, lined up the aircraft with the centerline and smoothly rolled the small Piper down the center of the wide, long runway. We parked in front of his friend's facility that housed corporate jets in huge, clean hangars, a pilot shop and leased office space. After the tour, we sat briefly with the owner, who was as ancient as the vintage aircraft on display. Watching the two men, I knew that something like this big commercial enterprise had been Forrest's dream. He seemed more sad than jealous that fate had never made him like the slender, savvy gentlemen who sat across from him, making a joke about doing something wrong somewhere along the way.

On our flight home neither one of us said much as we flew between blinding snow showers. Forrest Barber gracefully steered the aircraft with slight movements of his hands and feet, while his eyes focused on a point of blue sky just short of infinity.

At Miller's we parked the plane and saw the hangar door open. Unsuccessfully, Frank was attempting to start a small tug he had recently bought. The Skyhawk's one-hundred-hour inspection was complete, and he needed space for a friend's aircraft. A couple of times Forrest called out for him to wait and that we'd give him a hand. Frank glanced at us and pulled on the rope once more after making some minor adjustment with the choke. We all jumped as the engine roared to life and the handle flew out of Frank's hand. As the machine lurched dangerously close to the nose of the Skyhawk, with its handle pointing at the ceiling, Frank grabbed its top and briefly danced with the machine while Forrest yelled to turn it off. The zany jitterbug ended when Frank smacked a small lever on top of the engine with his foot.

Forrest said his friend from Columbus probably never danced with a two-wheel machine powered by a lawn mower engine.

"Of course not," Frank said. "Someone else dances for him."

15

PIONEERS AND THE FREE MARKET

IN THE EARLY eighties, charter and corporate flying were stagnant and the airlines were laying off pilots. In my neck of the woods, you had to either be ex-military or know somebody to be hired at a Fortune 500 company. Executive Jet Aviation changed all that. By the late nineties, two billion dollars was being spent on new aircraft from Raytheon, Cessna and Boeing. Free market capitalism had hit the afterburner stage.

Founded in 1964 by retired Air Force Brigadier General "Dick" Lassiter, Executive Jet Aviation (EJA) began with the purchase of ten Lear 23s. Formed after the Air Force's Special Air Missions Squadron (flying the President, Vice President, members of Congress), the company became the civilian answer for safe and professional travel for the wealthy. Early board members included movie icon Jimmy Stewart and radio and television star Arthur Godfrey. Later, Paul Tibbets—the military luminary who piloted the Enola Gay and dropped the A-bomb on Hiroshima— would be named president as the company entered its second decade.

Jimmy Stewart lent EJA that quality of the ordinary man performing the extraordinary, the citizen soldier of World War II. The world learned that Stewart's movie persona of the average guy struggling for his family and country was true of the man off screen, as he flew one dangerous mission after another across the English Channel into Germany. Between missions, Stewart lived an ordinary soldier's life, no extra perks, no pulling strings.

The energy of these men launched a company that pioneered jet charter in the 1960s. Early on, it even gave a tutorial to the FAA on how to conduct flight tests in business jets.

In the mid-eighties, Executive Jet Aviation became a pioneer again. Former Goldman Sachs executive Richard Santulli bought the business in 1984 and two years later started the concept of fractional ownership. This allowed a customer to purchase a fraction of a jet and keep all costs lower. With a fleet of the same model aircraft, having the same paint and interior, it became less likely for an owner to be grounded by unexpected maintenance. Owners had to only pick up the phone with a minimum four-hour lead time and be able to write the monthly check for maintenance fees and hours flown. Lear and Falcon jets made up the fleet until the late eighties, when Mr. Santulli purchased eight Citations and put Cessna's Wichita plant back to work.

For the next quarter-century, new opportunities opened up for pilots and all aviation-related business enterprises: sales, office staff, dispatchers and meteorologists. Cleaning and catering companies sprang up along with limo companies and aircraft maintenance centers. Manufacturers like Beech, Cessna and Gulfstream received large orders. In 1983, two brothers who owned a family restaurant close to the Teterboro Airport started catering about a dozen flights weekly. By the late nineties, Rudy's Catering covered the numerous airports in the New York and Washington D.C. areas, providing meals for hundreds of flights daily.

* * *

Flying for the Corbis ended when I started at Executive Jet Aviation in 1989. With the flights staying mostly in North America, Mexico and the Caribbean, we picked up our passengers and then made grooves in the heavens to deliver them to their destination, fighting with air traffic control to fly as the crow flies.

It was a time when a single-sheet resume and a twenty-minute interview with the chief pilot was all that was needed to get hired. I had thought the interview process had gone well. We were talking about our interests outside of aviation when I mentioned that I was a bass player. The chief pilot paused, grew serious, saying, "I can't hire you." In shock, I suffered through a longer pause, before he added, "I just hired a bass player this morning—a mechanic. I'm sure one bass player is enough."

* * *

By the end of the 1980s it was a dream to be at the controls of my first corporate jet, a Cessna Citation S-II, skimming the present, riding the crest of atmospheric waves, aware that the jet engines were turning with the force of miniature suns. I relished the power and smoothness of high altitude flight, no longer stuck in the lower altitudes battling the elements. But having to leave home every few days and live out of a suitcase for six days was unsettling. I told this to Frank Corbi, who said, "Well, the bigger the plane the bigger the suitcase, or maybe in your case, the faster the plane ...." I came close to leaving EJA.

The older pilots, mostly ex-military, were accustomed to the long stretches away from home, but their habits didn't rub off on me. These men had flown in the Strategic Air Command strapped into seats of the B-47 or B-52 for periods up to twenty-four hours. Later, as civilian pilots, they kept their military polish, referring to charter flights as missions and often ready at the hotel, dressed in uniform, shoes shined, bags packed, even when no flights were expected. One Korean War vet told me that the passengers he flew were like the guests that came to his house for a weekend visit. "Of course I grab their bags, show them to their rooms, see if they're hungry, what I can do to make them happy."

I admired these pilots. They taught me forbearance, staying ahead of the aircraft, committing radio and navigation frequencies, high and low altitude routes to memory.

I also enjoyed their stubbornness, the political incorrectness of these men who flew in the Strategic Air Command, piloted Sabre jets in Korea, or navigated the "Hump" over the Himalayas during World War II. Their many hours in treacherous weather, dog fights, testing and research would bring greater efficiency and safety to commercial aviation; their service to our country kept us free. When one of my captain's stubbornness overpowered common sense and anger arose, I was shown another side.

Landing one night at the Columbus airport, a veteran flier from the Air Defense Command, who had flown the F-101, started yelling when I exited the runway to the north. "Don't you know where the hell you're at? Which way to turn? Base is on the southside!" When it occurred to him that I was right, due to airport construction, he stewed for a couple of days and finally apologized at dinner, saying how hard it was for an old dago like himself to admit he was wrong.

Earlier that day, the captain had pulled out a picture of his wife he kept in his wallet. An old photo showed a dark-haired beauty. He stared at it briefly and smiled, a ritual, I thought, performed in many places of the world over many years of travel. That night I jotted down this experience alongside the practical details of the day's flight and quietly decided to stay with EJA. Difficult hours lay ahead: brutal early morning shows after only a few hours of sleep, long days of flying; reading through a complicated IFR departure followed by a clash with a difficult crew member. But no matter what beating the road delivered, I couldn't turn my back on this new world, seeing the soulfulness of another's life, like the pride and humility of a veteran pilot and his unabashed affection for his wife of many years.

Months later, after filling up a notebook on aircraft performance, icing, turbulence, storms or amazing sunsets, I did what most people did who drove through the sky a lot and scribbled—I became proud of my bad poetry. But it felt good. Flying and writing have supported each other, dovetailing journeys where nosey cab drivers and stubborn old veterans were never in short supply. The goal has been to put in a good day's work and return to my hotel room, not full of loneliness or regrets, but alive enough to write down a new feeling, a rush of thoughts or a moment of beauty that passes by so quickly.

16

GOING TO WAR WITH JIMMY STEWART

UNLIKE AUDIE MURPHY, who went from Medal of Honor recipient to famous actor, Jimmy Stewart went from famous actor to war hero and then back to beloved movie star in the 1946 film *It's a Wonderful Life*.

Not long after winning an Academy Award for *The Philadelphia Story*, Stewart enlisted in the Army Air Corps in 1941. Once in uniform, his superiors were reluctant to send him into harm's way. For two years he was an instructor on the B-17 Flying Fortress and the B-24 Liberator, where intense training all too often wiped out friends and students. When he finally got his assignment as commander of the 703rd squadron in the 455th bomber group, he would cross the English Channel on some twenty bombing missions inside Germany.

Jimmy Stewart grew up in Indiana, Pennsylvania, on Philadelphia Street. His family held hands and prayed before dinner. I found a picture in my research that showed him visiting his family after the war and instantly recognized George Bailey and his family from *It's a Wonderful Life*. The character George, like Stewart, is masculine and tender.

Jimmy Stewart understood Western Civilization's gift of

freedom deep in his bones. I had seen his Norman Rockwell face reflected in many Americans throughout my life, especially the two bar owners from Kent, and my friend and teacher, Frank Corbi.

Frank had made a comment years ago that we never followed up on. He had told Alan that in the late forties, Howard Hughes and Jimmy Stewart flew into Wright-Patterson Air Force Base. I don't know if Frank ever met Stewart that day, but I like to imagine the anonymous soldier meeting the famous one. Frank's manner was self-effacing, like the actor's, humble about his achievements, proud of his service. The two men shared an unmistakable love for aviation and had honed their analytical skills for flying and problem solving.

I know Stewart met many fine men like Frank Corbi during and after the war, but I like to think that he had the good fortune of shaking Frank's hand and seeing in Frank's eyes that same glint of toughness and love of country he so finely projected.

17

LIPSTICK AND ORANGES SUNSET

HEADED TO CALIFORNIA in the Cessna Citation, we watched the sun fall below the horizon, a lipstick-and-oranges sunset. The red-and-gold light filtered into the cockpit, softly illuminating our hands and face. The greater part of sky and earth lay in darkness. Often, this slash of red lipstick and band of orange appeared above the haze level at the higher altitudes. At times I thought I was looking at the background of all happy endings, or the celestial imprint of some greater force—the constancy of dream and nature. This sunset was at Charles Lindbergh's back on his test flight from California to New York and his voyage to Paris.

In order to break in his ship, Lindbergh flew over mountain, desert and the Great Plains. After a stopover in St. Louis, he continued across farm and woodlands of the Midwest then finally on to New York. It was fitting that the first pilot to fly New York to Paris nonstop across the cold Atlantic should do it alone and with the blessing of sunset, forest, mountain and river. Only a running leap from coast to coast could have delivered success.

Lindbergh's aircraft evolved from the mud-pie ship of the Wright Brothers. Its airframe and engine were products of a quarter-century of innovations, including a world war. Even the blocked windshield (due to an extra fuel tank) never detracted from the Spirit of St. Louis's aesthetic imprint on the American imagination. Its classic form ranked alongside the Learjet and the Fender electric guitar.

As a teen I first read Lindbergh's story in his book *The Spirit of St. Louis*. At a large, heavy desk in my parents' basement, I traveled with the explorer during his heart-stopping moments of engine roughness and painstaking navigation. But most agonizing was his battle to stay awake. I felt guilty, putting the book down and heading off to bed while my hero dealt with the eternity of hours and minutes. After he landed at Le Bourget airport, and he and the plane were safely at rest, I believed the whole world slept that night.

Perhaps one of the forces behind his success was the red-and-gold sky—color and light squeezed into the atmosphere, a laser pointed at the head and heart. This sunset obliterates the blue-domed sky of daytime, allowing the emergence of islands, new continents and uncharted seas.

Buried in Hawaii, Lindbergh overlooks the ocean, facing the twilight sky. A pioneer stationed on our furthest Western frontier, he travels toward that sunset, that colorful mystery surrounded by night.

* * *

Like explorers, pilots move among strangers, drop into new places and often spend nights away from those dear to us. We are beset with the tedium of long journeys until some invisible force opens us to a chance word, an unusual sunset or the geometry of desert and mountain from forty-one thousand feet.

One of our captains enjoyed venturing onto the hotel's roof at the end of the day. He wanted that vista, another perch, the confusion of freeways and buildings of an unfamiliar place spread out before him like an early American explorer climbing a ridge along the Missouri River and witnessing a world breathtakingly new.

My own explorations begin unexpectedly. I might be seated as a passenger on a crowded airliner, looking into the eyes of a tired flight attendant, when a thought emerges that brushes against the world. Inwardly, I turn and see a lush valley, the path of a river, or hear the words of a stranger. The sublime returns, the birth of that invisible force.

18

ROCKLAND, MAINE

AT THE START of my tour we were to fly four people out of Waukegan, Illinois, to Rockland, Maine. Only two of the passengers knew we were going to Rockland; the other two, a husband and wife, believed that we were flying to Stuart, Florida. Friends and family planned to surprise the couple with a journey to the town where the man had proposed forty years ago. The setup hardly impressed me—I was accustomed to flying wealthy folks for a multitude of reasons. An energetic man in his late fifties with a head of silver hair went over the plans to keep the couple in the dark. I mentioned that our route would take us over the Great Lakes.

"Don't worry about that. My wife and I will keep John and Elaine busy. They'll never notice." The man spoke with the assurance of someone who had been directing people successfully for a lifetime. "What about the weather at destination?"

The three of us stood in a huddle next to the plane. The captain answered him.

"Well, the ceiling and visibility is a bit low at the moment," Bill said. "But Rockland has airports north and south of it that we can use for an alternate."

The man winced. He trained his eyes on something in the distance, as if he could summon the desired results out of thin air.

"Damn, that won't do. Their children, friends, nearly a hundred people are already there. I understand the weather, the minimums you fellas have to follow—but what a letdown if they have to drive an hour to get there."

"We'll do our best. The weather is forecast to improve," Bill said.

"How soon can you give me an update?"

"Once we get settled at altitude, we'll contact flight service."

"That sounds good. You know Stuart is a little farther—"

"In my briefing, I'll mention the strong tailwind we're expecting," I added.

The man smiled and walked away with the confidence of a general assured of his men's morale.

"I sure want this to work." Bill's face tightened as he surveyed the hazy morning sky of late August.

I lacked his sense of urgency—the weather would cooperate or it wouldn't.

"Looks like they thought of everything," Bill said as the limo driver pulled alongside the aircraft and popped the trunk to reveal four sets of golf clubs.

The silver-haired man helped us. "We do a lot of golfing in Stuart." He held up one end of a bag while Bill struggled to wedge it into the tail baggage compartment. The man's wife, a petite woman, wore jeans and a white blouse. She stood at the wing tip and smiled as the three of us grappled with the golf bags.

When the couple arrived, we boarded the Citation and I started the briefing. But I had never checked Stuart's weather. Was it raining? Cooler than normal? Had they kept track of Florida's weather for the past twenty-four hours? I had no trouble lying. It was not having the facts that was bothersome. The anniversary couple had on shorts, so I went with fair skies and eighty degrees. Both couples smiled approvingly.

Twenty minutes into the flight, the silver-haired man popped his head between our seats.

"It'll probably be a half-hour before we get a weather update," I said, lowering my headset volume in order to hear him better.

"No, no, don't worry. I just came up here to watch you fellas closer. I'm still like a little kid when it comes to flying—and I've been doing it my entire life. I've owned some type of airplane for the last twenty years."

I took off my headset, and Bill nodded that he'd take care of the radio calls. "Are you a pilot?"

"I took a few lessons but it wasn't for me. It's too compelling, too absorbing. I could never give it the attention it requires. I've got my business on my mind sometimes twenty-four hours a day. But I envy the view you have from up here—there just isn't enough time in a person's life to sit in every seat."

The man glanced over the panel in time to see us break through the cloud tops. We were divers coming up for a breath, once again able to breathe blue sky and sunlight. By surfacing together, I sensed the man's vitality, his affection for his friends. My cynicism faded.

"If you could come back, say an hour from now, with an ETA and the weather in Stuart?" the man asked.

"Not a problem. But when I do that, passengers have the habit of glancing out of the plane."

"I'll shove a golf magazine in John's face, get Elaine's attention with an old story about the four of us. I know how to run interference."

"When we're in the descent, entering the traffic pattern, they're bound to look out."

"That'll be perfect. I expect them to recognize the coast of Maine. Believe me, that'll be perfect."

Thirty minutes out of the Chicago area, we leveled off at four hundred and fifty knots.

"One hour and twenty minutes to go," Bill announced. "Why don't you give flight service a call? Check Bangor, they're only thirty miles north."

The news was discouraging.

"Five hundred feet and a half-mile," I said.

"That's not going to work. What'd they say about Augusta?"

"Worse. And it's almost time for my phony update."

The two reporting stations, one north and the other south, indicated the likelihood of poor weather at our destination. Rockland's AWOS (automatic weather and observation system) was out of service.

"It may be time to widen our support base." Bill's intense look was softened by his words. "Time to ask my best friend for a little help."

For a moment I thought Bill was hinting at the possibility of divine intervention. In the next instant, I realized he was referring to his father, who had recently passed away.

"I don't make it a habit of asking for his help; I'd like to think I can get through most days on my own. But this is different. Important words were spoken forty years ago," Bill said as he looked out across the sky.

The weather had improved at both reporting points. With an increase in temperature and no cloud deck, the atmosphere was slowly drying out.

"I wish the AWOS was working at Rockland," Bill said. He shifted in his seat and stared at his attitude indicator. "Let's keep an eye on this. The command bars aren't matching up with my heading." He was quiet for a few moments, glancing over the panel, studying the clouds beneath us. "We need to get those people to their celebration."

"And the prayer?"

"I've put in my request." Bill smiled. "How about lobster in Rockland, Maine?"

"Sounds good. I'm off the radio. Time to go lie to the passengers again."

It was a relief to find them deep in conversation, ignoring me. And the silver-haired man was right. No one glanced out the window.

As we began our descent and the ocean came into view, we could see a low fogbank north and south of our destination. We hadn't sighted our airport in the thin haze.

"Let's hope it isn't very thick," I said.

"It sure looks better than that other stuff." Bill pointed to a section of coastline south of the airport's location.

By seven thousand feet, green rugged hills emerged from the haze. The discussion and the occasional laughter from the back of the airplane ceased. I hadn't time to turn around and check on the passengers. Fifteen miles from the airport, the visibility was five to six miles. I called out the items on the landing checklist, and we both leaned forward, searching for it.

"Let's just pass over the field, and I'll start my downwind leg over the ocean," Bill said.

Rockland is on Penobscot Bay. The city and harbor came into view, and moments later we sighted the airport. I made a check for other traffic then turned to look at the passengers. I saw the anniversary couple holding hands, their arms extended across the aisle.

Bill landed the plane with a solid thump. When I got up to open the cabin door, the man and woman still held hands. Their wet faces reminded me of divers who had just surfaced with their treasure.

I opened the door to the noise of a celebration. The couple's grandchildren surrounded them, and a young girl clung to her grandmother's side during the long embraces. Amazed, the husband and wife spoke quickly, describing when they realized they weren't in Florida. The silver-haired man helped us with the luggage and clubs, gave instructions to the van driver and then insisted that Bill and I stand in front of the Citation for a picture.

Across the ramp, another one of our planes had carried in relatives from the Southwest. The pilots approached me with sheepish grins—a pair of half-hearted party crashers. The older one shook his head and launched into a tirade against the company, oblivious of the moment at hand. Then the younger pilot said, "They've been working us like dogs. How about you? Are you finished here?"

"I think so," I said.

"Well, we've got to ferry over to White Plains. Dispatch has to make sure they work us our fourteen hours." He looked around and said, "Ain't it great to have money?"

"Ain't it great to have love," I added.

* * *

From my hotel room, I watched a ferryboat return from the islands. At the close of this day I couldn't imagine being anywhere else, even in my own home. I laughed as I unpacked my clothes. The day had gently wrung out my soul. My skin was warm and dry, and I felt as though I could look into the heart of any day of my life.

19

COMMAND AUTHORITY

I HAD A vacation after the flight into Rockland, Maine, and my new captain was on standard rotation, just off a four-day break. I hadn't flown in three weeks, so we took extra time pre-flighting before launching our first flight of the day. Late thirties, sandy-haired and handsome, Steve said, "I know when I come back from vacation I always miss something obvious, like forgetting to lock the baggage door. Let's take it slow."

That afternoon after we ferried into St. Louis, I was unpacking at the hotel, reviewing my progress since earning my private pilot's license fifteen years ago. My upgrade to captain in the Citation was only a few months away.

From my hotel room overlooking Lambert Field, I was thinking of the pilots who had influenced me. It had been their humor, their insight that lightly tapped the back of my hand as I moved the throttles forward, a tap of confidence, a playful nudge to move forward on the loneliest of nights.

I had a perfect view of the airport. Airliners and corporate jets took the runway, each producing a roar on takeoff that paid tribute to thunder and hurricane winds. I thought of Frank Corbi, who flew as maintenance chief on the early jet aircraft. He once told me how the other mechanics begged him to explain over and over again what it was like, how jet aircraft were different from the piston ships of the first five decades of flight. Smooth, he would say. The way you fly in a dream.

The next morning, Steve and I flew two passengers into Oklahoma City, about five hundred miles farther west.

* * *

"It has to do with command authority," Steve said. "Right now you're doing the greater part of the work, and doing a good job. Hold on a second. I'll be right back." Steve went into his room and came out with a couple of chairs.

I had waited patiently the entire day to hear Steve's thoughts on upgrading to captain. Before we sat down I leaned over the balcony and imagined a herd of buffalo trotting down the four-lane highway. Somewhere in the northern part of Oklahoma, the officials had released about a thousand buffaloes to roam the prairie.

We were on the second floor balcony at dusk, outside Oklahoma City. Several miles from the hotel, slow-moving airliners made their approaches under clear skies and calm winds.

Steve sat then swung his legs onto the balcony rail. "It's simple—I carry all the responsibility." He brushed a strand of hair from his eyes. "Everything good or bad goes directly to me and then filters to the copilot. It isn't a situation of equality. Think of all the extra work you do—flight planning, taking care of the passengers, cleaning the interior of the airplane."

"I don't mind any of that."

"That's good. But that's just the groundwork, and you've got it. Now it's time to oversee an entire flight. That's the command authority I'm talking about. You've got to start playing more at being captain. When you're flying, direct me to do whatever needs done. Sometimes, when you're in the left seat, you reach over to dial in a frequency or look up a power setting. Have me do it. Sometimes I think you're flying single-pilot again."

"It's the check runs—a lot of internal stuff, like setting up my own procedures in that nasty old twin I flew."

"Well, start to see the pressure from the outside. The pressure acts on us from the outside; it's steady and it never lets up. That's why I get paid more and get to wear that extra stripe on my sleeve. As copilot, you're playacting, playing at captain when you're flying. Act the part, and the upgrade will come much easier. There're headaches every day with passengers, delays, calls from the chief pilot when things start to crumble. That's why I delegate so much work to you. I get the brunt of all the weirdness when things don't go smoothly. You can get into trouble, but unless it's something big, the punch grazes you but catches me right in the chops."

Steve continued, "You never operated as a two-man crew until now. Ninety percent of your flying has been alone—Mr. Solo. You flew for a company that trusted you implicitly; you made all the decisions, did all the flying. A totally different climate. When you work a two-man crew, the label of captain has a bigger responsibility. What you do reaches back through a set of procedures that are more formal than a single-pilot operation. There's a different set of traditions."

I thought about my early years of commercial flying from Sal's Comanche to Corbi's twin. And night check-flying was equivalent to the Pony Express: one pilot, one airplane and a ferocious timetable to be met, passing the bags of checks to the courier or to the next pilot. Other than a six-month check ride, I was alone, grading my performance, always practicing and trying to perfect my skills.

An airliner turning final approach flashed a red position light and smoothly began its descent. Steve watched for a moment then started a story.

"I had a friend, years ago. This guy upgraded to captain but never really filled the job." Steve lowered his head and brushed a few ashes off his shirt. "He was a great person, one of these people everyone likes. But a strong copilot could walk all over him."

Steve watched the flow of airline traffic as he spoke and put out his cigarette in the glass ashtray he balanced on his stomach. "A lot of the pilots at my old job came in through a merger. Some of these guys were merciless. I told this friend to watch out, put some distance between himself and those jackals, take command whether they liked it or not. His easy manner continued, and it finally killed him."

"An airplane accident?"

"No. He was using an electric drill at home, for the first time;

thinking he was some kind of electrician and hit a two-twenty line. He died instantly."

Steve's face relaxed. It seemed as though he was finished with his story. He started smacking another cigarette out of the pack.

"A few days after this, all the pilots received a mimeographed picture of an electric drill in their boxes. And that wasn't the end of it." Steve's eyes were riveted on another chunk of smooth aluminum gliding toward the runway. "A few weeks after his death, his wife received a book in the mail—Bob Vila's *Basic Wiring*."

"Incredible!"

"We knew the guy. But the company did nothing."

"Someone catch up to him on a dark street? You know the saying? 'He needed killing.' "

"Nothing like that. About a year after the incident, he was taxiing out to the runway and had a complete seizure."

"The first one?"

"Yeah, lost his medical and never flew again."

20

MECCA OF THE AMERICAS

"TAKE A CAMERA," Frank had said during a brief phone call, shortly before my first trip to Mexico. "Nobody around here gets a chance to see much of the world." He paused and then said, "You'll be thankful to get back home, of course. But while you're out there, pay attention. There's a lot to see."

I stuck my camera out the back window of the cab. I was attempting to devour the buildings, the alleyways, the faces of Mexico City. Carl, my captain, ignored the clogged streets and dark faces. He asked Angelo, our driver, if there was somewhere we could pick up something cold to drink.

We were on a main thoroughfare crawling with taxicabs and hundreds of VW Bugs. Angelo assured Carl we'd find a corner stand soon. Men and young children approached us selling everything from cigarettes to wiper blades and furniture. The car next to us was getting a wash. When it had to move a few more feet, several boys followed with buckets of water to rinse off the soap.

In the States, a traffic jam like this would have been full of angry faces and blaring horns, but these motorists exhibited a strange calm. Angelo smiled and pointed to an old church slowly sinking into the soggy ground of the ancient lake this city was built on.

"Where can we stretch our legs? Look around?" Carl asked as he fidgeted with the door handle.

"At the National Palace, you get out and I wait. They sell cola there."

Angelo already had our twenty-five bucks for the tour, and I mused over the prospect of being stranded in a foreign city of eighteen million people.

I spotted a man going from car to car, knocking on windows. He carried a plastic jug and some kind of small stick.

"Angelo, what's this guy trying to sell?"

"He's a fire-eater. Pay him. He swallows fire, right before your eyes."

"Damn, won't he get arrested for that?" Carl pulled his chin close to his chest, protecting his throat.

Angelo shrugged. "That is how that man makes a living. Is bad for his health, so the authorities tell people don't pay him for his services. Maybe he finds different work. But nobody put him in jail for trying to live."

Carl tightened his chin against his neck. Trips to Mexico were a nuisance for him, and he detested having to deal with U.S. Customs on the return flight. He asked if every day was this hazy. Angelo laughed, saying it wasn't haze, but a fine dust that prevented the Virgin's supernatural beauty from blinding her beloved people.

Angelo parked the car along the curb. "The Square of the Three Cultures. And those boys, they sell Pepsi." He rattled off the different cultures present, and I thought he referred to the third one as Modern Bucko.

Carl seemed no happier out of the car. In his short-sleeved shirt, his muscular arms were tense, anticipating conflict. His blue eyes searched for a glimpse of his own land. A skinny teen sold us Pepsi in bottles. Carl took a swig, stared at the bottle and grimaced. The ritual failed to make him "feel at home."

I talked rapidly, excited about being dropped into the thick of another culture as we wandered about the enormous plaza of the National Palace. But Carl just shrugged his shoulders and kept turning his head to keep Angelo in sight. I had never seen him so reluctant to explore a new place.

When we returned to the car, Angelo said he was taking us

to his favorite sight—the shrine of the Virgin of Guadalupe. We argued that the extra time and distance might get us in trouble if dispatch needed to pull us out of Mexico City. Our arguments were useless against Angelo's excitement.

The flower-filled median was the runway leading to the temple of the Virgin. I sensed that we were being pulled into Mexico's magic center. Mary was in reach of millions of Mexicans; every shameful life, every unforgivable sin could be cleansed at this Mecca of the Americas. Angelo remained with the car as Carl and I headed up the steps to the Virgin's home.

An endless parade of people climbed the steps with us. Some groups of poor Mexicans were stalled out. They passed bits of food amongst themselves, took pictures or simply conversed. One family led an old man up the steps.

Inside the church, my hunger to devour the images of past and present was insatiable. Shamelessly, I took pictures while Carl stood guard near the entrance. I was in a high-ceilinged cave with old people materializing out of dark niches. The altar was cluttered with gold and candles; the cloth that had been marked by the miracle was stretched above it. When the priest began communion, a young woman knelt before him, cradling a massive bouquet of flowers. Finally Carl grabbed my arm, saying it was time to leave.

Outside, he asked me to take his picture. He didn't smile but had the look of a man who sees the barbarians piled against the garage door while his wife wonders why the electric door motor screams without working.

Neither of us said much to Angelo on the way back to the hotel. The fever broke, and I had run out of film. I was sure Frank would tell me to be better prepared next time. Passing Alameda Park, I watched two lovers huddled on a bench, encircled by screaming children in the midst of some game.

"We must be entering the Pink Zone," I said to Carl a few minutes later. The Pink Zone was Mexico City's version of Rodeo Drive. The armed guards leaned in doorways with pump shotguns or slowly paced in front of businesses with drawn Uzis.

"These fellas are serious about their business," Carl said.

I didn't say anything. But Carl's remark made me wonder if we still had such men to protect our "pink zone" with such ferocity.

* * *

The Spaniard had married glamour to the Indian face of hard angles and obsidian eyes. Angelo was genetically grown from the same Spanish-Indian forest, but he was too lighthearted to pose mysterious and macho in front of a jewelry store with a machine gun. The world was transparent from his perspective. He was captain of his clean old cab, the Virgin his consort. When he laughed, the heat of millions of people cooled into fog and beautiful shadows.

We met at seven o'clock for dinner in the hotel's restaurant. As Carl approached the table, his eyes shot past me to someone walking toward us. Earlier at the front desk checking in, we had run into an American, a pilot that he knew. Carl wasn't anxious to talk, made some excuse, then referred to the man as a "real strange bird" once we were on the street.

"It's Gary," Carl said, "the guy from this morning."

We exchanged greetings, and Gary sat down and lit a cigarette. Gary's neck and face grew red, anticipating the nicotine and story he was itching to tell.

"Carl, these people are brutal. Someday they'll squash us like an overripe fruit."

Carl registered one emotion with his eyes and another with his mouth—amusement tempered by revulsion.

"Jesus, Gary, you gotta get into it right away? Can't you tell us something simple, like, where you're flying to next, have things been slow, busy?"

"When I'm in a place like this, the only thing that matters is to watch these folks. They have vitality, patience. They're the enemy."

Gary's neck was swollen and red. He inhaled into his neck where it seemed another pair of lungs had taken root. I expected him to sprout gills. But he smiled as he scanned the menu. "I suggest the T-bone steak." He looked at me and winked. "Make sure this stud doesn't fly you into a volcano."

Carl mentioned the airlines hiring again, but Gary ignored him. Gary was a scout. He traveled alone. He smelled treachery, armies massing on the border, new plagues, the advance of killer bees. His tan sport jacket was wrinkled and dirty.

"I was at Chicago Midway and this Lear salesman was prowling around, trying to get the operator to trade in his old Lear 23 for a new 35."

"EJA sold off the Lear 23s by the early seventies," I said. "They stuck with the 25 and 35 series for their better handling and range."

Gary eyed me, amazed that I'd interrupt him. He continued, speaking directly to Carl.

"I heard he had been hanging around for days, chain-smoking with a severe look. Then I realized he was out to grab all those old 23s. Most of them had crashed—nearly fifty percent. The company wanted to pick up, buy, steal every Lear 23 and bury them in the desert. And this salesman wasn't just fighting the operator, but the ghost of Bill Lear who loved that first aircraft. Bill traveled at his side, losing his room key or changing the dials on his traveling alarm clock."

"Well, that was a lot of airplane for guys coming out of piston twins," Carl said.

"Lear wanted it that way. He wanted people to ride in a slice of his own imagination. And that's a dangerous place."

"Well, that's enough of that. Gary, when do you leave Mexico City?"

"Thursday. I wish I had something to drop on these people. Maybe a neutron bomb. I'd wait for the dust to settle then come back to this hotel. I like it here."

"Jesus, you're too much." Carl managed a smile. He appreciated the thought of dropping things on certain people.

Neither Gary nor Carl ate much. Carl ate slowly, almost in reverence. Gary stabbed at the meat, more for dramatic effect than for sustenance. My steak was delicious. I expected a steak to taste great in Wyoming, not in Mexico City.

Outside our window, an Indian girl, perhaps seven, dangled a large wooden puppet from her small hands. She moved the puppet's arms and legs to arouse interest in the people walking past. No adult accompanied her. Gary watched her and found his last foothold.

"They'll never evict that kid from this spot. Even though this is their Park Avenue, every hustler, including this kid, will always be outside our window. The day they give her the bum's rush is the day there'll be a revolution."

A few minutes later, Gary left our table. We watched him corner the manager and a table of customers like they were a bunch
of old friends.

"You know, this place brings out weird notions in people like
Gary. He's all right. But this place has a mood—something I'll
never be able to figure out." He paused and stared at his empty
plate. The same tension from our afternoon walk gripped him.

The next day our flight wasn't scheduled for departure out
of Mexico City until late morning, so I let dispatch know that I'd
be leaving the hotel for a walk. I left the camera in the room and
walked among the rich and poor, the ugly and the godlike. Of all
the emotions manifested, self-pity was absent. Someone could
have died right in front of me without a scintilla of regret for
themselves.

I turned the corner and came upon a man and woman lying on
the sidewalk near the curb. Hundreds of people passed in a matter
of minutes, yet no crowd gathered to taunt the sleeping couple,
nor did the authorities show any interest. As I approached, I noticed that they were sprawled out on a large piece of cardboard.
They were dressed in black—the woman in a formal evening gown
and the man in a tuxedo. A film of dust ran the length of the man's
jacket sleeve. They were young and attractive, of the world, but
not a part of it. Those of us passing took short glances.

In the lovers' dream, the streets of Mexico City were fuller
than any of us could have imagined.

* * *

By early afternoon we had landed at a desolate airport with
our single passenger. At that time I had only been to Cancun
and Mexico City, both having modern facilities, long runways
and taxiways. Here, at this border town along the Rio Grande,
the narrow runway had no parallel taxiway, so we had to swing
around a hundred and eighty degrees and hurry down to a ramp
area with just enough room to get turned around and hopefully
not blow down the small wooden building.

There was no telephone, no services, just a shack with a couple of chairs. The guy that greeted us said we could get a ride into

town, something to eat. My God, what a place—we had made a lonely moon landing, and there was no one to applaud us.

The guy took us into town in an old pickup truck. I've never seen such poverty. He pointed out a place to eat, but I just told him to keep driving; I didn't want to step out of the truck. Animals were wandering in and out of shacks, kids playing naked in the streets. I was reminded how good we have it.

We sat back at the airport for hours. No AC, hot as hell and the two of us sitting in this shack on the only two chairs. Baking, drifting off, I heard a commotion—cars, horns—it sounded like a hundred radios tuned to a hundred different stations. Carl jumped and ran outside. I looked out the hole in the wall where a window used to be, and hundreds of Mexicans were converging on the airport in cars and trucks, with women, children, goats, dogs in tow. We both went straight for the airplane.

They started driving up and down the runway, banging into each other, sometimes three cars abreast. Somebody set up a generator and pretty soon we were hearing mariachi music blasted over large speakers.

A car race?

For the next three hours, they ran up and down the runway passing bottles of tequila from car to car. I thought of the NASCAR drivers we occasionally flew. Were their promoters aware of this untapped market? It was a miracle no one was run over. Some drivers loaded up their junkers with as many people as they could fit. I saw guys jumping from one moving truck to another.

Luckily, the Virgin is their patron saint—a brown-skinned Virgin with a cluster of stars arched over her head and the loveliest of smiles.

When the passenger arrived, we had to clear the runway. We got in the truck and began driving up and down it, yelling for the people to clear out. Our passenger didn't seem to mind the delay. He said to take our time—he was in no hurry. Christ, some people. I guess with a lot of money, you lose your nose for certain kinds of danger. But what a mess—pieces of transmissions, nuts and bolts all over the place—it had to be cleaned. We couldn't take off with all that shit cluttering the runway. The airport manager and the two of us spent an hour throwing stuff off to the side. The cars had been disintegrating for hours. We walked the five-thousand-foot strip until it was clean. Then the Mexicans set up another party-on-wheels, a quarter mile away in an unpaved parking lot. You could hear them screaming and banging into each other, and the dust cloud they created made it almost impossible to breathe. Our passenger just sat outside the shack and went over some of his notes. I don't know, maybe he was going to buy the place.

A lot of partiers returned when they saw we were getting ready to go. Carl had the storm window open, and it became spooky quiet once the cabin door was shut. The mariachi music was still blasting, but the Mexicans had really quieted down. Then, as soon as Carl started the right engine, they started screaming and cheering.

I couldn't hear them anymore after the left engine started, but I could see from their faces and their arms going crazy that they were cheering like we had won the World Series!

The passenger was getting a kick out of all this and asked us if we'd make a low pass after takeoff. We started down the runway with hundreds of cheering Mexicans on either side. Carl had to make a short-field takeoff in order to clear the speakers at the end of the runway. We came back around, made the low pass and finally headed home.

A few minutes later, climbing to only six thousand feet for our short flight to clear customs in Laredo, I contacted Houston air traffic control and got our clearance. Carl leaned against the head rest, breathing a long sigh. He turned to me and studied my face for a moment, saying, "I've never seen people so excited over nothing."

21

GOD IN THE TREES

THE DUAL TV sets positioned at opposite ends of the empty bar were off. A radio station, piped through hidden speakers, was now playing Andy Williams's "Moon River." Earlier, on the phone, Alan mentioned that he had helped his dad set up a new stereo system in his office. Frank had christened the new technology by playing Big Band CDs all morning. Alan said his dad had a little story for each song, remembering the airplane he was assigned to or an outing with his young wife. Although the Beatles monopolized my teen years, I enjoyed a lot of the same music Frank did. The deepest-felt tunes were the standards I had grown up with, especially Sinatra.

The waitress approached with the coffeepot.

"Are you going somewhere exciting?" she asked, sliding the cup and saucer closer to herself as I strained to hear the last verse of "Moon River."

"My captain says everywhere we go is exciting," I answered, letting go of the tune.

Her body was a flesh remake of a Venus figurine—all hips and breasts. Her giggle was a long vibration originating in the bones, and her smooth, oval face remained serene.

"I'd like to travel. See new places." She poured the coffee and left room for cream.

"You'd find it exciting for about a year. Then you'd start dreaming what most pilots dream about—living right above their business."

"I know, I know, the 'grass is greener' stuff. I'd still love to try it. My grandfather traveled a lot after the war, out west—a bunch of different jobs, mostly on ranches, until he met my grandma in Albuquerque. He sure made an impression on me. Wow," she said, with a lot of feeling. "He's been gone a long time. But I got his stories." She grabbed a few dirty dishes from the vacant table next to me, and before she headed for the kitchen, added, "He liked his back porch too."

I almost called to her, but she had disappeared. My common-sense rap felt paltry against this young woman's desire to follow her own dreams, encouraged by her grandfather's stories. Why shouldn't she have the spirit-wise lyrics of Johnny Mercer and Henry Mancini's diamond-soul melody "Moon River" to inspire her?

I sighed. Maybe she too had caught some of the song's beautiful words about "dream makers" and "heartbreakers." And the fabulous second verse—*Two drifters, off to see the world, there's such a lot of world, to see ....*

No other tune played after "Moon River." The faded music left a deep quiet in the room until the cook walked out, grabbed the remote, aimed and the televisions lit up with news from the PGA tournament. I took a sip of coffee, shook my head, tempted to unplug the boxes.

When the TV narrator mentioned a pro golfer whom I sometimes flew, I turned my attention to the program. His face filled the screen. The waitress came out from the kitchen, drying a glass, watching as well. The pro talked about Harvey Penick, a golf legend who died shortly before the young golfer had won the Masters. He spoke of Penick as a friend, mentor and a second father. "When you know good people, it's hard to go wrong. When you know the best, well, that's the finest." He read Penick's own words on the game. I missed some of it. But what I heard were phrases like, "The golf course is holy ground. The sense of God in the trees. It was home."

The waitress and I looked at each other, exchanging smiles. Both of us had found a little corner of holy ground that morning.

22

DC-3

WAITING FOR OUR passengers at the Louisville airport on a pleasant summer afternoon, I decided to get outside and walk the tarmac. I had hit the books on company and Federal regulations for an hour inside the pilot lounge and needed a breather. Like Steve had emphasized in Oklahoma City, the culture at Executive Jet Aviation stressed the upgrade, the promotion to captain. There were no "professional" copilots. Everyone was expected to think and act as a captain from their first day on the flight line.

On the ramp sat a DC-3 in fair condition, marked with blemishes, smudges of oil and dents. A large plastic bucket caught an oil leak from the left engine, and its bulbous nose pointed skyward. One of our captains and an FAA examiner I knew had flown the "Hump"—a treacherous route over the Himalayas from the Assam Valley in Northeastern India to the Yunnan province in Southwestern China— during World War II, carrying supplies to the Flying Tigers and the forces of Chiang Kai-shek. Both men had told stories of a slow, warm-blooded plane constantly dogged by violent storms over the mountains and Japanese fighters. Today, DC-3s that dropped paratroopers on D-Day are still flying.

From a pilot's perspective, the DC-3 generated romance and adventure with its strong wing, big radial engines and tail-dragger configuration, sitting on its tail with its dolphin nose pointed at the sky. Even though the DC-3 flew in both World War II and Vietnam, it didn't look like a war bird. It was like our citizen soldiers in the European and Pacific theatres—strong, humble, yet ready to serve. While Frank worked on staying alive in Cabanatuan in the Philippines, the DC-3 delivered supplies and troops all around the world.

This old DC-3 taxied out of the pages of an aerodynamics book, the perfect aircraft to demonstrate the lifting force with its long fat wing. The radial engines that pulled the ship through the air massaged the entire airframe, renewing its molecular strength and flexibility. Unpressurized, it remained close to the planet, touching each foreign mile with its shadow. It was an airplane resting under the great tree of Newtonian physics.

I circled the DC-3 a couple of times and resumed my walk, making a beeline for the aircraft I flew—a Cessna Citation. Unlike most jets, it had a straight wing and a rounded nose where two pitot tubes for airspeed measurement protruded like catfish whiskers. It was the antithesis of the predatory, sleek and fast Learjet. The Lear's swept wing outperformed the Citation wing—less drag therefore more speed. But the straight wing gave the Citation better handling characteristics, adding to its friendly, inviting look, like the DC-3.

I walked around the Citation, admiring it, reviewing its performance, and my heart quickened, seeing myself soon climbing into the captain's seat.

23

LONG NIGHT

AT LAGUARDIA AIRPORT, general-aviation aircraft were parked at a remote site named Five Towers. I was getting ready to go to the plane with coffee and ice and pick up the clearance when the girl at the front desk said the authorities had just closed the airport to all departures and arrivals and had shutdown access to our parked aircraft. All she knew was that a plane had gone off the runway.

Rod, my captain, asked about getting out to the ramp later that evening and securing the aircraft for overnight. She had been told there'd be limited access by the third shift, near eleven. He called the company and we learned that a DC-9 had skidded off the runway and was hanging off the pier, partly in the water. No one knew if there were fatalities or injuries. I watched Rod lower his head in a silent prayer for those onboard the airliner.

With normal operations shut down for hours, we decided to leave the airport and get something to eat.

We bundled up in our London Fogs and stocking caps and left the Marine terminal. The parking lot and road leading in were crammed with cars, taxis and buses. We saw a group of people running across the tarmac, shouting back and forth, a wild hunt for the downed aircraft. We saw emergency vehicles racing erratically, lights blazing, seemingly as befuddled and directionless as the thrill seekers.

A man and woman flew past us, and the man noticed our uniforms. Still running, he yelled back that the pilots had left the scene of the crash. "No one knows anything," Rod countered, shaking his head at the man's blood-in-the-water excitement. A cold rain fell, and I buttoned the front of my coat. Once off the airport property, a heavy downpour made us duck inside a bank doorway. When it let up, we ran the last two blocks bursting into the restaurant and nearly running over an elderly couple. Pointing to an available table, our waiter announced, "Captain goes down with the ship!" I wasn't sure if this was a statement of principle or eagerness to hear bad news.

Rod said to me, "Maybe the crew finally slammed up against their max operating speed; hit their personal *Vmo*." He gave me plenty to think about.

Vmo was a technical term for the max operating speed of a jet aircraft. This was the first time I had heard someone use it for the pilot. I began thinking about my own limitations, especially with my upgrade approaching soon. Inside the restaurant I attempted to dry my head with a cloth napkin, trying to raise my flattened hair with my fingers.

They could only have been going one hundred plus when they decided to abort, but Rod said it didn't matter, that the takeoff speed was part of that *Vmo* envelope, and that every phase of flight happens at a higher speed. After a couple of years of flying jets, I felt comfortable with the speed envelope. But there was the next plane, something larger and faster that might shove me outside my personal max operating speed. I thought of my Uncle Gus's *Vmo* of approximately one hundred and twenty miles per hour. His speed brought him delight, adventure and friendship. Yet I knew miserable jet pilots who despised their work and couldn't get a mangy dog to accompany them to dinner.

Rod said the problem was when the pilot's *Vmo* didn't match the airplane's. "A pilot can fly a two-hundred-mile-per-hour airplane like a champ. But put him in a small jet doing four-hundred-plus, and the airplane eats him alive: navigation, communications, letting down in a busy terminal area and still having to fly the airplane!"

I thought of Tom Cole's comfort, his mastery of flying at cruise speeds well below that of jets. And Tom never had to work in a two-pilot setting. He sat alone at the controls.

"And it's not just speed," Rod continued. "Sometimes it's moving from the right seat to the captain's side. Everything comes at you faster when you take on greater responsibility."

The waiter returned with the menus and recited the list of specials. He lingered for a moment, forlorn, searching our faces for some lead to bring up the accident, perhaps wishing to join the crowd racing toward the tragedy.

"Hey, Bud," Rod said. "You're going to lose your cigarettes." The waiter pushed the cigarette pack deeper into his pants pocket.

"My name is Amandi." He recited his name slowly. It was clear he didn't like being called Bud. "Amandi hears from radio that someone dies in the water."

"Well, it's going to be a long night," Rod said.

"Sort of like an election—the news dribbling in over the hours." I handed the menu back, ordering a giant burger and a salad.

"You know, Amandi, this menu reads like a list of temptations from the Old Testament," Rod said, and the waiter grinned at hearing his name. He shouted at the cook as he walked away.

"Long night. Many die."

* * *

Back at LaGuardia's marine terminal, Rod and I were confronted with survivors wrapped in blankets, media foot soldiers and scuba divers who walked about bare-chested, their rubber suits peeled down to their waists.

Rod found a vacant couch in the pilot's lounge, and I wandered through the rotunda, where an enormous mural depicted man's dream of flight. One of the images resembled Icarus. But this Icarus looked successful for the moment, unaware of his fate.

I stood next to a newscaster and listened to him prepare for a live broadcast. His voice was nondescript. When it came time to perform via the phone lines, a deep, smooth voice with perfect diction wrapped itself around New York City. After his two-minute spot, he dropped his radio voice and began talking with some crony at the station. "Hey, you're not going to believe this. The half-dozen people missing—they're not in the river, they got out of the wreck and walked off the airport ... Hell, fast enough that no one saw them leave ... That's right, they never talked to anyone ... hailed a cab or called someone in their family to pick them up. And the guy that died didn't drown ... Probably a heart attack. They couldn't get to him fast enough."

24

THE WHITE BOX

IT WAS THE week between Christmas and New Year's. Our ground-school instructor at Flight Safety in Toledo was over sixty and within months of retirement. He closed the classroom door and began a litany of his life's sorrows. There were only two of us in his class, and I wondered which of us had the power of absolution. He talked of physical ailments that might send him out of the room without notice. Then, there was the story of the good son and the bad son, and how the company had been beating him up, coercing him into working the holidays.

He capped his tribulations with an explanation of his terrible skin condition. After World War II, he had been assigned to fly a four-engine transport through the top of a mushroom cloud. This was the atomic testing at Bikini Atoll in the Marshall Islands. His plane had been lined with lead shields. "We didn't know any better. They told us the shields would protect us from the radiation. There was little physical sensation other than some turbulence." At the end of his testimony, he sent us on a ten-minute coffee break.

I was anxious to begin the instruction for my type rating and upgrade to captain in the Citation S-II. The company had knocked a day off the normal training schedule, expecting us to finish all the ground and flight-simulator training in less than seven days.

I looked at Greg. "Do you think we'll finish in time?"

Greg had a habit of pushing his glasses back to the bridge of his nose before he spoke. "The way I see it, we're going to have to direct this guy minute by minute. It's a good thing we don't have him for the simulator. He's so easily distracted, we may be here until he retires."

Greg and I had flown together over the past several years. With his thinning blond hair, glasses and prominent belly, he was an unlikely model for jet jock of the month. But his quick instincts and flair for piloting a high-performance aircraft were undisputed. As '93 came to an end, I was glad to be finishing the year and upgrade with him.

By the second day, we were on track. Greg and I knew the material well enough that the instructor only had to skim over each aircraft system. He finished each lesson with a few more personal anecdotes that we ignored. On the third day we began our simulator training with a different instructor. After flying the Citation straight-winged jet for two years, I was now to get my type rating in a several-million-dollar flight simulator. The type rating would give me the credentials to act as a pilot-in-command. I looked at the sealed white box sitting atop long hydraulic arms, wishing that all of this could have been accomplished in the actual airplane.

An array of hoses and cylinders rested on the floor beneath the white box. Our sim instructor pushed a button, and the bridge lowered, connecting to the catwalk. A rope ladder on the simulator was added in case the drawbridge broke.

Greg pointed at the coiled-up rope ladder. "Aren't you worried about pirates, especially over the Caribbean?"

The young instructor smiled, saying, "Sharks are a problem too."

The catwalk encircled the windowless box. In the first small room, the instructor sat behind the pilots at a state-of-the-art console. There, he created the parameters for normal and emergency flight conditions. Other than his instruction, or playacting as an air traffic controller, we paid little attention to him, pretending we were in the actual jet, suspending disbelief.

The cockpit replicated perfectly the cockpit of the Citation

S-II that I had been flying. However, the dark windscreen reminded me that I was to be interred in an electronic tomb for the next four hours.

Greg had previous simulator time and suggested that I take the left seat for the first session. When the power was applied, the windscreen presented a ghostlike tarmac with a large hangar off to my right. The instructor emphasized this was to be a simple lesson to get the *feel* of the simulator without any emergencies thrown at us. "We'll go up to fifteen thousand, try some steep turns, then come back and shoot a few approaches and landings," he said.

The throttles and switches moved and clicked normally as I fired up the engines and watched the gauges come to life. I was cleared to taxi to Runway 20. Initially, the plane moved fine when power was added to overcome the make-believe inertia. But when I attempted to turn, the unreal response of the rudders became noticeable. I was steering for a taxiway off my left when I careened into the fake grass of the simulator world. I complained to the instructor, and he magically transported me to the beginning of the runway. I now peered down its full length into a clear night. Anxiously, I awaited takeoff clearance while overhead the position lights of other aircraft moved in real time.

I overcontrolled the sim during the takeoff roll and at rotation pitched the nose too high and wallowed close to the stall. A full stall was that precipitous moment in flight when the string was cut, the lifting force of the wings evaporated and the aircraft returned to the earth like an old Buick dropped off a cliff.

The instructor poked his head between the seats. "Don't worry. No surprises today. You've got her under control."

My rate of climb ranged from a couple hundred feet a minute to over two thousand. Power had been set but I couldn't seem to control the pitch attitude (nose up-and-down movement).

At dinner that night, I complained a lot and ate little. "Greg, I'm wondering if I need a career change."

"Everyone gets beat the first time by the sim," Greg said, cutting into a large steak with easy, fluid strokes.

"I used all of my energy to complete a couple of steep turns. Tomorrow, emergencies start getting thrown at us. I'll be exhausted in twenty minutes."

"You're not flying the airplane. This is a game—a game with all the potential screwups we could never practice in the real world. Slow down a bit, use the autopilot more often until you get settled."

"But it's in that unreal world that I'll pass or bust my check ride."

Greg ignored this, pushed his glasses toward the bridge of his nose and continued to speak disparagingly of his initial performance in other flight simulators. It was difficult to imagine him performing poorly.

My steak arrived a few minutes after the waitress had brought Greg's. It was overcooked and tough. I looked again at Greg's juicy steak and asked him what he ordered.

"A filet. Always go with the highest grade. I haven't eaten a bad steak in years."

He wiped the corner of his mouth with his napkin and set his fork down. He held on to the knife.

"It's all about corrections," he said, pointing the blade at me before laying it down. "We're constantly making corrections in flight. The sim as well, just different pressure, degrees of movement. But whether it's the sim or the plane, you're picking up a wing when turbulence drops it or making small changes in power and pitch as you roll down an electronic glide slope through rain and fog, real world or sim world."

He leaned forward.

"What's dangerous in the real world is becoming complacent, being too comfortable, and then having to overcorrect. *That* gets us into trouble. If I'm exhausted after hours of flying with demanding passengers, and I'm slow in picking up the localizer, I'll find myself banking roughly to align the aircraft with the runway centerline and maybe cross into the flight path of another plane."

Greg eyed my tough-looking steak and shook his head.

"If I don't scan the menu, look at the specials, I could end up eating another lousy meal. And if I fail to inspect the catering order, my passengers might end up eating *their* in-flight meal without utensils. Believe me, awareness is a fast-moving stream of small corrections."

As the hours passed in the simulator, I became more adept. One evening I remembered my days as a student pilot. After a flight lesson full of mistakes, I would walk to my car crestfallen, not knowing if I had the strength to continue my instruction. Watching the planes take off and land, I thought of ways to tackle a problem, tracing a maneuver in my mind, imagining the necessary pressure and smoothness to execute it properly. Then I would go back and rent the plane for another thirty minutes or an hour. Other times, I was almost home when I would turn the car around and head back to the Chagrin Falls Airport for more practice.

Greg and the instructor had an intimate relationship with the white box: They acted as a pair of friendly spirits sent to help me understand her mysteries. While in the right seat, Greg performed his copilot tasks with ease. "You'll see, after the steep turns it'll all come together. Make me work for you."

Passing through ten thousand feet, I was able to stabilize the rate of climb at fifteen hundred feet per minute. At fifteen thousand feet, I attempted to hold my altitude with little jabs of the control wheel. I didn't fly an airplane in this manner and disliked a contraption that required such obvious mechanical inputs. All flight control movements in a real airplane were accomplished with pressure, rather than a mechanical motion. In order to maintain altitude throughout a steep turn, it was necessary for the pilot to apply extra back pressure on the control wheel when banking more than thirty degrees. The sensation, under real conditions, was a pressure (G forces) that pushed the pilot against his seat. I felt no pressure while banking the white box. By forty-five degrees of bank, I started losing altitude rapidly. I overcompensated, began to climb and leaped through fifteen thousand feet. I struggled to get back to altitude. Greg suggested keeping the miniature airplane on the attitude gyro a few degrees above the horizon. The trick worked. Later, when it was Greg's turn to fly, I watched him effortlessly command the simulator through several steep banks. His physical movement was barely perceptible. His corrections were smooth and immediate.

* * *

By the time of my test, I had uncovered the old secret of dispassion. When I stumbled in a maneuver, I quickly recovered, made the correction, and checked my feelings of anger and doom. Greg used the maxim "Don't look back" in order to maintain energy and trim the emotions.

I passed the check ride and received my first type rating, allowing the move to the left seat—the captain's seat.

25

SURPRISE ATTACK

TWO WEEKS LATER I was ferrying the Citation S-II for my first flight as captain. Adding to my butterflies was a problem-child first officer who was difficult to work with and close to losing his job.

We ferried from Dayton, Ohio, to Lakeland, Florida. We were picking up five people in Lakeland and carrying them to Miami, returning to Lakeland by eleven that same night. Except for the slight chance of a scattered thunderstorm or rain shower, the weather forecast was good. I was familiar with both airports.

We escaped the frigid temperatures in Ohio and found Florida in the low eighties. My *difficult* copilot cooperated with every instruction, acting professional and demonstrating skill in his radio and navigational work. The two of us talked little once we began the flight. I concluded he was aware of his uncertain position with the company.

En route, I contrasted the days spent in simulator training with the actual ship. The true link between virtual reality and the folklore-soaked hills of the Appalachians that I presently flew over had been the emergency training. I looked at the engine-fire switch that might never illuminate, grateful for the chance to bring the throttle back to idle, push the red switch and fire the extinguisher bottles in the white box. Just getting the sensory feel of a thrust reverser deployed in flight, especially after takeoff, was invaluable.

Greg had been right: The unreal conditions had delivered slices of reality one could never practice in the real airplane. The few emergency conditions in flying that required an immediate response were practiced repeatedly in the simulator. Most in-flight problems demanded an unhurried reading of the checklist, a simple command-and-response between the pilots and a dose of common sense.

On the ramp at Lakeland, everything went smoothly. Within thirty minutes we were set to go. I even remembered to make sure the catered meals came with plastic forks and knives.

Lakeland was a small airport with a control tower. An active control tower allowed us to pick up our clearance before taxiing, enabling us to come under radar coverage immediately after take-off. Another advantage of a control tower was the regulation of traffic on the ground and in the immediate vicinity of the airport.

Since we were to have a few hours on the ground at Miami, I called my friend Carol, who lived in South Beach. I gave her the ETA into Miami.

I was in the plane when our passengers arrived, a few minutes early. The father of the family stuck his head into the cabin, look-ing up and down the Citation as if amazed that he could afford the luxury of his own jet. He motioned for me to stay in my seat. The few strands of hair floating above his head could have been transplanted from a thin cirrus cloud. His young wife and two teenage sons accompanied him, giving a running commentary on each other's foibles. He rattled off questions, never waiting for my reply. One son drummed on his brother's back with a rolled-up magazine. He stopped the percussive attack to inform me that they were going to their favorite restaurant to celebrate their dad's birthday. I was glad to have such a relaxed, boisterous group of passengers for my first flight as captain. We had two bottles of champagne on board, and when the door closed, a war cry exploded from the back of the airplane.

During the takeoff roll, the uneven pavement transmitted a series of shocks along my back and legs as we accelerated. The takeoff came as a surprise attack, the suddenness of being airborne, of shooting energy into the sky.

Air traffic control kept us at flight level one-eight-zero. I had my copilot check on the passengers even though their loud voices told me they were fine. He came back and said that they needed us to call ahead and confirm their limo. In the distance, several thunderstorms were spaced along Florida's east coast like a herd of prehistoric animals with blue-gray underbellies and rugged crowns glowing pink from the setting sun.

On approach to landing, my body connected with the muscle of engine and wing. I controlled two miniature suns with the throttles and banked thirty degrees to align with the runway. I skimmed the runway in the landing flare and applied steady backpressure to the wheel, resisting the downward movement of plane to pavement. The main wheels gently bumped the smooth concrete. After leaving the runway and performing the checklist, taxiing felt like a walk home.

The lineman directed us to park, and the limo was in place. Our passengers were headed to Joe's Stone Crab. Before the father jumped into the limo, he reminded me of their sliding departure time.

"Ten or eleven. It's hard to say with this group. By the way, do you like crab legs, seafood?"

The air was warmer, more humid than Lakeland. I stood next to the aircraft, rolled up my shirtsleeves and found the evening star. It was easy to believe that twilight rose from the ocean. Darkness had movement and purpose like the sun.

I watched the parking lot for Carol. I told my partner my plans and entrusted him with preparing the plane for the return trip. One of the women working the desk approached me, smiling.

"Are you guys all set?"

"We're all set with the plane. But I'm going to need directions to a restaurant nearby." I looked at my watch. "Story of my life. I'm down to counting minutes."

"Well, there's several places close. What about a crew car?"

"I'm getting picked up."

"You like Mexican?"

"Sure."

"Then I'm going to send you to my favorite place."

We walked inside, and she drew a simple map. Usually, I

hated having to drive anywhere while on the road. After flying, I wanted to be chauffeured. But I picked up the map and forced myself to listen to her instructions.

"She's late?" asked the woman.

"Always. She wouldn't be Carol if she showed on time."

I started to head out the door when Carol rounded the corner. Being late was one of her gifts. She was laughing, saying she was sorry. She wore her waitress outfit—short black skirt, white blouse, large earrings that might have been fashioned from tableware. Her long black hair was still moving as she hugged me.

With the windows down, we raced to the Mexican restaurant.

The place was packed, yet we were quickly ushered to a table. Our waitress indulged all of my questions about items on the menu, acting as though ours was the only table in her station. We decided on a dinner of appetizers. Carol ordered a margarita.

"Do you have time to show me your plane when we get back?"

I glanced at my watch. "There's a few minutes unaccounted for."

Except for a few well-placed cumulus clouds, the night sky was clear over Miami. The ocean delivered the full moon, and Carol's tanned body held the sun.

A couple of linemen and my copilot were standing outside the aircraft when we pulled up. Our passengers had just called and expected to be at the airport in fifteen minutes. Carol walked up to the plane, studying it quietly. She climbed aboard. After taking a peek at the cockpit, she sat down in one of the passenger seats. I stayed crouched in the doorway, half-listening for the passengers' arrival.

Carol began talking about the recent death of a friend. Death was something that happened up north, not in the sun-filled present, she seemed to be saying. She had come to Miami to worship the sun. She spoke of a trip to Trinidad she had taken and her longing for other kinds of beauty. I had to stop her when a limo entered the parking lot.

"I'll walk you to your car," I said, holding her arm as she climbed off the airplane.

* * *

When we were cleared for takeoff to the east, my aircraft lined up perfectly with the rising moon. Banking to the north, my thoughts moved around the safety and smoothness of our short flight back to Lakeland. There were a few storms between us and the airport, so I asked my first officer to handle the radar.

The passengers started singing in loud voices. They brought more champagne on board and had picked up some food for us. My copilot wasn't sure if they needed transportation. I reminded him that they had come in their own cars. He shook his head.

"I should've known that. How could I miss—"

"No big deal. You've got plenty to deal with."

He smiled briefly then pointed to a small target, the size of a dime, on the radar screen.

"It's about fifteen miles west of the airport." I tilted the screen up to get rid of the ground clutter. "We'll land in about ten minutes. If the wind's calm, let's see if we can get Runway 27."

The green target increased in size with an area of orange and red at its center, indicating an established thunderstorm. The weather was still good at the Lakeland airport and Tampa cleared us for a visual approach. The lighted runway seemed to be floating on a calm black sea. I ignored the occasional flashes of lightning west of the airport and concentrated on slowing up the Citation.

The tower was closed for the night. After landing, we taxied unaided, crossing another runway with caution. The lineman's twin flashlights guided us to an open area in front of the building.

The father thanked us again for the flight, handing us two Styrofoam boxes. The wife and two sons had just climbed down the steps when it began to rain. After asking my partner to escort the passengers, I closed the cabin door and headed for the tail-cone baggage area to get the engine plugs. As it started to rain harder, I slowed my pace. Within moments I was soaked. The rain was warm, and the days spent in the white box for my type rating finally made sense.

Back at the hotel, I sat on the bed with damp hair and plunged into the crab legs and shrimp cocktail. Maybe I'd take the Corbis up on teaching again. I felt the energy for a hundred different projects. I called the hotel operator and gave her my wake-up call. She had one of those voices backlit with the promise of laughter. She called me "honey" twice during the short conversation.

26

ROCKY MOUNTAINS

THROUGHOUT THE NINETIES I checked out in several other jets at EJA. Though many airports still overlapped, different aircraft promised different destinations. The small straight-wing jets allowed for landings at short four-thousand-foot strips like Harbor Springs, Michigan, whereas the Citation Ten allowed us to make Hawaii as long as forecast headwinds didn't exceed seventy-five knots. The years of riding into Aspen's challenging mountain airport in small and midsize jets ended with the Boeing 737. Of course, the rest of the world opened up flying a corporate 737. With each aircraft I was introduced to new places, encountering new people, listening in on the comical, the pithy; hearing the occasional insight that pointed to the ineffable all around us. Sky and mountain had a few things to say as well.

* * *

We flew over the Red River, extinct volcanoes, canyons, the Front Range of the Rockies and the Continental Divide. Canyons had been formed by an atmospheric power—an open hand, slightly cupped, slammed into the surface. Although the laws of geology suggest the majority of earth-shaping forces were internal (exceptions being surface weathering and gravity), the terrain out west suggests an aerial power: the influence of Olympus, the trademark of vastness and cities in the clouds.

The flight had been smooth and the view excellent for our passengers. The mountains had been visible for many miles.

On approach I caught sight of the Gunnison River curving around large snow-covered hills. The white and silver belonged more to the sky than the earth.

After we deplaned, one of our passengers, an attractive woman in her fifties, approached me with a few questions about my work. She had gray-streaked hair, a smooth face and perfectly etched crow's feet. With light-filled eyes, she took long glances at everything around her. When I passed her a cup of coffee, her fingers brushed the back of my hand. She told me about driving from Illinois to Lake Tahoe. After driving for hours on the flat plains of Kansas, she began to notice a long, dark cloud stretching the length of the horizon. "Is that a storm?" she asked her companion.

"Sugar, you've never seen the Rocky Mountains," her companion replied.

* * *

My captain and I rented a Ford Escort and headed north on route 135 to Crested Butte. Cottonwoods and icy creeks guided us to the new ski mecca. The snowfall was an overpowering sight. The base of thirty-three inches of snow had grown to one hundred and three inches. This was America's Olympus, where the earth worshipped sky and spirit and intellect sought control over the forces of gravity and erosion. Humans on skis became beautiful objects. Everything was speed, grace, the lines of a black Lamborghini. Skiers were snobbish Olympians, skimming the steep, frozen sides of mountains.

In Crested Butte, houses and stores were invisible, buried by weeks of snowfall. Some yards were square tracts of piled snow, six to eight feet high. Sidewalks had become alleys with walls of packed snow on either side, forcing one to look skyward at the winter peaks.

We ate at a place called Oscar's. All the stores had quaint Old

West facades, and I wondered about the town's age and its history. I asked our waitress how old the building was. She turned toward the bar and asked the boss. He yelled back "fourteenth century." The man was terminally grumpy. Perhaps his wife had gone to Zeus's bed a little too often. She ignored him. She thought that this particular building was probably the oldest in town.

She came from Chicago and was completing a one-year leave of absence from a high-powered public relations firm. "I don't know if I want to grow up," she confided. "Sixty to ninety hours a week in the peak season burned me out." Maybe she imagined that from the mountains she would see the solution to her problems.

As she moved among the tables, my captain commented on her good looks.

"Her body likes it here," I said. "But her soul belongs to the Midwest."

He smiled. "We need to overnight closer to sea level—richer oxygen levels. I'm starting to worry about you."

27

WALKING THE WALK

IN ORLANDO I often stayed at a hotel landscaped with exotic flowers, palms and a lake with a fountain at its center. It was already dark. As I moved around the lake, my body heated up, my stride lengthened, and I thought of Jim DeFore, a friend of my parents. He and his wife visited us on summer nights when I was in my early teens. After dinner, Jim would stand up from the picnic table and announce that he was taking his walk.

He was tall, mostly legs, and he left our backyard like a man called to defend his country. My brother and I nearly had to run to keep up. Mr. DeFore didn't say much, and he didn't slow down to accommodate us. He looked straight ahead as he walked, smiling, his eyes focused on some adventure unfolding in the distance. I can still see his face at twilight, a man given temporary possession of the sun.

My parents found his habit a bit odd and warned him that the police would probably stop us. When they did, Mr. DeFore would smile broadly at the officer, mention my parents and keep walking.

During these evening walks, the night never fully arrived. For every part of the landscape receding into darkness, some other part—a field, the side of a house—still glowed with an amber or reddish light. Twilight's electric heaven passed through us, and we walked with a giant who looked straight into the heart of a summer evening. Later in life I acquired something of Jim's rhythm on long walks, a sensation of being pulled by an outside force, a kind of flying.

Jim DeFore died recently. My dad visited him shortly before his death and found him content, without complaints. The death of his wife, and the loss years ago of two of his five children—one to violence and the other to disease—were tragedies that never crushed him. During my dad's visit, Jim talked of his years as a pilot, of summer mornings and evenings as the best for flying, a time when the air is smooth and cool. As a young man, he had explored the land of Ohio and Pennsylvania from a few thousand feet above the ground, saying that the best view was just above the trees.

Long before Jim left the insurance company where he worked with my dad, he talked of driving a school bus someday. After he retired, Jim did that for fifteen years. His wife told us that the children loved him, that he learned each of their names and talked to them over the sound of the engine of faraway places and their own backyards. The children must have thought that he was a giant out of a fairytale, protecting them with his strength and kindness.

A few months after his death, I asked my father what it was like to work with Mr. DeFore. He said they walked everywhere. "Jim would park his car, and we walked the entire morning from house to house." When I commented that Mr. DeFore must have sold a lot of policies, my dad said that he was a mediocre salesman.

"People liked Jim," my father said. "Once we made it into the house, they didn't want us to leave. They'd bring out coffee and pastries, and we'd talk for hours. But not many of them ever bought insurance."

* * *

As I walked around the lake, I could see my dad's face marked with bewilderment and undiminished affection for his friend. What illuminates, finally, is Jim's passion, dovetailing over a lifetime to enter a single day of driving a school bus or going for a long walk after dinner. His gift to those near him was his energy— a fountain, diamond-bright against the darkness.

Jim DeFore walks into the next world with an easy smile, a prodigious stride and the road unfolding before him.

28

BIRDS OF A FEATHER

IN THE EARLY nineties I airlined to Kansas between tours and flew a Cessna 152 back to Ohio for the Corbis. While in Topeka I made the mistake of asking the cab driver if tornadoes were common. He answered in a gruff voice that I better not be inching toward "that *Wizard of Oz* crap." But I was. That movie was part of my emotional history—separation from everything we love, the dangers of the journey, the surprises, the battle to get home and finally arriving, hopefully a bit wiser.

Missing my wife and my own backyard whenever I left for a week-long tour, I tapped into that "wilderness" I had discovered years ago flying bank checks. I knew that with a good workout at the hotel, a great book in the evening, or dinner with the pilot I was paired with, peace and strength often returned, flooding me with warmth and certitude.

That night at the hotel in Topeka, I wrote down a few lines about the pissed-off cab driver and knew life to be an adventure, finely tuned by the craft of writing and swapping stories with Lewis and Clark on long, quiet walks. Writing cut through life's jungle and made roads that connected places of the heart. Sometimes, it simply found a door open I had believed was closed.

Perhaps heaven is spread out before our eyes, and we just

can't see it: the ordinary, backlit by eternity.

* * *

After the passengers left, I went back to the plane, finished the day's paperwork and checked the oil before calling dispatch. Halfway across the tarmac, I stopped and looked for the sky. The hangar lights blotted out the stars and the humid air of Baton Rouge had swallowed the upper atmosphere, eliminating the sky and leaving only blackness without dimension.

From the dark area of the ramp appeared a teenage boy cradling something in his hands. He approached me holding a medium-size crow. Without any introductions, he started talking about the eating habits of crows and their uncanny intelligence. I eyed the heavy beak, the too intelligent eyes, with some caution.

My copilot walked up and said that the map and directions to the hotel were in the car. He said nothing to the boy and headed for the plane to get his roller bag. I asked if I could hold the bird. In my hands I felt smooth feathers encasing a bit of air. Crows had always appeared as dense, heavy creatures, yet this bird seemed more like a thought than the scavenger I passed on the road. As my copilot walked past us with his luggage, he threw me a puzzled look, dangling the car keys in front of me like smelling salts.

The boy stopped talking suddenly and raised the bird to his chest. He looked at the creature as if communication had never ceased. Without so much as a glance my way, he vanished back into the darkness.

* * *

I was in the backseat of a cab, waiting for my copilot, checking my watch to make sure that we'd not miss the flight out of Columbus to New York to pick up our plane. Leaning my head against the seat, I started dreaming of Alaska. It would be my first flight into Anchorage, and dispatch said that we'd have at least a day off in the forty-ninth state. I started to say something about my partner's tardiness, but the cab driver interrupted me.

"I know how you guys operate. Wait until the last moment, jump in and the race begins."

"Are we holding you up?" I asked.

"No way. I like you guys. I hear plenty of stories in the five minutes it takes to get to the terminal. Then I have hours to think about it. Like that one pilot of yours, saw a flying saucer."

"One of our guys saw a UFO?"

"UFO—that's right. But he couldn't say nothing to nobody. Said he'd lose his job. I understand that. Who's going to believe you anyway? Besides, you're a pilot. You should only see what's really there."

"What did this pilot look like?"

The driver was silent. He glanced at me in his rearview mirror. Before he said anything, the back door swung open, and Jeff apologized for being late.

"Are we really going to Alaska?" he asked, flashing a boyish grin.

"So far."

"Great! You like titty bars? Best titty bar I've ever been to is in Anchorage."

* * *

A number of the younger pilots at my company built their hours flying in Alaska. Early in my career I imagined the thrill of bush flying, sailing over forest and river, nosing out distant locations. But after hearing their stories, I felt lucky that I never pursued the fantasy. Commercial and general aviation accidents per flight hours flown are numerous compared to those in the lower forty-eight, and the weather and mountains tend to swallow aircraft.

Over dinner one night, I learned that my copilot had spent six years flying out of Nome in an assortment of single and multi-engine ships. There are no roads leading to Nome, so everything and everyone must be flown in. I felt a twinge of loneliness listening to someone who broke from family and friends and lived near the Arctic Circle.

In his stories, Mark kept coming back to the annoyance of the tundra. That walking was a chore on the mushy earth. Soon, he got to the bears.

From his plane he once saw a grizzly running toward a herd of caribou. The bear bounding across the landscape was an impressive sight—*ursus horribilis* steamrolling through the meat department of the supermarket. Another time he witnessed a migration of polar bears moving in groups of two and four along the shoreline, savaging walruses, leaving a bloody beach of carcasses. He circled the scene a few hundred feet above the attack.

During this same migration period, the citizens of Nome were warned of a lone polar bear headed directly for the city. Mark wondered why the bear wasn't stopped earlier as he stood with a large crowd gathered at an intersection. Finally, the bear appeared on the street from an alley. Mark said he looked surprised and rose up on his hind legs, near ten feet tall and probably a thousand pounds. When it made a move in the crowd's direction, an armed deputy shot it.

* * *

Having breakfast at a small Colorado airport, I discovered that Anthony's dad had been a trumpet player for Tommy Dorsey and Xavier Cugat. Anthony and I had been flying for several days and most of our talks—instigated by me—kept returning to his years hauling freight in a Boeing 747. His dad had died when he was only three years old. "My dad was at the dentist and the dentist looked at him and said get to a doctor. When he made it to the office the doc looked him over and said he had two days to live." Anthony's father died forty-eight hours later from lymphatic cancer.

His mother died at age eighty-two. She was never sick and simply dropped dead, boiling a pot of water for spaghetti. A neighbor found her. Anthony said that all the gates and doors to the house were open. "She never had everything opened like that. And nobody knows why."

Everyone has a master painter rendering their lives—detail and color layered over a lifetime, with a final last touch or two. Sometimes the end is a painful flurry of color, like Anthony's dad, or a deft brushstroke enlivening the blush of a woman's cheek, opening all the doors of the house as water goes to steam and Anthony's mom goes quietly with a bit of mystery.

Later that morning, before our flight back east, Anthony told me his wife could read a person's physical and spiritual health. "She knows if they're headed for a sickness, who's an asshole or who you can trust. She can read paintings too, see a story in them, read an emotion, something underneath. Yet, with all this talent, she can walk out of a restaurant and have no idea where she's at, or how to find her car. I have to watch her constantly, or I'll lose her."

As we preflighted the Citation Ten and took a few moments to enjoy the view, I told Anthony that I had considered bidding on the Boeing 737. He smiled, saying that I'd have a blast flying it. Then he grew serious, warning me about flying in Europe, especially the Italian controllers.

"They're lackadaisical. You really have to watch their instructions. They'll send you and another guy to the same altitude, same fix, and think, 'it's a big sky, they won't run into each other.'"

Perhaps the problem is traceable to the fact that all Italians believe they're artists first, seeing their radar screen as an empty, dark canvas until it becomes full with the ever-changing clusters of planes, begging for their artistic touch.

Anthony also warned of continually flying the east-west routes, not only the flights to Europe but those from the West Coast to the Pacific Rim.

"Believe me, back in the airlines you'd go to a Christmas party and the east-west guys have prematurely aged. You start crossing six or seven different time zones, regularly, your body's gonna feel like it was sucked through the engine. Guys forty look sixty. It's horrible, but true. If you can, take the north-south routes and stay young."

* * *

After paying the cab driver, I headed for the plane. I had an early morning departure from El Paso. Looking at the hot, bare mountains west of the airport, I noticed an unusual stillness had descended upon the place. Normally, airports swim in a cacophony of jet thunder and high-pitched noises. But for a few seconds, my footsteps and roller bag were the only sounds, like a sci-fi movie where everyone disappears. Finally, human activity broke the silence, pushing the world into motion.

An hour later we were lined-up on Runway 22 when the tower canceled our takeoff clearance. A frontal gust from a storm south of the airport had created the potential for windshear. I set the parking brake, scanned the instruments and spotted a dust cloud perhaps a hundred feet high rolling across the runway. From a mile away, this whirling thing had a chunky, animal presence. Shortly after its passing, the tower cleared us for takeoff, delaying us only briefly while a force of nature lumbered by.

* * *

My plans for getting home early began to evaporate. Dispatch was concerned that a plane coming out of maintenance might be late for a noon departure from Bridgeport to Richmond. My copilot attempted to hide his disappointment and asked for the details of the potential flight.

When I told the giant limo driver, he shrugged his wide shoulders and asked to look at the plane. "We got some time, right?" When he smiled I counted only a few teeth.

Walking toward the plane, I scanned the morning sky for the moon and Venus. Venus was extinguished, and the moon had become less substantial than a high cirrus cloud. On the flight over, the planet and the crescent moon had looked like an advertisement for Cartier—cosmic jewelry in a sky setting.

The driver looked up trying to figure out what was so captivating. He never asked me what I searched for. He simply followed my movements, turning his massive body with the excitement of a child shown a new game. The man and his tuxedo had married years ago: the patches, the shine of the material, ancient food stains. Here was the guardian of woodland and highway.

Carefully, he negotiated the small steps leading to the cabin. Holding on to the sides of the doorframe, he paused, then entered the Citation. The aircraft settled and moaned as though it had been fueled to capacity. He never moved about the cabin, he just stayed bent over, leaning inside the doorway.

Slowly, he backed down the steps and sniffed the air in the direction of Manhattan. We both watched a DC-9 overfly Teterboro on a straight-in approach to the Newark airport. Then, he pointed at the Empire State Building in the distance and smiled. "If King Kong was climbing it now, I bet we could see him, all the way from here." He stared a while, letting his imagination fill in more details. "He wanted to live here, wanted the girl too—could you blame him?" he asked seriously, with a hint of sadness.

As the son of Kong walked across the ramp to his limo, I remembered the first time I saw the movie. It was at my grandparents and King Kong's teeth and eyes filled the TV screen. I was horrified, but couldn't turn away, even when the biplanes made their shameful attack. King Kong became the head of my childhood pantheon of guardians and monsters.

After the movie I walked into the backyard crying. My uncles laughed, saying it was just a movie. Years later I could finally articulate what I couldn't then: The planes had killed a king—a king with a world heart.

This driver, this son of Kong sat in his limo with the window down, elbow resting on the door, eyeing the world like it just came to existence. He scanned Manhattan looking at the city he loved and longed for his king to take his rightful place on an island of giants.

* * *

The main lobby at the Westhampton airport was small, with dark wood paneling and a Christmas tree in the center of the room. The tree was strung with toy drummer boys producing a mechanical version of "Oh Come, All Ye Faithful." The young woman closed the door halfway so I'd be alert to my passengers' arrival, yet still have some privacy.

After finishing the cup of hot chocolate the woman had made for me, I called for our release while my first officer carried the catering and newspapers out to the plane. As she figured out the landing fee, she mentioned that a friend who had never tasted eggnog was coming over that night. She talked of making it from scratch and adding rum.

It was already dark and a light snow was falling. On his way back inside, the first officer said a van with the luggage had arrived, but no passengers. The driver said they had decided to extend their visit to eleven o'clock. Christmas Eve would be spent above the clouds on a moonless night. Walking past the drum tree, I glanced toward the office. The door was partially open and the young woman was dancing by herself, completing a pirouette, her full dress still in motion.

29

AN EVENING IN DES MOINES

"YOU MUST HAVE some new stories," Alan said. "We haven't talked much the last few months."

"I always have stories from the road." I stood in the kitchen, phone to my ear, looking at the backyard, anxious for a ground hog to make an appearance so I could shoot him from our second floor balcony and use him as fertilizer.

"Maybe you should come down here for pie and coffee with dad. Of course he's not here right now—he's in town buying up the store, some deal he saw at Walmart. You better have pictures. Dad will go nuts if you don't."

"I'm hot and cold with the camera. Mostly cold."

"Just keep your eyes open."

"Your dad prefers photography. But I miss too much when I'm carrying a camera."

"You took great pictures in Mexico."

"For me it doesn't tell much of the story."

"Hey, what about this girl you've been flying with?"

"That's Joan—"

"Any pictures?"

"It wouldn't do any good."

* * *

Thirty miles out of Des Moines, we continued our descent through twelve thousand feet. The city appeared as a geologic intrusion—a compression of human culture against endless miles of farmland. From our position, nature was asleep. The river angling into and out of Des Moines was a strand of a dream that momentarily formed the city and then continued its deep slumber as it passed into the countryside.

Joan sat upright in her seat, scanning the area for traffic, answering the instructions from air traffic control. She spotted the airport, and I gently banked the airplane to position us for a straight-in approach.

Several miles from the runway and a thousand feet above the ground, we entered the last stage of flight where the riches of the land bared themselves—beauty in the details, Satan's offer to Christ in the desert.

Clumps of trees, small rises in the landscape materialized into view. The runway presented itself as a long sliver of consciousness, a tame river that provided a safe transition back to the shores of the planet. I eased the Citation jet onto the runway and did my best to gracefully lower the nosewheel. A good landing on the mains would be ruined if I forgot the nosewheel was still a foot above the concrete.

After I shut the engines down, Joan scrambled from her seat to open the cabin door for the passengers. No matter if she lacked sleep or food, Joan was energized by people. She fell into quick conversation with the passengers as she handed them their luggage. I said little except to thank them for riding with us.

Outside the city limits of Des Moines, our hotel was wedged between a fast food restaurant and a car dealership. Joan hated spending time at hotels and finagled a crew car whenever she could to look around town or just go for a drive. I told her I needed more downtime before I was in the mood to explore. But she reminded me that downtown was only ten minutes away.

It was early May. As we entered the city limits, I noticed a heavy band of clouds approaching from the southwest. Joan suggested we make the state capitol our first stop before the storm hit. Passing through downtown, the traffic was light and only a few people appeared along the streets and crosswalks. The city seemed more ethereal than the countryside we had recently flown over, a condensation of human will that created large office buildings with canyon-size shadows and wide avenues.

At the capitol grounds, Joan and I split up. I roamed through the park area where dignified monuments and bronze plaques represented the Civil War through Vietnam. In a small alcove of trees and bushes, I came upon a bust of Christopher Columbus, dedicated by the city's Italian immigrants. I wondered if they might be planning to give Columbus some company with twentieth-century explorers like Sinatra or DiMaggio.

I spotted Joan admiring a tall monument. Lost in reverie, she glided around the obelisk dedicated to the war dead, her movement shutting out the world. I remembered our walk through an ancient cemetery in Boston and her meditation among the headstones. She had yelled at me when I walked on the graves.

We left the capitol grounds in silence. As soon as Joan started the car, she became energized with the prospect of dinner. "You probably want to find a place on the river."

"Just park downtown. We'll find something."

We were on the street for only a few minutes when we spotted a restaurant with an outdoor patio. I picked a table next to the sidewalk. The waitress assured us of a place under the large canopy if it started to rain. Joan smiled at the possibility.

Near the restaurant, a massive building faced the statehouse at the north end. Cloud fragments in advance of the thunderstorm shot over the building while glancing rays of the sun illuminated its bone-white exterior. Joan looked over her shoulder in admiration.

When a sudden gust lifted our napkins, I was already standing with my coffee cup. Within moments the rain swept down the boulevard. Under the canopy, a couple helped us drag a table and extra chairs from the mouth of the storm. They asked us to join them until the waitress had a chance to dry off our table. I had noticed them earlier, flirting and holding hands. Joan made the introductions.

Helen offered me a dry towel. When her husband Jack found out Joan and I were pilots, his smile grew.

"So what airline are you with?" he asked. He was one of those people who took a real delight in anything new.

"Not an airline. We fly corporate and charter," Joan answered.

"Oh, you mean the smaller planes," Helen said, "the ones with the propellers."

"Props are for boats." Joan was pleased to get the chance to use her favorite one-liner. "No props for us. We're married to those airplanes that go suck-bang-blow."

Helen raised her drink as if to toast, insisting that Joan give us a detailed explanation.

"It's simple. The air being drawn in is the suck. That air is squeezed, compressed and forcibly introduced to a flame in the can, where you get the bang and combustion."

"Let's hear more about the flame," Helen demanded.

"It's really very simple. The compressed air and mist of fuel is shot with a flame that's been alive since the engine first lit off. The ignited, expanding gases are channeled back to the turbine blades, forcing the blades to turn at an incredible rpm that drives the fan at the front of the engine."

"Ah, we're back to the suck portion of the engine," the woman said, grinning.

"Hey, you know, you resemble Amelia Earhart." Jack turned to his wife and she nodded in agreement.

"She has a lot of Amelia's virtues, except one," I said.

They both waited for it, while Joan smiled and kicked me.

"She takes a lousy picture," I said.

"I don't believe that," Jack said, having fallen under Joan's spell. "She's beautiful."

"True," I shot back. "But I've seen pictures of her. Every single one is lousy."

Luckily, our table was ready, stopping Joan's kicks and ending my remarks. A waitress brought our food and drinks, and we toasted the couple and settled in, just beyond the storm's fury. Corners of the canopy peeled back several times, and Joan let out a war cry every time the storm crested with an exceptional downpour.

"I don't know what future there is for Tom and me," Joan said, suddenly serious.

"I thought you two were happy."

"Well, he is. Christ, the guy is nuts about me. Who wouldn't be?" She laughed.

"Is the thunderstorm forcing you to confess? The happy couple?"

"He thinks I'm perfect." This threw both of us into a fit of laughter.

"I'll set him straight."

"I've tried all along. I let the devil in me pop out all the time—and he just smiles. It drives me nuts. How can I be with someone who doesn't see me? Doesn't know how to put me in my place?"

"If I dated you, I'd always carry a pair of handcuffs."

"I can walk all over him. And he wants to marry me."

"So, what's your response?"

"He's never asked."

"How can you be so sure he wants to marry you?"

Joan gave me an incredulous look. She straightened her shoulders and rose a couple inches taller in her chair. "Are you kidding? I can get on the phone right now, and he'll fly out here tonight. I just have to give the word. He'd marry me on the sidewalk in the middle of this storm. But he's afraid to ask. He knows better."

"I'm confused. Maybe you need someone like the guy in Greensboro. Remember, the fuel guy you fell in love with after five minutes?"

"Oh, that's just fantasy. Tom really loves me."

The storm thinned to a few distant rumbles. Neither of us said much as we watched the sun lacquer the boulevard with a reddish-gold light. When I looked again, there was only mist, the cooled-off streets and the coming night.

30

SOUTH FLORIDA

PEDRO, WHO WAS one of our company's youngest copilots, suggested a Cuban restaurant in the neighborhood where he had grown up and his mom still lived. He drove the crew car while I got a leisurely view of South Florida. On my right were several cruise ships at anchor in Biscayne Bay. These gleaming, city-block-long ships were the modern version of Charon's boat that carries the recently departed into the underworld.

"We can go to a fancy place where the setting is beautiful—the food's good but expensive." Pedro's easy smile and clear eyes told me that he was back on his own turf.

"I'm going to follow your lead. This is your town, you're driving." My excitement was as broad as the sun that swiped the Miami area with its eighty-five-degree heat. The second day of our tour placed us in Pedro's backyard. We were off duty for the next twelve hours. Dispatch couldn't even talk to us until nine in the evening.

"Then we'll go to Molina's. We'll stop by my mom's house first. She'd love to go with us."

His mom's small house, pink stucco and tile roof, faced a playground and a deserted baseball diamond. I stood by the car while Pedro climbed the locked gate. He seemed surprised at the

Beware of Bad Dog sign with its hand-drawn Labrador wearing a spiked collar.

"She doesn't own a dog," he said, shaking his head at the smiling Lab. His mom's house was compressed on either side by other single-story homes. The emerald patch of grass and well-maintained bushes gave it a singular air of hard work and beauty.

"Nobody's home. Even the guy in the back who rents from my mom is gone. Do you mind if we stop back later? I know you want to get to South Beach."

"I don't care if we drive around your mother's neighborhood for the rest of the day."

On the way to the restaurant, we passed other homes of brick and pastel shades, fantastic plants crowding the yards. I saw only a few people: an old man standing in his front yard with the mail in his hands, a few children on bikes, and a man washing his car and the suds rolling on a thin stream of water into the hot street.

At Molina's we were seated at a corner table, and except for us, I heard nothing but Spanish. I pointed to items on the menu and Pedro carefully described each dish and the fondness Cubans have for these combinations. He suggested the plantains instead of the yucca. I opted for the mysterious yucca root.

Our waiter was a tall, older man with short gray hair at the temples. His tight potbelly acted like a cat's tail for balance. He turned, walked, tuned into our conversation with sudden grace. His prominent belly seemed linked to invisible ball bearings. He spoke entirely in Spanish, waiting patiently for Pedro to reveal my choice for lunch. I decided on a plate of roasted pork with rice, beans and yucca. The Cuban coffee I was served was perfectly sweetened.

Except for a couple seated near the center of the restaurant, the place was quiet, with a couple of servers leaning against the wall near the kitchen door. The electricity from the busiest hours still lingered near the white tablecloths and straight-back chairs. The ceiling fans lazily circulated the cool air.

The food arrived in three separate dishes: a bowl of soupy black beans, a plate piled with rice and a larger dish of cut-up chunks of pork. Except for the yucca, Pedro had the same. I found the fried plantains sweet and delicious. I never asked, but the white yucca appeared to have been boiled. It was a fibrous vegetable with an earthy taste.

I asked for a second cup of Cuban coffee and our waiter seemed amused. He glanced my way as he made a comment to Pedro.

"He doesn't often see people order the espresso one cup after another," Pedro said.

"Let him know that you're driving." I didn't want it for the buzz, I simply loved the taste. However, when I finished the second cup, I felt wired to every household appliance in South Florida.

The bill came and I grabbed it before Pedro had a chance. "This is on me."

The waiter understood. As he passed me, he lightly tapped my left shoulder.

"He tapped you." Pedro was surprised. This barely noticeable, quick tap made Pedro rise in his seat and lean toward me. He was on the verge of saying something then smiled and settled into his chair.

On the way to his father's house, we passed small groups of Cubans displaying signs, waving the nationalist flag. They were protesting the latest government decision to return the rafters to Cuba.

"They're going to try and shut down Miami next Tuesday." Pedro spoke as an outsider. His heart understood the cause but the progression of his own life had given him another perspective. "My views have changed a bit from my parents'. Don't be surprised if the conversation runs into politics."

"Hey, I want to hear it, I've got my own opinions. But today I don't have the energy to spout my half-baked political ideas. Today, I just want to look and listen."

With the air conditioner blowing, we kept the windows down, enjoying a wind that pushed up from the first circle of hell where virtuous pagans tended flower gardens.

"You know what I miss the most living in Ohio?" Pedro said, "The sun. I adjusted to the cold winter pretty quick, but I couldn't take all those overcast days. My wife nearly went crazy with depression. It's hard enough to move away from your family. But no blue sky for days on end? We do better now by getting out to the movies, visiting friends. That's helped both of us."

"Well, I love those overcast days. I grew up in Ohio. The moody skies mirrored my moodiness as a kid. I feel more energy on cloudy days. Endless days of sun just flattens everything out. Shreds up your energy, your purpose."

"You must really hate this place."

"Not at all. The weather is too violent down here with thunderstorms and hurricanes. The beautiful, boring weather is constantly interrupted."

This delighted him. He started laughing as we rode the exit ramp off the freeway. The sun was forever buried in Pedro. It was the best place for the sun to be, inside one's self, a solar Holy Ghost. If called upon, it would rescue him and his family from Ohio's winter or other mundane terrors.

We pulled into the short driveway and the car lurched forward as Pedro threw it into park. The car nearly filled up the front yard, crowded with flowers and enormous plants. A couple of faded flamingoes stood in the white gravel of some ancient ocean. Pedro's stepmother opened the door. She hugged him and politely nodded in my direction. She was past the age of ever being pretty again, yet her dark features and silver-streaked hair were strongly female and handsome. She was a matriarch, not cut from stone but from the flesh of generations.

The three of us walked into the family room at the rear of the house. Pedro pointed to a comfortable chair. From where I sat I could see more lush plants and several trees protecting the house in a jealous embrace. A sliding glass door, to my left, led to the backyard. His stepmother handed me a glass of ice water and she began talking to Pedro in Spanish. Pedro's first language made him more sober, like a father making inquiries after a long day at work. After a few minutes, he broke into English and shed the seriousness of their talk. He explained that he and his stepmother held different views on the people fleeing Cuba.

Pedro kept surfacing from their talk to see how I was doing, or if I needed anything. I told him I was perfectly content. When he suggested we take a look at the backyard, time, responsibility, even movement had little meaning; I simply turned my head and found myself outside, awake to another summer vision.

"This is our mango tree." Pedro introduced the tree like a beloved grandparent.

I gently grasped one of the unripe fruits. "What a burden this tree has. Such a small tree for this massive fruit."

"My father says you can hear the mango tree sigh after all its fruit has been picked."

"Then it must moan for months."

Pedro shook his head. "That sounds like something my mom would say. You two should get along well."

The backyard was enclosed on all sides by a tall wooden fence. The afternoon heat felt like a second skin. I stopped in front of another tree that occupied the center of the yard near the fence.

"My grandmother planted this lemon tree thirty years ago. She lived a few blocks away and came over all the time to take care of it." Pedro squinted, looking at the tree's crown. "This one is the family favorite. We can't even swear when we're near this tree."

"It's a beauty." I could make out dark-green fruit. The sun's power seemed capable of ripening the lemons by late afternoon.

"This here is the heartbreaker." Pedro walked slowly toward the stump of a tree with a monstrous plant growing from its severed body. "Remember that bad hurricane that ripped through South Florida? It took out my avocado tree. I guess we should feel lucky. Some of our neighbors lost their homes. My dad used to mail me the avocados and mangoes when I lived out of state. I thought of this tree as my own, like having a dog or a cat. I used to love just looking at it."

The lush, tentacled plant had a fierce presence. It had the look of something dropped from the hurricane, a force of nature that fed on the energy of the decaying tree.

The patio screen door slid open and a man with a full head of gray hair emerged from the cool shadow of the house. He silently called Pedro with a smile. Father and son embraced and I was introduced as we walked inside.

His stepmother said goodbye and left for work. I took my same chair. Pedro told his father that I was his captain. His father gave me a nod of respect and asked his son to sit next to him on the couch. Once again, I was ignored in a pleasant way as the two of them spoke slowly in Spanish. His father's arm was stretched across the back of the couch; his hand would turn, exposing his palm, as if to take Pedro's words directly into his body. He lowered his head as his son spoke, and slowly brushed his hair. I remembered what Pedro had said about his father, the struggle leaving Cuba, living in Spain for several years to qualify for citizenship, and then coming to America only to have his credentials as an engineer disallowed. Pedro was spared the hardship. He grew up in the midst of summer—a good home, clothes, college, the pursuit of dreams.

Pedro said his father's life had made him old before his time. Sitting across from his dad, I watched a man who recaptured his vitality on a daily basis. He was slightly taller than his son, his short-sleeved T-shirt highlighting his muscular build. When he reached for his water glass, it was a slow, graceful movement. He was the kind of man who knew that if a great burden drenched you in sweat, the evening would eventually come, a moment of stillness and relief. His face registered something inextinguishable. I never found out his age, and in my thoughts I disagreed with Pedro. He hadn't become old before his time. His time was now.

When we got up to leave, Pedro's father came to my side and asked me about our evening trip. I told him it would be a short flight to Gainesville. "I like evening flights. There may be some isolated storms, but they're usually easy to circumnavigate." I also mentioned the fine job his son was doing as copilot. We shook hands, and as I turned around to follow Pedro out the front door, his dad lightly touched my left shoulder.

His father stood at the door and waved as we climbed into the car. Pedro shook his head as we slowly drove away.

"Let's stop by my mother's house. She'll talk your ear off. I felt bad that we excluded you so much."

"It's odd, but I felt welcome. I usually get pissed when people ignore me—not this time. The waiter, and now your dad, gave me a little tap. What's that about?"

"Acceptance, part of the family," Pedro replied.

We approached the empty baseball diamond and spotted his mom's car parked in the driveway. The door opened by degrees as we climbed the steps of the small front porch. A woman who rubbed her eyes like a child waking up, met us. Her first words were a complaint. The ends of her black hair were wet and she smiled in a girlish way, pointing to a couple of chairs for us. Pedro's mom had been struggling with a flu bug.

"Mom, where's the dog?" Pedro asked.

"No dog, just a sign, cheap security."

The living room was spacious and neat, larger than I expected. She hugged Pedro and began talking to us of her troubles. Layoffs at her factory were imminent, and she spoke candidly of her money fears.

Pedro interrupted. He wanted to know what she thought of the new immigration policies that had the Cuban community ready to shut down Miami in a few days. "I know they want to come here for the jobs, the food. But what a mess there'll be if we let all the rafters into this country."

Her hands caressed the top of her legs down to her knees. She wore black shorts and a sleeveless white blouse. She looked up and smiled.

"They're not leaving because of food or even some miserable job. Would you leave this country tomorrow if you lost your job? No, of course you wouldn't." Her compact body sensually expanded as she spoke. She leaned forward to rub her calf, massaging herself as if to drive away her illness. Her large breasts pressed against her legs. "They have no freedom. That's why they leave and risk their lives." Without hurry, she straightened herself. Another smile emerged, one more enigmatic. Her girlishness mixed with maturity.

"They're leaving a place where they can't even speak up in their own backyards. The drabness of their lives is secondary. Now Castro's people, the ones in the party, they have a purpose in staying, even in hard times. They move with the ups and downs of jobs, material things. But these rafters don't leave because some products become scarce. We can't refuse the people searching for their freedom."

"But we need to do something different." Pedro's tone was respectful. "The embargo, all the hate toward Castro has changed nothing in Cuba. Are all these demonstrations just for revenge? To cut off the head of one man and shove it on a stick?"

His mother shrugged. "Honey, get me a glass of water. Would you like something to drink?" she asked me.

"Water would be fine." I sat across from her, admiring the youthfulness that mingled with her middle years.

"You don't mind hearing about politics?" she said.

"Not at all, it's different the way you talk about it."

"It's not always cordial. But he's my son. I'll listen to whatever he has to say." She folded her arms across her lap. She looked directly at me then scanned the room, intent on pulling some feeling out of thin air.

"We Cubans mix all of our passions. But today I fear getting old more than anything else. Things are better now for women, even older women. I grew up in a time when things were more limited. My regrets come and go. It's the fear that's so troubling. I hit forty-five, and I became afraid of everything. They're the same old problems—money, your children, your health—but then you start thinking what will happen twenty years from now? How will I work, will there be enough money? Maybe a mole appears on your stomach, and you can't remember ever having that mole. You exhaust yourself in fear. My only defense is to squeeze everything I can from each day." She extended her right arm and squeezed an invisible rope before her eyes. I could see her getting hold of something plantlike and full of juice. "I don't know why forty-five. But for me, that age made my heart tremble."

When Pedro returned, he asked if the family was going to have its traditional pig roast over Memorial Day.

"Of course. And thank God your uncle will be cooking. It always turns out beautiful when he cooks."

"The real skill is timing the drinking with the cooking," Pedro said. "Start drinking too early, and you burn the pork."

"That's why your uncle is such a genius. He can be drinking all day, yet he never forgets when to add to the fire or turn the pig."

"Fred won't be around for Memorial Day, but I took him to Molina's. He had the pork, and he loves black beans."

Pedro's mom got up from her chair and walked into the kitchen. She returned with a brown paper bag. Inside were two large cans of Cuban black beans.

"Just heat these up. Make some rice or meat with it." She hugged me. A few minutes later, we said goodbye and headed for the airport.

That night we curved around a few isolated storms. The air was smooth just beyond the areas of heavy rain and lightning. The remainder of the tour was evenly paced. Pedro and I didn't have any early wake-up calls. We averaged four legs of flying a day and our passengers were a tad friendlier. Perhaps this beautiful, broken world had mended slightly after our long afternoon in South Florida.

* * *

Back in Columbus, we finished our paperwork and got our release to head home. I was in the parking lot when Pedro walked up as I threw my suitcase in the backseat of the car.

"I hope to fly with you again," he said. "If you're ever in town on reserve, give me a call. My wife can cook the same food you ate at Molina's—even better."

31

CAPISTRANO

YEARS AGO A flight crew was arguing about the existence of God when they failed to notice they were picking up ice and subsequently lost pitch control. They went heavenward at high speed and then nosed down, aiming for that other metaphysical location. Finally they got the ship under control and returned to our home base to tell us about God and aerodynamics.

A similar, though less threatening experience, happened with me and Leon. The few times we flew together we talked intensely about many things so that several times we missed an ATC hand-off, and I had to scramble through a high-altitude chart to find a nearby frequency. Leon stayed cool and collected because he was cool and collected until his big-union, East Coast persona was activated. He was horrified that management and the pilots got along decently. "They should hate you!" he charged. "I hate them! Always will. If they laid the greatest contract at your feet, you walk away."

He turned to me one night and said, "The pilots at this company are goofy."

"How's that?"

"You're too happy, even when you're working hard."

"We got some miserable people here. I could introduce you."

"Well, there's not enough of 'em. If the company tells you to run out and put oil in the engine, you guys with a million other things to do run out and do it with a dopey smile. Hey, you don't run, you don't put oil in the engines—you stand your ground and tell them you're not a mechanic. Tell 'em, 'Get the damn mechanic out here! That's his job, pal, make him work.' "

I made Leon work that night after another one of his "goofy discussions" distracted us from hearing repeated calls from the controller. We were out of range for communicating on our last assigned frequency. I asked Leon to find a workable one. He opened the chart and sighed a few times as he perused it like the morning paper. He was in no hurry.

A transplant like so many Californians, Leon grew up in Philly and could shift seamlessly through emotions, but always with the energy of a downed power line, dancing, throwing sparks. He could have passed for Robert De Niro's character in the movie *A Bronx Tale,* yet could drop back into California cool in an instant—laid back, a hip spokesman for good weather and blue ocean. He embodied East and West Coast with flair. His West Coast persona smoothly emerged one evening when talking about his wife's lack of interest in working or doing anything productive. He shrugged. "She just hangs out."

Leon lives in Capistrano—lovely name for a town. For me this town's name embodies Southern California better than Los Angeles. Other Southern Cal names conjure magic and beauty, but only Capistrano sits at the crossroads of heaven and earth, a spirit-filled Hollywood of swallows and Zorro, the place where all good people of Los Angeles go to when they die.

32

A VISIT

FROM MY HOTEL bed I watched the storm pound Miami. After several days of flying, I had the day off and was looking forward to a long morning and a leisurely breakfast when the phone rang—it was my mom. She and my dad wanted to drive down from West Palm Beach and have lunch.

A few hours later, my parents walked into the hotel lobby, tanned and smiling. I hadn't seen them since Christmas. They had been coming down to Florida for the past twenty years, leaving a few days after New Year's and returning home in early May. After hugs, I complimented my mom on her lively blue pant suit with a light blue blouse.

"So, what's new?" my dad asked.

"Well, management's going after one of the guys. I don't know the whole story, maybe a pissing contest with one of the managers over one of his flights, maybe some regulation broken. I don't know for sure. Rumors. Don't have many details. I just know it looks like he's leaving the program, and that would be a real loss for everybody."

"Can't he go to someone, appeal his case?" my father questioned.

"There's always the union. But Doc didn't want to pursue it.

Maybe things just piled up for him."

"Things aren't piling up on you?"

My mom said nothing, only watched my expression.

"Management has treated me well," I replied. "No complaints."

My dad looked surprised. "Why do they do it? Go after someone?"

"Sometimes they have to. It's their job. You were in management when you sold insurance."

"I didn't go after someone who didn't deserve it."

"Your father needed to go after some of those men," my mom added, "they were lazy."

"Mom's right," I said. "Dad, unlike you, our management folks don't get out of the office very much."

"Your father did both—worked at the office and went out knocking on doors with his men," my mom said. "He worked long hours."

"I know," I said. "But our managers spend most of their time in the office. They have a lot of stress and no release that flying would give them. They don't have what dad had, going out to meet people; talk with them. A lot of satisfaction in that. If we have a good flight, smooth ride, passengers happy—and it happens more often than not—we go to the hotel feeling satisfied. Management doesn't get that type of satisfaction."

"They start acting like animals," my mom volunteered.

"Sometimes," I answered. "They're decent people, but their relief sometimes comes from tracking down and nailing someone."

"That's too bad," my dad said.

I told my parents about a recent incident with Doc. He and the Ohio State University hockey team were airlining home and found themselves grounded at Dulles due to weather. One of our flight attendants flying with Doc said that one player would steal a seat when another player got up to visit friends or go to the restroom. When the athlete returned, he found his seat occupied by the prankster, not willing to give it up, taunting his teammate. This played out a few times until Doc intervened. He walked over and put his hand on the bully's shoulder, saying, "I've been watching your stunts. Game's over, go back to your seat."

The noise level dropped and the flight attendant held her breath, until the kid stood up without a word and returned to his seat. The students began to cheer. Our flight attendant said she couldn't believe what he had done. She told that to Doc when he sat down. Doc said, "I'm a father. And I wasn't going to watch that crap go on without saying something."

"I see what you mean about this friend of yours," my dad replied. "Seems like the kind of man you want around when there's trouble."

"You're right. He'll be missed."

After lunch, walking my parents out, I glanced at the sky and told them to get going. "Beat the next storm." They didn't seem concerned. Nearing their Lincoln Town Car I was struck by its soft, but brilliant whiteness. It outshone everything else in the parking lot. It looked heaven-sent.

I waved as they slowly drove off. Smiling, my mom returned the wave as my dad focused on the traffic ahead.

The low clouds raced overhead, shredding themselves, warning of the next storm, while my parents in the elegant Lincoln headed back to their second home in West Palm Beach, safe and happy.

33

UNCLE SAM

ONE EVENING I called home and learned that my Uncle Sam had died. My mom sounded drained, but relieved, thankful that Gina, my niece, had helped Sam through his final days. His last night was bad, with a lot of thrashing, kicking the covers off, yelling for his wife. My mom had told him to let go, that his parents and wife were waiting for him. He mumbled, and she wasn't sure if he understood.

My Uncle Sam, who could complain, whine and feel sorry for himself with the best of us, had rejected the feeding tube in the last weeks of his life and had regained a dignity that had long ago slipped away. Once again, he was the tough uncle of my youth—funny, bigoted against all, in love with his nieces and nephews, getting me a job at the factory where both he and my aunt worked all their lives.

That was the summer of '69. I was young, lazy and full of myself, but it didn't matter to my aunt and uncle. They drove my friend and me to work every day and protected us from other workers who wanted to bone-crush us for screwing off and avoiding our responsibilities. We even tried to educate the masses on the coming revolution and the horrors of capitalism. We refined our pitch on one young college kid from Cleveland State. He wore heavy-rimmed glasses and wanted to know if everybody would get uniforms when that glorious day arrived. Fortunately, we never changed anyone's mind, receiving mostly yawns and a few "You gotta be shittin' me, that's commie talk" from the more wise employees.

One afternoon on the drive home from the plant, my uncle spotted a man lying on his back, surrounded by a group of people. I can see the grassy knoll, a man not moving, a sunlit day, a large tree in the background and my uncle yelling: "Jean, look, a dead man! A dead man lying in the grass. Goddamn, Jean, he's dead!" We were rounding the corner, my aunt driving cautiously like she always did and Uncle Sam hanging out the window, pointing. That man was all of us someday: a few people in attendance, life in motion on all sides, eternity poking through a bright Friday afternoon.

My Aunt Jean had passed away a few years earlier than Sam, leaving my uncle in depression. She was his support, almost a slave to his needs: cooking, cleaning, running his bath water and, of course, driving him everywhere while he hung out the window lambasting the world. But she still kept her joy in life primed, not prone to moodiness like her husband. Whenever she greeted us, we saw an intensity of love, a brightness in her face and smile that never dimmed.

My gracious, smiling aunt and my fun, loud-mouthed uncle who scared us when he could—both gone now.

Today, I felt his courage at the end. Also the peace he must have felt. He told my niece that he had "a date with God."

I recalled his brazen remarks, his tough-guy stance that was truly tough at times. In his middle years he started a mini riot at a softball game when a player on the opposing team flipped off his brother's wife for some comment she yelled from the stands. When the cops arrived, Uncle Sam was directing the riot. The cops zeroed in and arrested him first.

I admit I enjoyed his mean remarks too. I could hear him yelling at us from the couch in their beautiful apartment on tree-lined Corlett Avenue, laughing and teasing us about drinking his strawberry pop, or getting into his favorite sweets. I should have remembered this before he died, but I didn't, seeing him as a scared old man limping toward death. I wish I had visited him in the last month of his life and told him of the happiness he had brought me.

Today, I feel the release, the new journey that death brings. I believe my uncle knew for certain that he would walk again with his wife and brothers, hug his parents, walk the old neighborhood of his youth. I believed that he and my Aunt Jean would once again snuggle close, watching a football game as the snow fell, glistening. And I was sure that he'd keep his date with God.

* * *

It's the middle of the night, and I'm away from home and have this dream. I'm at my grandmother's, alone, with a fear of something just outside the door, a catlike presence ready to pounce and tear. When I look out the window, I see my grandmother walking up the driveway, supported by her daughter and sons. My Uncle Sam has his arm around her, an attempt to protect her. Going outside, I tell everyone that grandma likes sleeping in the basement and that a bed is ready.

My relatives are all over the house as if gathering for a family picnic. Some linger in the yard. I move through the rooms, saying goodnight. It's a summer night and the basement's a perfect temperature—cool, without being chilly. I see my grandmother in bed, and I know she's come from the doctor and that the end of her life is near. I talk to her, and because it's a dream, what I now write comes from an immense feeling and only a vague memory of the words spoken. But some words do return as I stumble out of bed at two in the morning and clumsily grab pen and paper.

I lie alongside my grandmother and believe she's asleep, putting my arms around her. She stirs slightly, and I feel as if my arms encircle all my family's sorrows and joys. Dreams can do that sort of thing. I tell her that I love her with all my life. And my grandmother responds, from my dream and the many years since her death. She says faintly, "and I love you also, more than life, more than life."

34

THE WRIGHT BROTHERS

JIM STOOD BEFORE our class, detailing his heart attack of six months ago. The day before he went into the hospital, he had been raking leaves when every muscle in his body became exhausted. Of all the details we heard over the next ten minutes, that picture of him sitting down, wiped out by an unknown force, hit me the hardest.

It was the second day of recurrent ground school and Jim paced before our class of a half-dozen Citation Ten pilots, his eyes bright as an explorer gazing at storms on the horizon.

Moving away from his near miss, he told us that as pilots we probably had one of the best jobs in the country. He said that we got thrown into situations dealing with the super-rich and the young girl working the desk and headed for college, some business maverick or rock-solid CEO. And what about that view, he asked rhetorically. I agreed with Jim on the view from the cockpit. Sometimes, after a descent through dark clouds, we witnessed a verdant landscape in the Blue Ridge Mountains after a rainstorm, or on approach, skimmed the infrastructure of a major city on a day when the sun pounds across glass, steel and cement. There was nothing diminished about the view from the cockpit. If anything, it was a reminder of the vastness of the country, how much of the eastern half was tree-covered and the big Western states were primeval, with mountain, volcano and high plains desert.

By the end of the nineties, Executive Jet Aviation had grown to the point where I was paired up with a different pilot nearly every tour. The same was true for recurrent training at Flight Safety International, the training facility in Toledo, Ohio. Chris from Columbus was my sim partner. He was tall and confident, an early icon of the airline pilot. After looking at our five-day schedule, we both wondered about the temperament of our sim instructor.

The next day we met for breakfast, and I learned that Chris was weighing the pros and cons of leaving for the airlines. Over the years I had watched many of the younger pilots take their excitement and expertise elsewhere. Chris knew he'd never make airline salary at our company, but had stayed for several years with the hope of better pay and retirement benefits. However, what the airlines couldn't match was the variety of experience, in the air and on the ground.

That afternoon, Chris and I were leaning against the railing that overlooked the indoor bay area as five simulators slowly rose, fell and rocked for twenty out of twenty-four hours daily. Our sim, a twelve-million-dollar Citation Ten that cost only a few million less than the actual aircraft, pitched and hummed atop hydraulic legs, fed power by thick, black cables connected to computers. Its sophistication and likeness in handling to the actual plane was a far cry from the first simulator I flew for my initial upgrade to captain.

Pete, our sim instructor, greeted us, and we spent the next twenty minutes in a small briefing room, going over our training syllabus and enlightening each other with gossip. Pete seemed easygoing, helping us to relax. Our six-month recurrent training always carried the possibility of busting the check ride and, in the more rare circumstances, busting it a second and third time and losing your job. We were pleased to discover that our laidback instructor was scheduled to give us our check ride on the last day.

The cockpit of the sim was identical to the actual aircraft, except for the instructor who sat behind us at the control console. The sim sessions were normally four hours long, with the pilots exchanging left and right seats (captain / copilot) at two-hour intervals. As Chris completed his initial airwork of steep turns and stalls, it was evident that a graceful pro worked the controls.

Pete asked me to take the yoke and told Chris to close his eyes and lower his head. The game was to put the plane in an unusual attitude, then have the "sleeping pilot" open his eyes to a steep dive in progress or a high, nose-up attitude close to a stall. It was a matter of situational awareness—recognize the problem then recover. Our instructor chuckled at the mild maneuver I had given Chris. The next time I plunged into a steep, inverted dive. Smoothly, Chris rolled the wings level and gently pulled out of the dive.

What followed next was a series of emergencies, unexpected for the first day. As one system after another failed, Chris was left flying on the small, back-up flight instruments. He kept pace with each loss of hydraulics and electrics and calmly let me know what he needed from the checklist.

That night at dinner, we both laughed at our smashed expectations.

Chris relished the variety that came with the job: the places, the people, the assignments that fell into our laps, unlike the airlines where one would be stuck for months flying the same schedule, dropping into the same airports. Staying at EJA also allowed him and his wife the chance to move back to the Carolinas and be with family.

Although it would be a shame for the company to lose Chris, I felt lucky to be at a job where I went on the road or to school with such high-caliber pilots.

The next day, thirty minutes into the two-hour segment, I got an aborted takeoff call from Chris at one hundred miles per hour. Brakes, throttles, speed brakes—all emergency memory items (no time to read a checklist)—were executed while Chris added the unusual call to shut down the left engine. I did it immediately since he said that the throttle was frozen in the takeoff position. This emergency scenario didn't exist in the checklist. Our instructor was laughing, saying that most guys go off the runway because they simply bring the power back to idle and aren't aware that the affected engine is still producing takeoff power.

"This just keeps getting better and better," Chris said in deadpan fashion. "Can we switch to daytime?"

The company insisted that the simulator training be conducted under a night setting. Even though the sim's daytime graphics of terrain and buildings had improved since my first sim, there's also a psychological reassurance of seeing outside. Yet it was the sim at night that best mimicked the sensation and performance of flight. One particular flight condition, eerily duplicated by the simulator, was an actual approach to minimums in calm air and fog, a long glide back to terra firma, scouting for the brilliant approach lights. Several months earlier, I had discovered another similarity between the real plane and the sim.

On a night flight from Cincinnati to Chicago Midway, we entered the initial approach phase and discovered that the flaps were inoperative. I knew that O'Hare had longer runways and we changed destinations. The Citation Ten matched the flight simulator's performance for a no-flap landing, using almost fifty percent less runway than the book numbers indicated.

* * *

At dinner, Chris informed me of his class date the following month with American Airlines. It was midway through the week, and he was close to making a decision. The chance to fly the big ships, fly for the airlines, was pushing him out the door.

I told him that was a good enough reason to leave, yet he seemed embarrassed at revealing his boyhood dream. I related the story of my dad asking me when I was twelve what I wanted to do someday—fly in South America and write books, I confidently said. Chris understood, smiled and the discussion soon circled back to the Carolinas.

He had grown up in North Carolina on Roanoke Island, next to the Outer Banks. He started drawing a map on his napkin. A bridge connected the mainland to Roanoke, a narrow, north-south island and the next bridge connected to the Outer Banks. Chris said that there had been two Indian tribes on the island, the one comfortable with the white man and the other antagonistic. Chris said that those sentiments were still alive today, a North-South split of pleasant versus grumpy. When I mentioned the Wright Brothers, he smiled, saying that at the turn of the century he had a relative who had given Wilbur and Orville a hand.

Chris's great uncle was part of a life-saving station, an early version of the Coast Guard. They were stationed to the south of Wilbur and Orville's test area. Their job was to scan the sea for boats run aground. When the brothers needed help pulling the Wright Flyer out of a makeshift hangar, they would put a potted plant in the window. When the guys saw the plant, they'd walk up the beach and help out. The best part was his relative happened to be an assistant to them. He was the guy who took that famous shot of their first flight.

I shook my head in disbelief and heard our ground instructor's voice: "I think you guys have the best job in the country." It sure felt like it as I looked at Chris, lit up with pride, saying that the Wright Brothers had set up the shot with their camera and Chris's great uncle had taken it.

Some shot, I thought. The Wright Brothers knew the picture was for posterity, but how could they have planned the capture of such an elegant moment in time?

That photograph has always seemed wistful, not just because of the charm of its low-tech, black-and-white nature, but because it encapsulates so many dreams. Although they were adults at the time of the momentous event, there is a flavor of boyhood adventure. The one brother, the chance-taker, lies prone on the beautiful contraption while his older brother runs alongside with such emotion that he seems that he could fly as well. Then there is the flight itself, away from the observer. Even at the beginning, we are waving goodbye.

A number of years ago I flew the president of a small computer company from Kent. For years this man had owned a series of different planes—turboprops, exotic twin-engines that were fast and maintenance prone—for the sake of his business, but more importantly, because he loved to fly so much.

One summer evening, the boss and I were watching a lineman tow the plane back into the hangar, talking about our next flight. From where we stood, we had a view of the planes at takeoff, climbing toward the southwest, piercing the twilight sky. He turned to me and said, "The most beautiful thing about flying is the takeoff; I could watch them for hours." We paused for a few minutes, watching a departing airliner, enjoying its graceful bank and farewell.

* * *

Chris and I completed our training and wished each other good luck outside the simulator. Pleased with our performances, Pete talked with us about our future plans and asked Chris to stay in touch if he went to the airlines. Before we left his office, Pete mentioned Ernest Gann's *Fate is the Hunter*. Chris nodded, saying he had always felt part of that tradition.

After a few weeks and no word from Chris, I ran into him at the Teterboro Airport in New Jersey. He told me he was taking the plunge starting in two weeks.

I congratulated him and found out that the relative who took the famous picture was John T. Daniels. Today, a memorial to the first flight at Kitty Hawk bears Mr. Daniels's name.

He started to walk away then stopped. "Hey, did I tell you, this is my last day? I've got one more flight in the Ten over to D.C. I'm gonna miss that airplane."

That evening I had a flight to San Francisco. Other than moderate headwinds, the trip would be a pleasant five hours and ten minutes, with good weather expected in the Bay area. Near the end of the flight, I got up to stretch and one of the passengers asked if everything was going well.

"You guys aren't going to fall asleep up there?" Her smile was part serious, part teasing. "When you opened the curtain I felt all this heat from the cockpit, and I started to get worried."

"The heat was from all the talking we've been doing up there for the last couple of hours."

"I'm always worried that something is going to happen to the pilots," she said, blurting out the information as though she had been waiting, holding it in until now. "When I'm on the airlines, I break out in a cold sweat."

"You seem to be doing fine."

"Oh, I love the little jets. They get going so quick. I mean they make sense, like they're meant to fly. It's the big ones I can't stand. I have dreams about taking the controls."

"Where are the pilots?"

"I don't know, they're gone. It's a dream, you know, not a lot of explanation."

"Are you successful, I mean in the dream?"

"I guess. I never crashed. But then I've never landed either. I'm on top of a 747, lying flat, and I've got my arms on a long bar and I'm steering the plane by twisting the bar."

"That sounds like a version of the Wright Brothers. Orville was lying prone too."

I described the John T. Daniels picture of the Wright Brothers's first flight, but she was too excited with the terror and the thrill of piloting a Boeing 747.

Back in my seat, we reviewed the Quiet Bridge arrival into San Francisco. It was a clear night, the conditions well above minimum standards. With the airport and traffic in sight, I started my turn to place us slightly north of the extended runway centerline. The other traffic was a Continental 737, landing on the parallel runway. Both of us were cleared for the approach to our respective runways and required to maintain visual separation. Even though the controller staggered us slightly, we could literally fly alongside each other, wing tip-to-wing tip through touchdown. I decided to increase my approach speed so as to pull ahead for a little more room. After a smooth landing a few minutes later, we taxied to parking and shut the engines down. On the tarmac, my copilot and I said goodbye to the passengers, and I told the woman she was going to have to land that dream plane someday.

"I know," she said. "I'm not afraid."

35

ONE WITH NATURE

DURING THE NINETIES, a charter pilot named Ed Bones flew into Miller Field several times a month. His boss owned a furniture factory in Indiana and one in Ohio. Bones was the wrong name for a middle-age guy with a paunch who laughed easily. Frank appreciated his business. Ed always bought fuel, sometimes a quart or two of oil, and spent plenty on food. His only sin: He fed donuts to the airport dog. Frank confided to me that wasn't smart and often made the same point to Ed.

I was sitting with Frank and his grandson, Nick, having a cup of coffee, when Ed's voice came over the Unicom.

Ed's voice traveled from the office radio to the nearly empty restaurant, the steady, calm voice of an aviator. For all of Ed's earthy quirks, his voice was that of a professional, not a hint of the prankster while airborne. It was an extension of his short arms and fat fingers that skillfully moved switches and smoothly regulated throttle, mixture and prop controls.

The July wind was light. I ran outside with Nick to watch Ed land. It was ten in the morning, humid and my shirt stuck to my back as I ran.

Frank caught up to us as Ed turned a short final.

"Grandpa, where's he going to land?" Nick pointed at the

gleaming aircraft a quarter mile out, its nose pointing away from the runway.

"He's a got a crosswind from the right," Frank said. "Don't worry, Nick. He's lined up with the runway. It's just where you're standing. I love watching this guy land."

Within moments the twin Cessna was over the numbers of Runway 27, making a graceful flare and touchdown. Ed used about two-thirds of Miller's three-thousand-foot runway.

After shutting down in front of the restaurant, Ed spent a few minutes writing in his logbook, looking up and smiling at us on the ramp. Parker arrived, expecting Krispy Kreme donuts. The large mutt was one of the airport dogs rescued by Frank's daughter, Cindy. Ed was sure the animal wouldn't eat any other brand, declaring so from the cockpit. He walked onto the wing to an adoring crowd and a patient dog, sitting on his haunches. Ed made a motion, pretending to throw a donut and Parker darted into the grass and then stopped, looking up as if the sky had swallowed his treat. Ed reached into the backseat, grabbed a glazed donut and tossed it to him.

"You shouldn't be feeding him all the time," Frank said.

"I like feeding animals. I believe that if I build up enough good graces with the animal kingdom, they're less likely to devour me after I've crash-landed in the Everglades and a big old gator's climbing up my wing."

"Are you hungry?" Frank asked.

"I'm still thinking about that Sea World project you were gabbing about last month," Ed said, stepping off the wing, tucking in his wrinkled shirt. "After these investors spend a ton of cash, are they going to put up with skiers jumping past their living room windows? Screaming motor boats, stunts and whatever the hell they do? I thought you wanted some nice, quiet, out-of-the-way places."

"Ed, the skiers won't be there forever," Frank insisted. "But for heaven's sake, you just got here, relax a bit; tell me about your flight, your family."

"Hot and bumpy, and my wife's leaving me."

"I believe what you say about the flight, but your wife's true blue."

"Nailed me again," Ed said. "That's why I love coming here."

"Fred, you must know a whole bunch of rich people ready to plop down a buck fifty for property and a cottage?" Ed asked.

"I wouldn't dare approach one of my passengers with a business scheme."

"Well, maybe if you had the right introduction, a way to set the stage," Frank chimed in.

"One of our pilots tried to sell a share of a trailer park to a movie actress, and she almost bit his balls off."

"I know *your* man is a perfect candidate," Frank said, looking intently at Ed.

"Well, I haven't said anything yet," Ed confessed. "He's got a lot of irons in the fire. Fred, what about your pilot buddies?"

I started to say something, but the conversation ran all over the place between Frank and Ed, leaving me stranded.

Raising his voice, Frank said, "As a matter of fact, the nice young lady from Sea World has agreed to renegotiate on a summer-by-summer basis."

Ed sighed, looking at the hazy sky. "Frank, you've exhausted most of your negotiations in this lifetime, all that's left are renegotiations." He glanced down at the grandson. " 'Renegotiate,' Nick, is a term your grandpa loves to use when hashing over some dubious scheme. Another word he likes is 'wash'; it normally follows the renegotiation period. And of course in Corbi business lingo, the worst scenario is a failed renegotiation followed by a 'wash' that leaves no other recourse but to utilize an 'out.' That's when things have really gone to hell."

Nick looked stunned but amused by Ed's reasoning. He asked if Mr. Bones was hungry.

"I sure am. Eat first, and then we'll check out your grandpa's project."

Nick yelled, "Yes!" and Frank agreed, saying that Ed would think better after a good breakfast.

Ed chocked the front wheel to keep his plane from rolling into the fuel pumps.

"Mr. Bones, you must really like Parker," Nick said, watching Ed clean up a plate of home fries and eggs faster than anyone he had ever seen. "Donuts are expensive."

"I understand his place in the world, Nick. And it gives me a clearer picture of our place. Animals belong to us. We can eat them or just have them for pets, or treat them to Krispy Kreme donuts. The Bible offers clear guidance on our relationship to the beasts," Ed said. "Look, I like clear guidance. That's the reason I'm a pilot and not a liberal high school teacher, or part of the nature crowd. Hey, kid, when you hear someone talk about becoming one with nature, you know what to say?"

Nick shook his head and waited eagerly for the answer.

"Look them in the eye and say the quickest, surest way to become one with nature is to be ripped open and eaten alive."

Frank rubbed his temples, head down, and Nick said he was glad to hear someone put down teachers. He asked what a liberal was.

"It's a perspective, a way of looking at things—boy, I'm gonna get myself in trouble here." Ed studied Nick for a moment. Behind his eyes I could see his mind at work, a searchlight for Nick's passage through a haunted forest full of aging baby boomers dressed in shabby Peter Pan costumes. "The first thing is to learn to think for yourself, able to say something's right and something's wrong, and don't duck the hard decisions by saying the world isn't black and white, because it sure the hell is." Ed waved both hands down in disgust. "But I'm not here to pour my beliefs into that miniscule little brain of yours."

"Then tell me about the gator climbing up your wing," Nick said. Ed always seemed to have a backlog of weird animal stories.

Ed pushed back from the table. "Hell, wasn't my wing, thank God. It was a friend who had an engine failure over the Glades. Pretty nasty moment. Well, my buddy was flying a single-engine Piper Arrow when the engine quit about thirty miles west of Miami, just swamp for miles and miles. He did everything by the book, airspeed, attitude, looked for the most promising section of terra firma to land close to. Then he approached his landing area nicely, skimming across the water. Now my friend was no seaplane pilot, but he knew to keep the gear up. Yet he didn't really know how much backpressure to use in the landing, so when he the lowered the nose too soon, the water grabbed him and flipped him on his back.

"He's hanging upside down, the cockpit filling with black water, and he can't get the door open. Seatbelt off, he pushes with all his might and finally the door budges, and the next thing he knows he's at the surface crawling onto the wing of the plane. There's an island, maybe a hundred yards away, and he thinks about swimming until he sees the water alive with serpents and gators. Now, picture this: surrounded by swamp creatures as far as the eye can see and you're soaking wet, sitting on a portion of wing that's not submerged.

"Well, he prayed the authorities were looking for him since he had filed a flight plan. A flight plan will save your rear end, unless you're doing what your grandpa does all day—fly in circles around the airport, admiring your local treasure, not going anywhere. Where was I?

"Oh yeah, my friend's pondering his fate, when a big old gator swims onto the wing and starts to crawl up. This guy didn't even have a shoe he could throw at the monster; he took them off after the emergency landing. Inch by inch the fat bastard made his way up the wing and—" Ed paused, eyeing Nick's dessert.

Nick, caught up in the story, didn't even notice the piece of apple pie à la mode the waitress placed in front of him.

"Then the gator just stops and slides his gnarly ass back into the water."

Frank was enjoying the story as much his grandson. Ed continued. "Before nightfall, my friend's rescued. Do you think he'd survive a night of hungry gators and snakes?" He looked at Nick, who had found the dessert, shoveling it in, his eyes on Ed. No answer came, so Ed answered, "Nope. He might have survived the animals, but hypothermia would've been his doom."

Frank explained hypothermia to his grandson, adding that nature had a way of eliminating people quite efficiently.

"I've got the bill," Ed said, jumping up from his seat, scooting over to the cash register.

"Let's all take a walk out to the lake," Frank said, leaving the tip. "Nick, just leave your little radio here. I'll lock it in the office."

"Come on, Grandpa. It's a Walkman, not a radio. You don't have to listen."

"True, but it's the black bear sightings I'm concerned about. You don't want to be distracted by loud music in the middle of the woods, become a nice tender morsel for some hungry old bear." Northeastern Ohio had become the home for a small but growing black bear population, crossing over from Pennsylvania.

When Ed rejoined us, he pointed out the cracks as we crossed the runway.

"You better get moving fast on your cottage-lake idea, Frank. You're going to need some work on this runway in a year or so."

Frank said nothing, head down, thinking, pointing in the direction of the pond.

Ed walked behind Frank. "Now, Alaska in the sixties was a great way to build time for a pilot with a few hundred hours under his belt." He turned to see if Nick was listening. "Most of the pilots drank and the really stupid ones drank too much, including the operators. Weather, aircraft weight and balance were ignored as a matter of principle and manhood. And of course the accidents were numerous. Luckily, I soon found employment with a commuter outfit that had a semblance of respectability.

"The FAA hadn't much of a presence up there," he continued. "So we were on our own. You'd be long dead before the Feds got a chance to violate you for breaking the rules. I was no angel, but I understood aircraft performance and personal moderation. And, I wanted to live to see another day."

Ed had Nick's full attention, so that a couple of times the boy tripped over an uneven patch of ground or got swiped by a low branch. Once in the Christmas tree forest, Ed stopped and so did his audience. "Speaking of bears," he said, "the closest I ever got to a grizzly was at an outpost a hundred miles outside Fairbanks. The oil research post had been abandoned. We were no sooner out of the plane when a ten-foot-tall grizzly came crashing through a metal door. Why he didn't attack I don't know, but I guess he was more frightened than angry. We found cans of honey pried open and blood everywhere as the dumb ass cut himself over and over again to get at the honey.

"Now, a pilot I knew wasn't so lucky with bears. But I'll back up. Remember the drinking stuff I mentioned? The first time I met the unlucky guy he's doing shots and beers right before taking a couple of whores to a roughneck camp. I asked these ladies if they were really going to get in the plane with this guy and the one said, 'Oh, he only drinks beer when he flies.' "

Everyone laughed, including Nick, who showed a perfect row of white teeth.

"So they go and fly, and the whore—I guess I should say young woman—fell asleep. When she woke up, the rest of the passengers and the pilot were sleeping. She's looking out the window and the ground looks awfully close. So she yells, and the pilot wakes up, just as the engine starts to sputter. Down they go. He picks a patch of tundra and lands. Well, it was a week before they were rescued. The pilot made huge bonfires with the dry scrub and set most of the interior of Alaska on fire to get noticed. Now, what's the moral?"

Ed answered himself: "Don't drink and drive."

Again, everyone laughed. Nick's smile grew so that his eyes were full of light. He had entered the world of men.

"Now, I once heard of an Indian girl from Nome, getting the willies the first time she went to a place in the States populated with trees," Ed said. "She had gone to meet her boyfriend's parents in Seattle. What scared her was the possibility that a bear could be hiding behind any one of those thousands of trees. In Nome there are no trees, or very few. It's desolate, wide open to the sky. Could you imagine, Nick? A place like this would give her a heart attack."

Nick looked around at the trees, wide-eyed. Frank suggested they keep walking, but Ed said he had saved the best for last. As he started his story, the cry of a hawk made Nick jump and look skyward. The boy still smiled but nervously scanned the pines. He wasn't sure what kind of sound a bear made.

"The guy who set fire to Alaska," said Ed, looking back at Nick as we walked, making sure he had his full attention, "he's off flying hunters, roughnecks and whores and lands at a camp, drops off his passengers and leaves. He should have been home that night. The wife starts making phone calls to flight service, the charter office—nobody has seen this guy. So a few days go by, a full-blown search and they don't spot his plane until a week later, just on the other side of the lake he took off from. He never got out of ground effect. Nick, you know about that? If not, ask your grandpa later. So, he crash-landed in the trees, and got out alive only to be eaten by a bear."

Nick's mouth fell open.

"One with nature!" Ed proclaimed. He laughed without much sound, only his body shook and his eyes teared.

* * *

The pond's design flowed in a natural S-shape. Nick threw one rock after another, and Ed kicked around the shore, looking for arrowheads he said were certainly there. This little pond had always excited Frank, and now he talked nonstop about enhancing its natural beauty and increasing the airport's value.

"Why go through the trouble of building a bunch of cottages when you or Alan can build a beautiful place of your own—privacy, no neighbors?" Ed asked with a look of genuine concern.

"I like people," Frank said. "I don't want to live alone."

"The problem, Frank, your place is big enough for just one nice project, one home, like what Russ tried to do years ago. You know, a little retreat." He glanced at the abandoned log cabin at the north end.

"Why the hell would I want to come back here every night by myself?"

"Jeez, Frank. You got your wife."

"Well, hell, she needs more stimulation than just me and the woods. This place would really drive her crazy. She'd be drinking all the time. I wouldn't blame her. Who wants to drive through a dark forest across a runway just to get to the road to go buy milk?"

Frank stared at the pond. "If I can build a few cottages, get the lake enlarged and maybe your man interested, we won't be able to stop all the excitement for this project. If I'm successful now, I can be successful again."

"Knowing you, Frank, you'll give the best land to someone else."

"That shows everyone I'm being honest."

"Well, it's not a crime to take advantage of foolish people," Ed said. "If it was anyone else, I wouldn't care. I gotta say my peace. I like you Corbis. But, hey, you're a dreamer. Nothing wrong with that." He eyed Nick as he spoke. "I've had my own dreams, so I know the attractions and the pitfalls."

"It's worth a try," Frank said.

A large rock broke the water's surface.

"Come on, Grandpa, get a rock, it's fun," Nick urged, standing across the pond from him. His next rock landed so close to the bank that it sprayed Frank.

Frank yelled, "Stop filling my lake with rocks!" Nick went back to kicking up rocks with the end of his tennis shoe.

"They have a whole new crop of water skiers from the Akron area," Frank said, leading us back toward the runway. "They can practice here, hone their skills before moving up with the advanced skiers at the park. The young lady told me it's a year-by-year agreement. They'd like five years, but they're flexible. And if they become too much of a nuisance, they're out."

"What kind of deal is that?" Ed asked. "That girl believes her skiers will have a place for at least a few years, I'm sure. It sounds to me like she's getting screwed before she starts."

"Ed, those are the bare bones of the agreement," Frank said quietly. "These Sea World people want to renegotiate every year, and they like that. They like having an out. You can't blame them."

"You know, Frank, usually I can count on Alan to bring sobriety to your dreams and schemes. But you've got your son bamboozled as well."

Head down, Frank grinned.

"Fred knows this, but how 'bout you, Nick?" Ed asked. "Do you know that your grandpa has a magic touch with everything from lawn mowers to jet engines? But no magic with business—his deals usually benefit strangers, never him or anyone close to him."

Uninterested in replying, Frank pointed to the aviation junkyard, a small mound of discarded parts and wrecks from over the years. The crumpled elevator ribs from some plane rose out of the pile and smaller pieces—doors, windshields—were scattered near a large blue spruce, like presents around a Christmas tree. Ed followed us over.

Ed started to say something and stopped. Frank had center stage now.

Frank pulled a seat from the junk pile. It looked like the passenger seat of an airliner.

"This seat, I think, was used by Russ Miller on his boat. You see, Russ was good at a lot of things, but he was also just as lousy at a number of things." Frank lightly scratched the side of his head, a habit whenever he explained one of life's mysterious contradictions. "This man taught me to fly fifty years ago. No better instructor and a good mechanic, though his inventions were a problem. He got hundreds of people their private license. But get him out of the instructor seat and look out. With piloting he always had setbacks too. Remember what happened with the Seabee?" he asked, looking at me. "And the dog?"

Frank told the story and the three of us hung close, intent on hearing every word, even Nick, who kept eyeing the junk pile and the pines that could hide some wandering bear.

One of Russ's aircraft was a Canadian amphibian called the Seabee. Inside and out, it reminded me of a Jules Verne invention, probably from his novel *From the Earth to the Moon*, with its large cockpit and big levers and its ability to operate from land or water.

After the Seabee was grounded one summer with an engine problem, Russ and Frank finally had it running by late August. Unfortunately, it was black fly season at the Miller's cabin in the north woods. But Russ and his wife were both determined to spend a couple of weeks vacationing before summer ended. They packed the Seabee with a few essentials and brought along their small dog that slept peacefully on the backseat.

Russ was so excited when the lake and woods came into view that he lowered the gear instead of keeping it retracted. The water snagged it, flipping the Seabee on its back. Immediately, Russ released his seatbelt but had to slap his wife when she froze in her seat. Between the slap and the cold water filling the cockpit, Alice came to life and they swam to shore. The dog made it safely before they did and had already found a friend. The two mutts, unconcerned with the fate of the exhausted couple, were humping away, panting loudly.

"Russ took it personally," Frank said, catching Nick when he stumbled off a smashed wing. "He thought dogs were supposed to save your life. That's what he kept telling his friends for a long time."

* * *

A few weeks later, I was midway through a seven-day tour with a lot of short hops in the D.C. and New York areas, when I called Alan and found out that Parker had been killed. "Dad was right about the donut-eating dog," Alan said. "Stupid animal kept following every plane thinking it was Ed's—trotted right into the prop. Dad helped the girl, a student pilot from Kent State. He got her out of the plane and sent her to the restaurant. Of course, he cleaned up the mess and hosed down the plane. You know Dad, he took the cowling off and made sure the engine looked good, and then ran it up, checked the mags. The girl was horrified. And of course Ed was upset. He told dad his relationship with the animal kingdom needed some rethinking. What's that all about? I guess I'd know if I was here that day."

I started the alligator story when Alan interrupted me.

"And my sister's a basket case," he added. "She's already talking about adopting some dog she saw wandering around Dad's house."

I asked about Nick.

"I was worried about him too," Alan said, sounding relieved. "But he seems all right. He's convinced that Parker just decided to become one with the prop."

36

STARLINGS

AFTER A FERRY flight from Chicago to Louisville, Kentucky, I took a walk to loosen up before going to the hotel. The next day there was a morning flight with three passengers out of the small Bowman Field. The runways were short and narrow, giving every pilot plenty to think about for either the takeoff or landing.

I had agreed to bird-dog a bit for Frank, keeping an eye out for another Cessna trainer or even a four-place cross-country ship for one of the regulars at Miller's. But as I started across the tarmac, I noticed the few aircraft tied down along the edge of the grass looked tired and neglected. Turning into the parking lot, I saw a stand of old trees, oaks and maples, squeezed between the buildings and the road. The broadness of the trees, dense with leaves and shadows, created a wooded isle surrounded by noise and commotion from the traffic and nearby businesses.

Returning to the tarmac, I headed toward a worn-out Lodestar, minus the engines. This twin-tail ship was full of starlings. The birds and their nestlings made such a din that it sounded like fast-turning props. I heard them in the wings and behind the exposed firewall. One starling shot into the opening of the wing tip with a large earthworm in its beak.

That night the starlings outside my hotel window had clamored well past sunset. When I pulled back the curtain, a security light illuminated a few in the grass and several flying out of the swimming pool under construction. The border of the cement pool was torn up. Standing in the grass was a brown ceramic horse, and in front of a well-trimmed bush was a three-foot high sitting Buddha, in light and shadow. A few other lawn ornaments encircled the pool, waiting for the water to flow, the construction finished and their world restored.

The next day I returned to the FBO to wait for the passengers. I asked the manager, an old man himself, about the island of huge old trees in front of his building, and he said that they were at least a hundred years old.

"The Standifords donated the land for the airport." He motioned with his arm toward the ramp and runway beyond. "At one time, this was mostly pear orchards."

He started to write something on the daily flight schedule in front of him then stopped.

"You think those trees out front are big?" The manager looked at me as though I had challenged him with my tree question. "My wife and I were in South Carolina, visiting her sister. I wasn't there a day, and they both dragged me out for a tour of some old plantation. We probably walked two miles, mostly through woods, then swamp. I'm going along with my head down, watching where I step, ready to call it quits, when I look up and there's the biggest live oak I've ever seen. Six hundred and fifty years old! Isn't that amazing?" He waited until I nodded in agreement. "The giant limbs started just a few feet off the ground. Boy, and that Spanish moss hanging all over it, you thought you had walked into a dream."

He smiled to himself, as though he could smell the earth and reach out and caress the trunk. I asked him about the Lodestar on the ramp.

"Oh, that thing," he said blandly, leaving his daydream. "That belonged to Howard Hughes. That was the second private aircraft he ever owned. Every few years, people from some museum come out and pump air in the tires and shine it up. The last time they came, the door was falling off, so they just rigged it shut with wire and duct tape."

"All for the starlings?"

"Those are Howard's starlings," the man said as he turned and answered the phone.

37

DEMONS OF PERFECT LANDINGS

ALTHOUGH I NEVER had a chance to take Frank up in any of the jets I flew, I did have the opportunity to take my father on a short flight from Willoughby, Ohio, to our base of operation in Columbus. It would be his first ride in a corporate jet, and I wanted to impress him with a good flight, especially the landing.

Pilots have a saying that any landing you walk away from is a good landing, but few pilots ever beat their obsession with perfect landings. Recently, I flew with a guy who nearly went off the end of a runway attempting to hold off the aircraft for the perfect touchdown. By resisting the downward movement, he inched himself closer to the surface in order to grease it on—the tires rolling smoothly onto pavement.

A few months earlier, I had confronted my obsession with perfect landings. Smoothly, I brought the aircraft onto the runway in calm air, crosswinds and turbulence, allowing me to walk alongside the Buddha, the two of us pinning roses in our lapels, wondering why the demons of perfect landings had troubled us for so many years. My fall from grace—a solid thump one morning—felt like a slap across the face, and I found myself back in the real world making good and bad landings and caring too much about the bad ones.

A Cessna Citation had received new paint and interior at the Willoughby shop, and a flight check was required since the control cables had been removed and replaced.

The Citation had many fine handling qualities, but not its landing aptitude. The stiff landing gear made it difficult to avoid varying degrees of thuds and bangs. As my copilot and I readied the ship for our twenty-minute flight, I wondered if I had ever told my father about the plane's propensity for terrible landings. I couldn't remember and now wasn't the time to bring it up.

After takeoff, I glanced back at my dad, who seemed unnerved by the few bumps during climb-out. I had been flying big shots all week, but my father's presence added the tension of a flight test.

A storm over Cleveland required a deviation. Cleveland Approach suggested a westerly heading, keeping us north of the shoreline. The controller said there were level-four cells in this mass of clouds that stretched forty miles southwest of the city, yet the skies were clear above Lake Erie. I wondered if my father was admiring the spectacle—if he knew the havoc this storm was creating in the Cleveland area while we peacefully flew beyond its fury.

Everything tested fine en route except for an erroneous reading on one of the engine instruments. Nearing Columbus, approach control asked us to reduce our speed. The Citation slowed up quickly once the aircraft was configured in the "dirty" position. Dirty was a good word for dropping the gear, flaps, and, if necessary, popping the speed brakes. The dirty configuration made the aircraft stable and slow for landing.

Dali's painting of a young Christopher Columbus stepping onto the New World was an accurate rendering of an aircraft before touchdown. Gracefully, the explorer's foot is poised like the aircraft wheels: a perfect moment before contact. I rolled the Citation onto the runway and lowered the nosewheel—my smoothest landing in the past six days. With the thrust reversers deployed, I increased power to the engines to decrease the landing roll. Slowing the aircraft with thrust diverted forward was the only instance when pilots and passengers heard the engines roar. It was the last "dirty" exercise.

* * *

The door seal hissed as my copilot moved the handle to the open position. A mechanic climbed into the cabin and whistled at the new interior.

On the ramp, my father thanked me for the flight and mentioned the good landing. I wanted to inform him that there were better adjectives than "good" to describe a perfect textbook landing in an airplane known for its stiff, straight gear and unwillingness to cooperate in the landing phase. But I lacked the energy.

Exiting the building, I decided to have a smoke. My father shook his head and asked me when I was going to quit then turned to watch a Boeing 727 on final approach. I thought of mentioning how dirty that airliner was at this very moment—gear and flaps extended—but, like my father, I admired its slow-motion grace, thankful for its safe return and wishing the pilot a good landing.

* * *

On the drive home from the airport, we sped past trees flowering, the earth upturning an emerald mine of tall grass. My father talked of cleaning the yard with his grandson. He was especially proud of a trailer the two of them were building to attach to the riding mower. These were pursuits that never connected me to my dad. I avoided physical work growing up and was never encouraged to work with my hands. Perhaps if we had worked together, taking him for a flight would be a less anxious experience and more enjoyable.

Next, my father asked for the latest company news. I mentioned the purchase of a dozen mid-size jets. He commented on the company's expansion, my opportunities, then turned to me and said that I should be driving a bigger car.

"I'm happy with my car," I replied.

"Well, you can afford it. That's a long drive you make down to Columbus. What is it?"

"Two and a half hours, door to door."

"You're much safer in a bigger car. If we were in something small, your mother and I never would have walked away when we got broadsided in the Cadillac."

"What about living simply, having less bills. You've been telling me for years to be frugal."

"We were frugal growing up because we had so little to begin with. All I'm saying is, you don't have any big outstanding bills and that it would be wise to treat yourself to a nice car."

"Well, I feel perfectly safe in my VW Fox."

My dad sighed.

"When did you get your first car?" I asked.

"In high school I bought it from a friend, a '37 Oldsmobile. It cost me a hundred and twenty-five dollars. That was a big deal then. Not many people in our neighborhood even owned a car."

"But they got along without one?"

"Sure we did. But we didn't feel like we were missing anything either."

My father's words surprised him. He smiled at the avalanche of old memories and talked about moving from house to house when his father got tired of a landlord or simply couldn't pay the rent. Or awaking to a very cold house and having to shovel coal into the furnace. And he talked of a father and son who left their homes for work every morning singing loudly, full-throated. Even after the father suddenly died, the son kept the tradition, walking down the sidewalk to work singing, until he also died young.

As my dad reminisced, I thought of all those mornings that he prepared for work with high energy, sometimes singing, or encouraging us to do better in school, as he slapped on aftershave.

"You know what I like recalling?" my father said. "Making a big fire on a summer night with my friends in an old vacant lot. One of us would bring a bunch of potatoes, and we roasted them. Potatoes never tasted better." My dad chuckled warmly. "That's really something, don't you think?" he asked innocently. "Of all the darn things to remember so well."

After dropping him off, I headed home. The wild flowers along the side of the road, tall with purple and white blossoms, spread deep into the woods. I caught glimpses of more distant colors. Like my dad, I had my own memories that I cherished.

* * *

In high school I ran cross-country every fall. The days were usually overcast. I could still see a runner several feet ahead and myself growing stronger as he struggled for air and broke stride like some doomed animal. Finishing each race, I experienced a pain that wounded my entire body. I can no longer remember the races I won or lost, only that I finished with hard-won grace. Without speaking, my father supported me as I pulled on my sweatpants. The traffic in the distance and the voices of my teammates vanished. I heard only my breathing and saw only my father against the October sky.

38

GLOBETROTTING

ON A FALL Saturday morning, dad had announced that he was taking me on errands and leaving my younger brothers home with a list of chores. At twelve I was the oldest he reminded them, as they howled at the unfairness of it all. Mom just shook her head at being left behind as the enforcer.

Dad's Saturday ventures often meant a trip to one of his brothers, my grandmother or the West Side market. My dad was always pumped up around his brothers. They talked loudly, even shouting in a friendly way over the next delicious meal their families were planning, or a house or a car they were looking to buy, confident of a good deal.

Years earlier, my father and I had a memorable outing searching Cleveland stores for the materials needed to build a racer. He finished it the same weekend, and it worked beautifully—a coasting thing with ball bearing wheels, handle brake, steering wheel and a small storage box behind the driver's seat for tools and spare parts. Shortly after it was finished, I sold it to the kid across the street for a dime. That broke my dad's heart. But he never tried to get the racer back. I made the deal and had to live with it, he had said.

* * *

Dad and I made our escape and took Broadway Avenue, the artery that connected our home in the suburbs with my grandma's in Cleveland. Broadway was lined with stores, factories, auto dealerships and a sand and gravel pit that is still there a half a century later.

The previous summer, the entire family was traveling this familiar route—including our two-year-old sister in the front seat. We were stopped at a traffic light behind a red cement truck admiring its great rotating drum when the driver's door opened and my Uncle Chick climbed out. My brothers and I screamed his name from the backseat. He had surprised us all.

He was a handsome, broad-faced man with a mustache, dark hair and eyes and an easy smile. He wasn't concerned about the traffic light as he sauntered back to our car like he was taking a walk at the beach. He stuck his head in the open window and he and my dad smiled at the unexpected rendezvous and Dad started firing questions. A few moments later, mid-conversation, Uncle Chick growled something at us boys, making us laugh even more. After saying a few things to my mom and reaching across my dad to smooth back our baby sister's hair, he gave a good-natured shrug to a final question of Dad's and said goodbye.

Uncle Chick would die in his fifties, a robust man with a fierce growl that entertained us and always got our attention. He'd die with a full head of hair streaked with gray, long before old age would ravage him. That day he climbed down from the truck, he seemed "forever," like the sun.

* * *

I was looking out the window, still daydreaming, when my father asked, "Have you thought about what you want to do someday?"

"Write books," rolled off my tongue with pride, "and fly over the jungles of South America."

"You're dreaming."

At twelve years old I believed I had a license to dream. Friends, books, movies, the exotic tale of my dad's brother riding a horse through Northern Mexico, all of it had triggered my aspirations.

"Why South America?" he asked as we passed the very sand

and gravel pit where Uncle Chick worked.

"Um, anacondas ... jungle ... uh, the Incas, Amazon River—panthers?"

"Traveling is fine, but you can read about South America any time." Working his jaw, taking a breath, he weighed his next comments and then blurted, "I enjoyed the places I got to see in the Navy, like Chicago, San Diego ... boy, what beautiful cities." He wanted to say more and caught himself. "Stick to your studies," he said with a shake of his head, mildly chastising himself for the outburst his dreamy son might hitch a ride to. "You need to think about college right now."

He turned onto Prince Avenue with its squat corner bar, where my grandfather often came for a drink before he died.

Although college was an eternity away, I had no problem with dad prepping me for higher learning. I enjoyed reading, being studious and had ambitions of going to the Air Force Academy. Showing him that no fights loomed over the college thing, I asked about learning to fly before I left high school.

"You get a good job and then you can learn to fly."

Years later I learned that he was even stretched thin with guitar and accordion lessons for my brother and me. But he never complained about scraping the bottom of the checkbook, or, later, the huge cost of sending us to a Catholic high school.

Before turning down the narrow driveway of my grandmother's three-story home—all floors filled with family members—my dad mentioned someone's kid headed for medical school. And once again he brought up his friend, a local lawyer whose son planned on following in his father's footsteps.

Parking the car in front of a small garage, next to an old pear tree, its leaves already changing, dad told me to think carefully about my choices in life. Stubbornly, I believed choices meant following your dreams. Years later he would admire my decision to start flight lessons, telling all his friends and family that his son was going to be a pilot. Also, being practical, he immediately took out an insurance policy on me.

As we both grew older we'd often sit down on his back patio when I was off the road. There, I'd tell him everything about the week—the passengers I flew, where I went, any problems with the plane. And if there was another aircraft on the horizon, he'd smile and say, "Boy, that's fantastic." He took the writing dream in stride too, no longer worried of failure since I was making a good buck with a great company by the mid-nineties.

During my career, I'd travel to Beijing, Hong Kong and Singapore. In Jakarta, Indonesia, with the formidable jungles of that archipelago, its smoking volcanoes and Komodo dragons outside my hotel window, I began writing a Christmas novella called *Saint Nick*.

Piloting over the lower forty-eight as well as Alaska and Hawaii, I scribbled for years at the end of the day, taking notes on a host of inspiring visions that would become *American Sky*. I flew in the Middle East and Europe and West Africa and had time off to explore Almaty, Kazakhstan, and Athens, Greece.

Ironically, I never made it to South America. Customer demands, dispatch needs and aircraft mechanicals constantly altered my flight itinerary. So the furthest south I ever flew in the Americas was Costa Rica, even though my company routinely flew over the Amazon jungle and into the cities of Brazil and Argentina. We pilots just called it "luck of the draw."

We were on the back patio when I reminded my father about our long-ago conversation about flying over the jungles of South America and never making it there.

"You can't expect to visit every place on the planet," he said.

Dad was right, only adding to the mystery of our Southern Hemisphere. For me, South America remains a boy's vision of foreign travel and adventure. It's a place to keep dreaming about, a place to keep reaching for. I like that.

39

PATCH OF GREEN LAWN

IN THE MIDDLE of the night, in some foreign city, I woke up after a dream about my friend's father. Before the dream vanished, I got to the desk and scribbled away.

I'm walking over to Al's home on the street of my youth, Woodlake Drive. His dad, Stan Czarnecki, is tall and athletic— the way I remember him when I was a teen. He's going to show Al and me some baseball plays. He's energetic, strong, relaxed, showing us a technique for fielding the ball. In the dream I burst with emotion, knowing that even though this moment has passed, it still remains fully alive in some corner of this big old world. I look around at the overcast sky and the trees starting to leaf, aware that it's spring.

The grass is green, wonderfully green, and Mr. Czarnecki is smiling now, walking across his front yard holding a bowl of fruit, sitting down to eat.

Before waking I hear a voice, say, "If we could push sadness away, we could live forever."

On Saturday mornings I often went to the Czarneckis for a big breakfast of eggs, bacon and toast fixed by Al's mom. His two beautiful older sisters often perched at the breakfast bar wise-cracking, casting looks of feminine wisdom well beyond their years.

Mr. Czarnecki covered many topics—sports, careers, older kids in the neighborhood that were driving too fast down the street and the occasional war story. A favorite of mine was when Stan was ordered to go and wake up another sailor. Stan yelled for the man to get up and then started to rock the guy's shoulder when a wild left hook nailed him in the jaw. Obviously a setup, a local rite of passage, embarrassed more than sore, Stan yelled in the fella's ear the next morning and then quickly sidestepped the flurry of punches. On the third day, Stan Czarnecki stood over the sailor, quietly watching him and then simply clobbered the guy while he slept. The sailor awoke dazed and hurting, with the big Polack standing over him, smiling, right arm cocked for the next punch, saying, "Wake up! It's gonna be a good day."

There were other stories, the stuff of nightmares, of Japanese soldiers boarding the ship at night stripped down and greased, stabbing men and eluding capture.

The story I remember best was about a major decision Al's dad made near the end of the war. Stopping in Hawaii for supplies, he said that he looked out from those beautiful sands upon the Pacific and weighed it against family and home. I never knew if he spent minutes or hours contemplating his next move. Seated in his kitchen, eyeing another future, his long pause made us feel we were contemplating the decision as well. Finally, slapping his leg, he returned us to the smells of bacon frying and coffee brewing, telling us that he turned his back on a life of travel and adventure, confident that marriage and raising a family were to be his destiny.

These stories were meant to enthrall, and they did. What I know now is that Stan Czarnecki was retelling the wonders of life at sea with all its danger and terror. He had been transmitting a part of himself, the explorer part that might give his son and me that extra kick in the pants to get out in the world and make something of ourselves.

Those Saturday mornings were a special time during the long haul of growing up. We enjoyed it immensely and learned about courage and steadfastness and humor that packed a punch. But like many men from his generation, we only learned of Stan Czarnecki's heroics after his passing.

As the USS Wren's chief petty officer stationed in the engine room, Stan's job was to ensure the men kept the engine running and the ship moving. The oil-fired boilers required around-the-clock vigilance by crew members, the firemen, who watched the water level in the boilers, and the oilers, who checked the bearings for overheating. Frozen, burnt bearings could not only stop the ship but signal the enemy with black smoke from its stacks, making it easy pickings for the Japanese. The crew's other responsibility was to keep sea water from swamping the red-hot boilers and exploding.

One fateful day an air attack damaged the engine room and set it ablaze. Through fire and smoke, someone had to close the valve that prevented cold sea water from reaching the boilers. When no one volunteered to make the crawl through the wreckage of twisted pipes and equipment, Stan—six foot four, two hundred and twenty-five pounds, with a forty-four-inch chest and twenty-seven-inch waist—made the belly crawl, stripped down to his skivvies. His only demand was that they keep the water hoses on him. Climbing over hot pipes, staying as best he could beneath the smoke, Stan reached the valve and wrenched it closed. He returned to his crew exhausted and "sunburnt" from the heat.

I did a search of the USS Wren and discovered that it was hit several times in the Pacific Theatre yet never suffered any serious damage, attesting to the courage of one man who prevented a catastrophe one afternoon and saved a lot of lives.

The USS Wren and the other ships Stan served on in World War II were Fletcher-class destroyers—fast, maneuverable and able to take a lot of punishment like the big Polack himself.

On watch one night in a terrible storm, Stan had to strap himself to the railing so as not to be swept overboard. Like Odysseus, whose crew tied him to the mast, ears unplugged, in order to hear the Sirens yet not follow them to his destruction, Stan likewise had to listen to a thousand symphonies of rage and seduction embedded in the storm. Perhaps over the cold, lonely hours, a singular melody surfaced—the sirens mocking him, tempting him to remain a seafarer, pointing to a Hawaiian shore and other exotic shores and oceans of the world. That night as the bow plunged deep and the waves broke high over the ship's mast, Stan kept to his job, his station, his duty and celebrated his twenty-first birthday with a can of tuna.

Mr. Czarnecki understood the dream of adventure, and he understood the American dream. He once told me that his job was to make sure that his kids would do better than him. If he accomplished that, he had accomplished his most important job.

Years later, after Al's parents retired and moved out, I still enjoyed the short walk to my friend's house. The neat yard with its pretty flowerbeds, brick well with rope and bucket, still was in good shape after forty years. It was as though every owner since recognized the hard work that went before and wanted to roll up their sleeves and maintain the tradition. The only real change was that one of the two oaks near the street—used as goal posts—was gone.

Sitting in the front yard, Al and I spent many a summer night listening to the men of the neighborhood talk about everything under the sun. The best moments were at twilight.

One such evening, Mr. Czarnecki gazed at the twilight sky and began talking about death, his own. Everyone listened. The only bird still singing was a cardinal that flew from a dogwood to the woods behind the house. But Stan Czarnecki wasn't watching the birds that evening—he was smiling, legs crossed, holding a beer. With a twinkle in his, eye he described what the process of death might be like. My dad and I just listened, and Al mentioned something about the soul. But Stan believed that his whole person would be making the voyage.

"It's going to be an adventure. I don't fear it. A real journey and no looking back."

Remembering this evening nourished my optimism toward life. I'd never forget a middle-aged guy, smiling at death, sculpting his own view of immortality on a summer's evening on a patch of green lawn.

40

WITHOUT A SCRATCH

I FIRST MET Jimmy Vecchio in the ninth grade. The Catholic high school arranged our classes by our smarts—starting at the top with 9A and continuing through 9G. Jimmy and I were in 9F. The low end didn't bother us since we knew that there was nowhere to go but up. And *up* for a fourteen-year-old was continuous adventure.

Early on, I'd recognized Jimmy in books like *The Catcher in the Rye*, except that he wasn't worried about letting a kid slip through the rye and over the cliff every now and then. In the movies, I'd see his energy in actors like Paul Newman in *Cool Hand Luke*.

In the tenth grade, he introduced me to Lenny Bruce's *How to Talk Dirty and Influence People*. Jimmy identified with the sharp-tongued hipster and passed the book around to our classmates until nearly every page was dogeared. When I mentioned it in our philosophy class, the priest let Jimmy read an excerpt. In one riff, Bruce talks about how he wrestled with the apparent hypocrisy of the rich church surrounded by poverty. Jimmy read the poor guy's punch line without flinching: "Raggedy ass guy won't go into a raggedy ass church. 'I live in a shit house, why would I go and pray in one?' "

If he wasn't pushing iconoclastic characters like Lenny Bruce, Jimmy encouraged those around him not only to have a ball but to unleash their talents. Whenever I mentioned flying, he'd stare at me with a big smile, asking, "Jets or props?" or at lunch pull out a book on Greek mythology and read about Icarus getting too close to the sun and losing his wings.

After a gym class, when a bunch of us had showered and started getting dressed in the locker room, Jimmy walked up to me and combed my wet hair into a Beatles style. "You see, you look good with your hair like that. You should try out for the next play." But that was Jimmy's ambition, not mine. He once told me how an actor could experience everything—love, death, adventure and still finish the day without a scratch.

In our science class, he sat behind me and gave me a shove when the teacher mentioned the cross-country season approaching. "Hey, that's something you'd be good at," he said, leaning forward in his seat. "You don't shoot your mouth off all the time. That means endurance. Christ, I'd die after a couple of minutes."

I joined the cross-country team and won Most Valuable Harrier the following year. Unfortunately, the football awards occupied most of the banquet and my coach, Mr. Mayforth, spaced out and forgot to award me the trophy. That same evening I imagined a chicken bone was stuck in my throat and had my parents take me to the emergency room where an X-ray showed nothing.

"Call the school paper and tell them how Mayforth screwed everything up," Jimmy said. "Those clowns owe you. Hey, you might get your picture in the paper." Jimmy enjoyed seeing himself in the school newspaper or yearbook, and made a point of showing up for photo shoots of clubs he never belonged to, his arms folded, looking skyward, gazing at something above, beyond arm's reach.

I had my driver's license but was unable to get the family car the way Jimmy did. I can't remember the model, but his parents had a boxy, small station wagon, one of those cars that a sixteen-year-old who combed his hair down across his forehead and wore penny loafers regarded as cool. Jimmy drove as if the next destination couldn't arrive soon enough for him. Leaning forward, his forearms resting on top of the steering wheel, he pushed further into life than anyone I knew.

Throughout high school, Jimmy befriended college-age kids whom I found intimidating. When we did get together, I endured the crowd, watching him flirt with every girl in the room, wondering if his charm was transferable. However, football players about to have their girlfriends swept away were not charmed. Only female intervention and fast talking defused potential fights.

The last time we were together was at my parents' house. We were both in our early twenties, smug and excited about a lot of things in life, especially music. Jimmy raved about Creedence Clearwater Revival, and I countered with Frank Zappa. Since I was on home turf with *my* records, I was able to torture him with one of Zappa's more complex instrumentals. Jim listened and I can remember him shaking his head, saying how CCR's music shot up from the ground, right through the soles of your feet, fire and defiance.

After high school our contact decreased to maybe a phone call a year. During these short conversations, Jimmy spoke quickly, excitedly, trying to explain a thousand new ideas, encouraging me to chase down my own dreams, learn to fly if that's what I really wanted to do. But before he went to work on the Alaskan pipeline, I started hearing stories from friends about his involvement with drugs, of deals gone sour. One summer's evening I learned that he had been murdered in Alaska. That night I walked the neighborhood for hours, thinking about him, thanking him with hot tears and looking up to see my friend falling through the sky, his wings destroyed by the sun.

Recently, while driving home from the Columbus airport after finishing a seven-day tour, I wondered what Jimmy would have thought of my career as a pilot. He might have laughed at my uniform, but I knew he would have appreciated the unending view of America from coast to coast. Dialing in a station I caught "Bad Moon Rising" just as it started. That scary, foot-stomping piece was the most forthright tune on the planet. For years I had heard this song yet only then did I sense its power—an act of sympathetic magic that protects by evoking what we fear. I pounded the floor with my left foot and yelled the lyrics out the window, hoping Jimmy could hear me. Speeding past eighty miles per hour, I leaned forward with my arms resting on top of the steering wheel and peered into the rich night, making it home without a scratch.

* * *

One night I dreamt about my high school friend, years after his death. Exiting one dream, I ran into Jimmy in the next. He wore a canary-yellow suit and a white shirt. Pressed against him from behind was a beautiful young woman with her head resting on his shoulder. Her arms encircled Jimmy. We talked of our travels, and I told him how much I still missed him. I woke up feeling the sadness behind my everyday life. No bitterness, just a realization that an overriding sadness seemed to extend in every direction—sadness at the quick of life.

41

B-52

Looking over Frank's shoulder, I watched the images of Alan and General Cardenas on the camcorder's small viewing screen. Frank took aim with a close-up as the general described his flights in the XB-49, the Flying Wing. Alan listened intently, slowly rubbing his chin. The general, short and robust, seemed to have the same energy now as he did over fifty years before when he flew down Pennsylvania Avenue at the behest of President Truman. The President—who was fascinated with the plane and wanted to buy some—cautioned the young test pilot not to run into anything.

The avenue was lined with trees, hiding several tall radio towers and the White House. Major Cardenas slowed to three hundred and fifty miles per hour and started his pass, looking for the towers. When the Dome suddenly appeared, he pulled up. Luckily, someone snapped a picture of the Flying Wing over the Capitol Dome, perhaps inspiring the mania for alien-invasion movies.

After the Capitol flyover, Cardenas started back to Edwards Air Force Base. En route, six of the Flying Wing's eight engines failed due to low oil pressure. The crew made an emergency landing at Winslow, Arizona, where they discovered that the problem wasn't in-flight oil leaks, which would have drenched the engines, but a low oil level.

Frank Corbi kept videotaping and explained that if an engine spit out just a teaspoon of oil, it looked drastic, like it was bleeding profusely. But oil wasn't blowing out the engines. They just hadn't been serviced properly to the correct level.

Although the transcontinental flight and low pass at the Capitol took place in February of 1949, by year's end Congress scuttled the Flying Wing after the plane broke apart during a high-speed taxi trial.

When the General walked off, Frank held the camera at waist level and reviewed his recent footage. Alan looked around in awe at the massive hangar full of jet fighter and bomber aircraft. I had finally made it to Dayton's Wright-Patterson Air Force Museum and the 27th Bomber Group reunion. Earlier that day I also got to see the suburban neighborhood where the Corbis lived in the 1950s. The streets and the brick ranch homes were familiar, an understated miracle of material progress and sweet reason. Alan had said, "I used to play with Gus Grissom's kids." He laughed. "All we did was run through the backyards on summer nights before their dad was called to Washington for the Mercury program."

* * *

In the shadows of planes like the XB-70, a forerunner of the Concorde, over a hundred guests listened to a speaker who had been interviewing POW survivors from World War II. He was writing a book to commemorate their service and sacrifice. Frank sat with arms crossed, smiling thoughtfully. Sometimes he raised his hand, palm up, moving it slightly as though weighing the speaker's words. He sat low in his seat, comfortably in tune with the speaker and the buzz of old friends who leaned over to say something. It seemed that his eyes grew bright with vivid memories of flight tests, crashes, amazing rescues, short, brilliant lives and long, satisfying ones, like his own. Once the speaker finished, Alan turned to his dad and asked him why Chuck Yeager wasn't there. Yeager was part of the Fighter Bomber Squadron but rarely made an appearance at the reunions.

I leaned over so I didn't miss Frank's explanation.

"His agent said that it wouldn't be profitable for him to spend his time with us," Frank said, sounding resigned to the inexplicable ways of the rich and famous.

Another speaker took the stage.

"He was a good pilot," Frank added, talking quietly, "But there were plenty of other pilots every bit as good. Some guys, well, things fall into place for them better than others. Some people can just do the right thing at the right time nearly every time. But we all worked hard, some of us died during that testing. He should be here. We don't begrudge him the money, all his popularity. But he should recognize the men who kept those planes flying and the ones who flew them, like Cardenas."

General Cardenas had piloted the B-29 on all of Yeager's flights in the rocket-propelled Bell X-1. The small aircraft, shaped like a .50 caliber bullet, was air-launched at twenty-three thousand feet. It needed a running start to perform its one mission: break the speed of sound, which Chuck Yeager did in 1947. The general once had to land with the X-1 still connected to the belly when the shackle mechanism failed during flight and couldn't be released.

There was a break. A few old acquaintances came by to talk with Frank, leaving Alan and me free to roam the museum.

We stopped in front of the XB-70. A white, futuristic ship with a swan neck and a cockpit that extended one-hundred and ten feet from the main landing gear, it resembled a sleek alien spaceship from the movies. Alan shook hands with Joe Cotton who stood in front of the supersonic bomber, looking at it like it was a favorite old book he could still page through.

"This plane never went into full production," Joe said. "It was a prototype for high-performance bombers, even commercial stuff like the Concorde."

When Alan mentioned his father's name, Joe smiled, saying he remembered Frank Corbi.

That night I learned that politics played the biggest role in removing the XB-70 from the production line. During a photo shoot, an F-104 got caught in the Valkyrie's wing tip vortices and slammed into it, resulting in both aircraft being destroyed and the two pilots killed. The Air Force used the accident as an excuse to get rid of the program.

When Mr. Cotton excused himself and walked off with a few friends, Alan mentioned that his dad always said good things about Joe.

"Dad said he was real methodical, not excitable—a damn good pilot. I don't remember seeing him as a kid. But then all adults probably looked the same to me."

"How long did you live down here?"

"Until I was twelve." Alan paused, looking at the plane like he and Grissom's kids had just stumbled upon it. He looked it over from nose to tail. "What a thrill it must have been to fly this. It's so beautiful."

I agreed and asked him if he knew its top speed.

"Mach three, and the nose heated to over six hundred degrees. Cotton and the boys may have hit that speed only once. There were a lot of problems. Ground stuff is what I remember. And I think they put a restriction on the speed when the skin started to separate. They couldn't figure out why. Hey, if we run into Joe again, we'll ask him."

We approached the B-52, and Alan just shook his head.

"Dad took a lot of movies for the Air Force from this plane. I bet I've only seen a handful."

The B-52 was a droopy-winged monster, able to drop a lot of bombs on the enemy. It wasn't exotic like the XB-70 or aesthetic like a fighter jet that could transition perfectly from combat to crowd-pleaser at a weekend airshow. This utilitarian hulk that operated during Rolling Thunder, over Vietnam, looked the part—all bomber, a deadly kin to the bombers of World War II.

As a flight test engineer, Frank and his crew experimented with severe icing conditions over the Pennsylvania Mountains and Alaska. But the initial testing was accomplished at Eglin Air Force Base in a cold hangar, still in use today. Known as the Climatic Laboratory, its enormous refrigeration systems were used to lower the temperature to as low as minus sixty-five degrees Fahrenheit. There in Florida they'd spend the day dressed in heavy, warm clothes, observing and recording the operational function of systems after the airframe, equipment and engines had been cold-soaked to minus forty degrees.

Alan and I heard our names and turned to see Frank filming us.

"We threw everything at this beast, and it kept flying," Frank said, pointing with his thumb at the B-52 as he kept peering through the viewfinder.

Cleaning the lens of his camera with a hanky, he started talking about a flight during the summer of '49.

"I was there to test new radio equipment."

His crew of the B-45, a four-engine bomber, had been assigned a six-hour ferry flight from Wright-Patterson to San Bernardino, California. At twenty-nine thousand feet over central Kansas, they encountered a fairly solid line of thunderstorms and had to deviate. Between the deviation and Frank adding more time for the tests, they had gotten low on fuel. As they tried to contact Forbes Air Force Base in Topeka, lightning hampered their communications, garbling the reception.

"How come I've never heard this story before?" Alan asked.

Frank looked at a blinking red light on his video cam, shrugged and continued.

"The radioman couldn't talk with the tower and our fuel was getting low. Then to make matters worse, the navigation receivers gave us nothing. We couldn't plot our position. We needed to communicate and we needed a steer," Frank said, referring to an older form of navigation where a ground receiver painted the aircraft as a lightning strike every time the pilot keyed the microphone, depicting the position of the aircraft on a screen, making it possible for the ground controller to assign headings. "Many precious minutes went by before we heard a voice saying he had a fix on us. A fella from Tinker heard us."

The operator on the ground was in the control tower at Tinker Air Force Base in Oklahoma. After plotting the B-45's position, the controller gave them a heading and started vectoring them toward the airport, where a short time later they landed safely.

"Where were you going to land if you didn't make contact?" I asked.

"It would have been an emergency landing in a cornfield."

"Or someone's house," Alan said.

"With all the heavy rain, low clouds and lightning, we wouldn't see the ground until we hit it."

Alan reminded his dad what he had told him years ago about emergency landings at night. Frank smiled and said that you got the ship configured: airspeed, flaps, controlled descent, lined up like there's a runway in front of you, and then, at a hundred feet above the ground you turn on the landing light. Frank paused, allowing the bleakness of the situation to sink in, even though we all knew the punch line.

"If you don't like what you see, turn off your landing light!" All three of us laughed, and Alan asked if there was more to the story.

"Of course there's more to the story," Frank said. "I haven't got yet to the best part."

The next day, Frank and his crew met the three servicemen who were manning the tower. The youngest looking one said that the crew of the B-45 was very lucky. Having completed their tower duties, they were closing down for the night. Almost out the door, one of them mentioned the garbage cans outside, against the building. For months they talked about painting the old rusty cans, and that night they decided to stay a few extra hours and paint them. One of the men suggested that they leave the radio on since they'd be within earshot if someone decided to call in.

"Saved by rusted garbage cans," Alan said, astounded by his dad's luck. He started to tease his father for not saying anything until now and then stopped himself.

"Great timing on part of those men," Frank said, smiling a big, forward-looking smile. "Actually, I'd call it coincidence."

42

FISH HEADS AND RICE

IN LATE WINTER of '98, I started to get into Frank's car and noticed the backseat was filled from a recent shopping spree. Besides his skills of mechanic, pilot and survivor of Bataan, Frank Corbi ranked as an expert bargain hunter.

He smiled. "Everything's from Sam's Club." I glimpsed a miniature compressor, packets of batteries and pens, cans of coffee and tuna. There were only a couple of filled bags; the rest was strewn across the backseat. I tried to figure out what was there, but he told me to jump in.

"It's like Christmas there," he said. "I can't help it. I see all this stuff, all the good deals, and I've got to have it."

I was armed with my tape recorder and a list of questions, hoping to add his POW experiences to the book I was writing. Before visiting Frank, I reviewed Japan's attack on the Philippines, only hours after Pearl Harbor. During the next four months of fighting, supplies dwindled, reinforcements never arrived and General King, commander of the American-Filipino Forces on Bataan, finally surrendered on April 9, 1942. The men were starving and suffering from disease and injuries.

After King's surrender, General Wainwright continued to occupy Corregidor, the island guarding the entrance to Manila Bay.

In order for the Japanese to make their assault on Corregidor, they had to remove seventy thousand captured American and Filipino soldiers from the Bataan peninsula. The march out of Bataan and the subsequent years of imprisonment began as a logistics problem for the Japanese and ended in a nightmare that took the lives of nearly seven thousand Americans by the end of the war. The march started with ten thousand U.S. soldiers.

I turned on my tape recorder as Frank started answering my questions. He confirmed the many reports of men bayoneted and shot if they straggled to the back of the line or off the road during the five-day march from the southern tip of Bataan to Camp O'Donnell. Frank watched as a Filipino woman was bayoneted, possibly for handing rice wrapped in a banana leaf to one of the prisoners. The Filipinos suffered over five thousand dead on the march alone; the Americans, six hundred.

As Frank named possible restaurants, he corroborated my latest data.

Hoping to eventually become a pilot, he had graduated as an airplane mechanic in 1940 from the Chanute Air Force Base in Illinois. Assigned to the 48th Material Squadron of metal workers, welders, and mechanics, Frank's unit was sent to the Philippines to support the fighter and bomber aircraft.

"I went over on a luxury ship, *The President Coolidge*, and later on, another so-called 'luxury' ship took us to Japan."

We stopped by an Italian restaurant that was closed, and Frank mentioned we were near where he had grown up.

This side of town was depressed and shabby; the homes looked neglected; the trees bare and lifeless for months. Winter tipped into spring. Frank turned onto North Liberty, the street where he was born in 1919 and would live until enlisting in the service in 1939.

"When I was a boy, I used to watch the planes from my backyard," Frank said. "The Argo factory wasn't far from my home."

"Argo? Never heard of it."

"Alliance Aircraft Corporation. They built planes before the Depression wiped them out."

He pointed to a shed in the backyard of his old house. "I used that little building for developing pictures." He maintained his love of photography with a laboratory of video and computer equipment in his basement, where he edited wedding pictures or transformed eight-millimeter home movies into video with sound. A guy like Frank could have been born on Lucky Boulevard.

* * *

After General King surrendered his forces, Frank Corbi had a trek of seventy miles to Camp O'Donnell in grueling, one-hundred-degree heat. The Japanese allowed the marchers to rest in front of artesian wells but killed anyone who made a dash for the cool water.

"There was no stopping, even if someone fell," Frank said, slowing down in front of another restaurant that was also closed. "That's why having a buddy was the real life saver. You watched out for each other, supported each other, or you dropped and never got up again."

I mentioned the rumors of MacArthur's return. Of course there were plenty of them, he said, and for a while, they lent hope. In Donald Knox's *Death March: The Survivors of Bataan*, a rumor circulated during the fight for Bataan that a black cavalry unit had landed in Manila to rescue the men. Frank pondered my information then shook his head. "That's nice, but I never heard that story."

Frank shifted in his seat, gazing left and right, perhaps expecting a familiar corner, small business or abandoned playground to trigger another memory.

Frank said, "A lot of disappointment with MacArthur leaving us there in the jungle with the Japs all those years—but what could he do? What's worse is they forgot about us a second time—no reparations. And boy we sure deserved something—prisoners, slaves working the docks and mines. A few of us keep writing, but the politicians are looking the other way, waiting for us to die off."

"That's a shame."

"You go and check it out with the computer. You'll see what I mean. That computer and Internet must scare the hell out of 'em. You can chase 'em down, build your case a lot faster. Oh, well, we'll see what happens."

Frank asked if I'd like to drive past the old Taylorcraft plant where he briefly worked and learned to fly after the war. "It's not far from here. Then I'll take you to my old-standby place to eat."

He guided the car along the city limits where older homes and empty lots transitioned into forest. Usually, Frank wasn't prone to talk about his experiences, believing the details of his imprisonment were personal matters of little interest to others. But at eighty, with many of his friends gone, there was a desire to make sense of a long life. A sandpaper company now occupied the long, narrow buildings. Woods and fields surrounded the business. Frank drove up to the spot where a new aircraft would get its final check before the test pilot took the controls. Both of us got out of the car, and Frank pointed to where the runways had been located.

"You know, I first saw my wife here. Her group built the wing, starting with just the spar. Another group covered them." Frank looked from the sky to the buildings and smiled. "Aggie worked at a restaurant in town as well. That's where I started talking to her. I was pretty timid at first, so I'd just come in and buy a pack of smokes, then leave. We didn't date very long. I had hot pants. Well, that's what we used to call it."

We got back in the car and drove to his favorite diner.

After a few months in captivity, Frank and the other men turned their conversations from sex and freedom to the talk of food—all the different foods they'd eat once at home. "You know, I kept a little journal of all the dishes we'd make for ourselves someday. There was picnic food, holiday food and the three squares."

I turned the tape recorder back on and asked Frank about his fish heads and rice diet.

"We didn't have it all the time, but when we did, it gave me strength. You know someone who wants to go on a diet? Put them on fish heads and rice for three months. They'll lose weight and stay healthy." Frank smoothed his napkin then added, "Sometimes during the march, they'd let us rest alongside the road and there'd be a little bush with flowers. When we got up to leave, every flower was eaten off that bush."

The flowers were probably abundant in vitamin C, great for the immune system, and possibly an early contributor to Frank's remarkable health. But Frank reminded me that at the prison camp, Cabanatuan, he contracted both malaria and dysentery during his internment. What saved him from dying of malaria was the quinine acquired by the medics.

When a mound of home fries smacked the hot grill, Frank glanced at the cook then resumed talking.

"Now, if you're already healthy, and have a good immune system, your best chance to maintain your health is with as little medicine as possible. You see, I believe medicine can make your body lazy, dependent. That little bit of quinine was a miracle, but I had other things go wrong with me, and no other medicine to depend upon."

His toughest hours were aboard the notorious Hell Ships bound for the Japanese mainland. Like many others, Frank hustled to stay alive in camp, where there was some room to maneuver, using wit and skill. But the cargo hold of his first ship was filled with men standing shoulder to shoulder, front to back. Even managing a breath might depend on a man's height. Frank said the afternoon before their departure the temperature was well over a hundred degrees. "Imagine that heat, then thrown into a hole of a steel ship." This first Hell Ship was the *Oryoku Maru*.

Frank paused before digging into his scrambled eggs. "Some men just went crazy down there, and there was nothing to do but kill them. Of course, our big problem was no water, and this made the men do terrible things. Some tried to drink blood."

In the camps, one could imagine how a man might live with hope. But the condition of men pressed into a hot, dark cargo hold, standing in their own filth, and hearing the cries of madness, was a horror that would only be wiped out by the atomic bomb. For the men who survived, the *Bomb* would be their black cavalry that comes riding over the ridge.

I took a rest from my questions and went to work on my omelet while Frank continued.

After the *Oryoku Maru* was badly damaged from an air attack, a train transported the prisoners to Northern Luzon in order to reach the next ship. Boxcars meant for forty men were packed with a hundred. Frank survived this ordeal where other men died standing up.

A torpedo disabled Frank Corbi's last vessel, leaving it to be towed the rest of the journey by a destroyer. Of the original sixteen hundred men that boarded the *Oryoku Maru*, only three hundred survived to reach Moji, a seaport not far from Nagasaki. Soon after reaching the slave-labor camp, Frank took ill and required three months to recuperate before he began working daily, unloading ships. The prison camp overlooked the harbor, so it wasn't uncommon to hear mines exploding below. During the night, allied aircraft would seed the bay with mines, and the next day Japanese mine sweepers and unwary ships set them off. Occasionally, news of the war came from the guards. In the closing months of World War II, these same guards talked in awe of an aircraft called the B-29 and nervously mentioned rumors of a secret weapon.

On August 9, 1945, the ground shuddered as it had many times before. Five days later, Japan surrendered. By the terms of the surrender, the Japanese had to provide for the safety and security of the American POWs. When Frank's liberation came a month later, he learned that the Americans, in the powerful, four-engine B-29, had dropped a new bomb on the city of Nagasaki. The explosion he had heard and felt had been detonated seventy miles away.

By train, Frank passed near Nagasaki, bound for the port and an American ship to take him home. He said as you neared the city, the trees furthest from the explosion had lost their leaves. The next group was without branches, until finally, the trees were gone. The burnt steel structures left standing leaned away from the center of the blast.

We left the restaurant and then drove to the hospital to pick up Frank's wife from her weekly dialysis treatment. Frank Corbi and Agnes Svoboda were married in 1948, raised three children and lived for the next twenty-three years at Wright-Patterson Air Force Base. Aggie wasn't quite ready, so Frank and I sat in the waiting room and talked about his time on the B-52.

"They tried out new things with the aircraft all the time," Frank said, referring to his work as a flight test engineer. "Today, someone would object, or try and sue. But you know, we didn't feel like guinea pigs. We knew what we were getting into. That was our duty." Frank added, "You accepted a situation and improvised."

When they wheeled Aggie into the lobby, she asked if her husband had been driving me crazy with all his stories. Not much, I said, adding that I couldn't be that critical of a guy who bought lunch.

It took some maneuvering to get Aggie in the front seat and her wheelchair in the back end of the station wagon. I was starting to get in when she warned me about all the junk cluttering my seat.

"Just throw it in back if it's in your way," she said, laughing. "Did he buy up the whole store?" Even after today's treatment and several years of illness, Aggie looked girlish and ready for a fight.

Frank defended himself, saying that he had bought some things for Aggie as well.

He started the car, and I had a chance to examine more closely the spoils of his morning shopping spree. Sitting next to this small mountain of gadgets, tools and food, it was like riding around town with Christmas in the backseat. The bearer of those gifts and his wife argued almost continually, on two different tracks—Aggie expecting her husband to be more sensible, thriftier in the future, while Frank insisted that he had forgotten some things and needed to return to Sam's Club the next day.

* * *

When I think back to that day, I wish now that I had pursued more time with Frank—more note-taking, more recordings over lunch. Hearing his voice today over the tape player, I'm reminded not only of the uniqueness of his life, but his voice as well. His voice is calm, comforting, without sorrow. A voice recalling nightmares that have slipped into history, a voice asking us to remember.

43

CATHEDRALS

AT THE START of the new millennium, I was recently married and had rejoined the Catholic church. Sue, my wife, had never stopped attending, while I had been absent for nearly thirty years. Her quiet passion for her faith was evident sitting next to her in the pew, her rosary held lightly, a straightforward look of devotion. When I looked from my pew at the other worshippers at Immaculate Conception, I often saw that same quiet passion.

It was wonderful to be in a solemn church again, paying homage to God, away from jets on takeoff, the earsplitting noise of the tarmac and egos colliding. The layperson reading might not always articulate a Bible passage with precision, a new piano player's tempo might falter, the cantor drift off-key, and the priest's homily not as inspiring as last time, but nonetheless, perfection abounded in a shared liturgy deeper than the ages. The drama of Christ's life, death and resurrection was played out in the humblest of settings, with a few precious drops of blood scooped from eternity.

Later in my career, flying to Europe, I'd walked through the greatest cathedrals and found them possessing that same humble quality of my church back home. The artistic genius that built Notre Dame Cathedral was in service of something greater than itself.

44

THE STREAM

DRIVING DOWN CANTON Road after lunch with Sue and my father-in-law, I spotted a Citation Ten on base leg into Akron Municipal airport.

"Watch yourself," Bernie said, chuckling, as I accelerated, both of us looking up as the jet angled toward Runway 25. From the backseat my wife leaned forward, tapping his shoulder, and said, "Hold on, Bernie. We're on a mission."

With Sue's help, I found the streets that led us to the airport on a beautiful September day in the fall of 2000. The plane was just taxiing in when we pulled into the parking lot. At eighty-seven, Bernie exited the car with some difficulty, but on his own. He wore plaid pants, a sweater vest, long-sleeve shirt and bolo tie.

A few minutes later, we were on the ramp talking to the co-pilot, who expected passengers soon. Luckily, we had a camera, and I took a picture of Sue and Bernie standing on either side of the plane, hands resting on its nose.

"I hope you have a lot of pictures of this ship," Bernie said. "It's a beauty. Who's that friend of yours that takes the pictures?"

"Frank Corbi. You met him at our wedding."

"Okay. I remember now. Has he seen this one?"

"About a year ago."

"You worked for him when you first got started," Bernie stated confidently.

"I sure did. And I know I've mentioned his survival of Bataan; his years as a prisoner of war. Just last week I heard another remarkable story from that time."

"Yep," Bernie said with a pained look, not interested in war stories on this sunny day. "He's a good man," he said with finality.

Before I could echo Bernie's remark, the captain returned and told us to take a peek inside.

"Okay, lead the way," Bernie commanded, negotiating his large frame up the narrow steps, admiring the interior with intelligent, peaceful eyes.

Sue had gone first, waiting at the top of the steps, and I followed in case he needed some support. Slightly hunched over inside, Bernie smiled at the state-of-the-art screens for aircraft control and navigation.

"Those are the TV tubes you've talked about," he said, pointing at the rich-colored screens displaying checklists, a moving a map and digital engine instruments. "Okay, that's good," he announced loudly, turning toward the exit, heading carefully down the steps.

Bernie never lollygagged, especially away from home. A direct question required a direct answer, and Bernie was finished. His phone conversations followed the same path. After stating the reason for the call or answering a question politely, he followed with, "We'll see you later," or, "We thank you for calling—over and out!"

Twenty minutes later we were back in Bernie's kitchen.

"You know, I've always wondered ... what I can't understand is how those engines stay running," he said, seated in his chair, arm resting comfortably on the table.

"That flame in the can is so intense, it just gobbles up all that compressed air coming its way, maintaining the fire," I replied.

"But if I hold up a match and blow on it, the flame goes out."

"True, but you can't do the same thing with a blowtorch."

"But the pressure of all that air across that flame."

"I'd call that flame an inferno."

Bernie smiled, thinking in another direction. "I was told once that the jet engine is a model of simplicity—a lot less moving parts than the old piston engine."

"That's right. The piston engine is always on the verge of tear-ing itself apart, like some people I know."

"I don't want to know who," Bernie said, amused, raising his arms as if surrendering.

"The jet-engine concept is simple: It turns and burns. And performance is incredible. The Citation Ten engine can push five times more air out the back than goes through the core engine for combustion. The core engine turns the turbine that turns the fan. Remember now, the fan is what we see looking straight at the engine of most airliners and corporate jets. And for every pound of air through the core, five pounds is accelerated by the large fan and blown out the back creating most of the thrust. The air the fan accelerates goes around the engine and never hits the fuel and spark—you know, the spark that never blows out."

"It's an engineering wonder," Bernie said with a catch in his throat. "But how many people know this, respect the knowledge and the men who built this?"

"Not many. From the Wright Brothers to the Citation Ten is an epic story that should be taught in school."

Bernie thought about that. He had never lost his boylike curiosity about the marvels of flight. Born in 1912, he grew up with the excitement of Lindbergh flying across the North Atlantic or a pilot crash-landing at Akron Muni, carrying whiskey from Canada during prohibition.

Finally, he said, "Well, write a book. But don't let it go to your head." As he rose from the table, he asked, "You and Suzie like some coffee?"

He enjoyed making us coffee. He told us to sit down, that he'd take care of it. His kitchen was unchanged from the fifties: linoleum floor, green countertops and an oak kitchen table. All the burners of the electric stove folded vertically at the back when not in use. Standing at the sink, filling the coffee pot, Bernie could see his backyard: a row of tall arborvitae, a large tulip tree and a jungle of moon lilies popping into view at the bottom of the window. His property, along with his parents' house next door and St. Matthews church, just a block away, had once been part of the Reymann farm. The family donated the property to the Catholic church.

His father and mother had moved into east Akron in the late 1890s. Bernie was the middle child in a family of sixteen brothers and sisters. His parents' hard work had built not only the farm, but two businesses—a foundry, where Bernie worked as foreman, and a mattress company. Although the Depression nearly cost them everything, the Reymann family still enjoyed a measure of security and prosperity that many in their community had lost, producing two priests, war veterans, successful businessmen and many grandchildren and great-grandchildren.

Bernie poured each of us a cup. I tried to help.

"Just sit down," he repeated. "I slept well last night. No dizziness."

"I can at least get the milk." I grabbed it from the fridge, taking a look at the backyard, viewing the third story of the original Reymann home, rising above the arborvitae. Currently, it was a group home for adult, mentally-challenged men.

"Bernie, I'm amazed at the condition of your parents' home. I forget when was it built."

"Nineteen-eighteen, fifteen rooms, brick and timber; it should last another hundred years."

"How about the barn?" I could see the roof from the kitchen.

"Built in the twenties."

"Wasn't the barn built with the house?"

"Of course," he said loudly, annoyed by my question.

"What happened to it?" Sue asked.

Bernie smiled as he left the kitchen, saying he'd be right back. He returned with a bottle of B&B and three shot glasses.

"What's the occasion?" I asked.

"You answered one of my questions today about flying, so I'll answer yours about the barn," he said, pouring the liqueur.

"I hope I did a better job with engine combustion than trying to explain the jet stream."

"Your explanation of the jet stream," he said with a scrunched face, indicating dissatisfaction with a turn of his hand, "let's call it adequate." His mild rebuke eased into perplexity. Shaking his head, pouring shots, he added, "I still don't understand how it's formed. Oh well."

Bernie and I had a running discussion on that high-altitude wind that wraps itself around the globe. He was puzzled by its creation, how it was sustained. I used my knowledge, read up on it, but my explanations had never satisfied him.

Bernie took his seat. We toasted his health then he pointed out the window. "Anyway, that's not the original barn. The original one was connected to the north side of the house. That was the European tradition."

"What happened?" Sue asked.

"Well, there was a three-hole outhouse connected to the barn, and the twins were in there—Cletus and Clem—playing with matches." Bernie wagged a finger, as if reprimanding his brothers. "One thing led to another, and they started a fire. The barn was full of hay."

"No time to put it out?" I asked.

"My parents didn't see it for thirty minutes," he said defensively. "When they did, my dad called General Tire and they sent their fire trucks. People were stopping on Canton Road getting out of their cars, helping us empty the house." Bernie folded his arms.

"Strangers?"

"Of course. They were just driving by. They wanted to help."

"So the fire trucks made it in time?"

"Oh, they made it. But it was raging and headed toward the house. The wind was blowing that fire right toward it. And in front of everybody, my mom got on her knees and started to pray, and immediately the wind changed direction and the house was saved. A hundred people witnessed this miracle." Bernie's voice cracked.

We sat at the kitchen table in silence, waiting for his final thoughts.

"The next day, my parents took inventory and nothing was missing," he said. "Those people who helped carry everything out of the house carried all that furniture and family stuff back in. Not a fork was missing."

On the drive home, Sue and I remembered the miracles that occurred throughout Bernie's life, especially the ones we watched from his small back porch.

Rabbits appeared unexpectedly, and the sycamore's bark measured the intensity of the coming winter. In early fall we'd examine the tree, especially its north side, and Bernie would peel off a hunk of bark showing its thickness then pull apart the layers before making his predictions. With his wife, Edna, Sue's mom, they cared for the yard daily, planting, weeding and occasionally sprinkling the gardens with holy water. One September, a sunflower bore so many heads that the local paper came out and took a picture. When Edna died in December 1988, a flower bloomed in a bed alongside the house. And the day of her burial the temperature was unusually warm.

Edna was Bernie's second wife. They shared their lives with St. Matthews and each other. Edna took care of the altar and the priests' vestments and Bernie mostly the yard and whatever chores Edna asked of him. Like that radiant sunflower, their life together was full and rich, which only added to the loss Bernie felt with her passing.

* * *

On the back stoop the topics were unending—family, politics, religion and back to the jet stream.

"If it's a river, I should be able to see it," Bernie stated one afternoon.

"Good point. Sometimes bands of high cirrus clouds outline the jet stream. And the anvil head of a thunderstorm points in the direction of the prevailing winds. And if it's high enough, it's in the jet."

We had framed two pictures of the tiny porch. In one, Bernie was gazing straight ahead, thinking out loud, the philosopher-king forging ideas mankind would employ for centuries. The other was of Bernie and his granddaughter Amanda, her knees pressed together, starting to blow a bubble with her gum, while Bernie looked on, bewildered.

From this perch he empathized with me when I had to leave for Almaty, Kazakhstan, for a special assignment in the Boeing Business Jet, an extremely fancy 737 designed for only eighteen passengers, with bathrooms, showers, a master bedroom, dining room table and a large plasma TV on the forward bulkhead. Although severe hearing loss in one ear ultimately prevented him from serving in World War II, he mentioned his month away at a summer military camp. There he learned to fire a Thompson submachine gun and dealt with the daily struggles of military life. "I was so homesick," Bernie said sadly, the past still raw. "I was just devastated." Yet when I finally had journeyed so far from home and was terribly homesick myself, I got this response one afternoon when he answered the phone: "Nobody misses you. And Suzie's found someone new."

Shortly after my return from Almaty, Sue and I had taken Bernie to lunch and returned to his house, planning to visit for a while. As Bernie grabbed a couple of lawn chairs for us, we got antsy, thought of what needed to get done and decided to leave and finish some shopping. For the few minutes that we stood in the bright sunlight, a life-giving wind swept through my father-in-law's backyard. The wind seemed to dive over the arborvitae on a mission from God, an airborne elixir. Later, I regretted our abrupt departure.

Bernie went to mass daily. When he was still able to walk to church, unassisted, he followed the same path through his yard around the east end of the arborvitae. On a later visit, near summer's end, Sue noticed that a dense patch of white clover marked the path that Bernie had walked for decades. Of course there was clover throughout the yard, but this grouping made a thick, well-formed path of flowers leading from the porch to the corner of his yard.

* * *

Near Christmas, 2001, we sat around Bernie's kitchen table with his son's wife, Tammy, and her daughter, Amanda. We just had set the table and poured shots of B&B when the lights went out. Bernie told Tammy to get candles. All of us stood up as our eyes adjusted to the darkness. The moment felt rich, creative. As Tammy lit a candle and we took our seats to enjoy the liqueur, the lights came back on. Bernie laughed, enjoying the brief interruption.

After ham and scalloped potatoes, I asked Bernie about his brothers who fought in the war. Without a word he rose slowly from the table. We followed him into the dining room, where a picture hung of his brothers in uniform. He said that Father Jim's B-29 was a decoy for the Hiroshima bombing, and the infamous twins were fighter pilots: Clem piloted a torpedo bomber and Cletus a P-38. Bernie mentioned that his brothers Vince and Richard were also in World War II and Tommy was in the Korean War. He said one brother was saved returning from a mission by the aircraft carrier's commander who, against orders, had lighted the flight deck so that the Reymann boy and other airmen could land.

"But it's my mother's prayers that brought them all back," Bernie concluded.

* * *

By summer 2002, Bernie started going in and out of the hospital often, and it became more difficult leaving for work. Yet I still believed he'd be with us for a long time, to share an experience or to answer any question. And when I told him of all-night flights over the North Atlantic or my first visit to Westminster Cathedral, he always had something to add, even if it was just his surprise, his enchantment with life itself.

Once I called from London, and my wife told me that Bernie was home again after several days in the hospital. She said that they had sat in the backyard and that the air and sunlight were perfect. They talked easily, unhurriedly, followed by long, comfortable silences. Birds landed a few feet from Bernie, who sat smiling in his brown pants, shirt and vest. She said it was so beautiful, so peaceful, that she cried on the way home.

That Christmas Bernie and the Reymann clan celebrated at his parents' original home after a thirty-three-year hiatus. Accompanied by friends, the descendants of those sixteen children filled the large home once again. The men who lived there were taken in by their families or other homes for several days. Bernie passed out candy canes with his brother Gil, ninety-six and wheelchair bound. Across the room, Uncle Cletus prepared a group of kids to sing a carol. "Listen to me. Sing good, not loud. There's a difference. And pay attention, or you'll crap it up."

Joining us in the music room was Father Al, a sarcastic, dedicated missionary who served in Central America for the better part of his priesthood. He pointed at the ceiling. "That was my parents' bedroom where my dad died. We're all standing around his bed, and my mom tells me to go get a priest. I reminded her that I've been a priest for ten years. She called me a fool. So I went and found a *real* priest."

Bernie couldn't make the short walk back to his house, so Sue and Tammy got the car. I stayed a bit longer before walking back in the deep snow. Halfway to Bernie's, I stopped to feel the cold and listen to the voices as the great old house slowly emptied of its guests.

Bernie was undressing in his bedroom when we barged in on him. With one leg in his pajamas, he was having trouble negotiating the other, reaching for my shoulder for balance. "It's hell getting old," he laughed. "Your reward for helping an old man is right there in the closet." He laughed louder when I screwed up the German word for a shot of whiskey and then grabbed the bottles off the shelf, pouring a B&B for Sue and me and himself a large shot of Canadian Mist, topped off with Mogen David blackberry wine. Bernie said the wine took the edge off.

* * *

Several months later the phone woke us up near midnight. Bernie had passed away. At the hospital I had a few minutes alone with him. I told him how much I loved him and how I'd miss our talks. In death his mouth hung open, not in agony, but in the desire to finish another sentence, complete another thought, ask another question. A few hours earlier he had enjoyed a cup of chocolate pudding.

A nurse told us that Bernie went peacefully—"No lie," she said. "He was agitated earlier, trying to take his clothes off. We'd get his clothes back on and play his music."

His music was Gregorian chants. When he was first admitted I had made the mistake of buying a CD with musical accompaniment. Bernie wanted just the voices, unaccompanied, and I rushed out and found it.

The nurse added, "When we checked on him again, he was settled down. And the next check, about fifteen minutes later, he had slipped away."

As Bernie died in April of 2003, his yard was just coming to life. The ground had warmed but the air was still cold. I took a walk with Amanda who, deft in the practice of loving and torturing her grandfather, now felt the pangs of real separation. The streets looping around Bernie's house, his parents, St. Matthews and a high school, roughly formed the boundaries of the old Reymann farm. Amanda and I walked this perimeter talking little until we were headed back toward his house. She said, "I wish Grandpa could come back as a teenager, so he'd be healthy again and not sick."

The following day we again took our walk. Passing St. Matthews, walking uphill, a strong wind plowed down the street, a real headwind that made us pull our coats tighter and bow our heads. "Grandpa sent the wind," Amanda said. A short time later, with the wind at our backs, we approached Bernie's house. Amanda darted in while I stood on the street facing the sun as it slipped toward the horizon, obscured by new houses across the road and the remaining woods where Bernie and his brothers had once played when they were young.

Bernie's front yard was steep, and the two flowering crabs with pink blossoms had been cut down years ago. Yet the unadorned brick house with its grass lawn, budding sycamore and evergreens, looked peaceful, content with the changes time had brought. Walking a few feet more, I spotted a stream flowing along the curb to Canton Road. Bernie's house sat squarely over an underground spring that once filled a trough for their animals. He said they had to harness and redirect it during construction to avoid damage to the foundation. But no damage ever occurred.

"Birds come often to drink and bathe," he once told us.

45

BROTHERS, SONS AND FATHERS

IN LATE SUMMER 2003, Frank and I met one morning at Miller Field for breakfast. Since Frank sold the airport in '96, it had been sold again. Frank was anxious to meet the new owner, confessing that his unfinished dreams had kept him away from Miller's.

I arrived before Frank and surveyed the runway with its asphalt patches and noticed that the Christmas tree forest appeared fuller, more foreboding. The cool wind seemed a harbinger of fall. I remembered mornings like these, getting a plane ready for passengers or a student, the deep silence before activity made the world conscious. And there were the summer fly-ins where either side of the runway was lined with planes, some of them aerobatic, like the Pitts, a small, fast biplane that ripped the air overhead like the sweep of a chainsaw.

On slow days when customers canceled, Alan and I often took walks, talking about the life of the airport and our own lives. When good friends of mine had moved out West and I was earning practically nothing, he gave me a pep talk on how I could save a few bucks, set aside the time and make it out to see my friends yearly. Since then I've never missed a visit.

Frank pulled up in his late-model white Cadillac. His spirits were good. Inside the restaurant, both of us looked around, trying to notice any changes, and Frank started talking about the new owner.

"Now I think this new fella may have some real potential. The last guy, the one that bought it from us, was always strapped for cash, and he wasn't around very much. The place died for a while. But now I think it's back."

I didn't recognize the waitress and neither did Frank.

"How long have you been operating here?" I asked.

"Too long," she said.

"Well, we'll pass the word along," Frank said. "You make a good cup of coffee, and I've heard the food is good too."

"You must know the same six people that come here. This is my last month. He doesn't advertise. He only fools around with those toys."

Frank laughed. "He's an ultralight man. Nothing wrong with that," he said after our waitress disappeared. "He has a vision, and that's what counts."

"I've never been very interested in ultralights."

"Are you kidding?" Frank leaned toward me. "The technology has moved a million miles ahead of where they were even ten years ago: new engines, lightweight frames, everything state of the art—wings don't fold up with a gust of wind."

"If I ever go back to flying small stuff, it'll be the Cub or Cessna 150."

We both glanced out the window, searching for aviation life in the form of a canvas motorized kite, the single occupant too big for the contraption. Even a one-quarter-scale-radio-controlled airplane whipping about, or an extra from a Pixar movie, would be promising, but nothing stirred the air.

"How is this guy going to do any better than the last guy who operated the place?" I asked.

"Well, what I heard is this new boy has some money." Frank grew serious. "He owns a couple of bars in Kent. I've heard money isn't really an issue for him. Time is. But not money. I'm hoping when we take a walk up to the hangar, he's there. I've got ideas that may help him." Frank smiled shyly at the waitress, who set our food down in front of us. I could tell he was reluctant to ask her more questions. But he waited until the table was set, and she asked if we needed anything else.

"Well, you could let the new owner know that Frank Corbi is here, and we'd like to chat for a few minutes."

"You'll have to track him down yourself. The guy's invisible. I don't see him until the rent's due. Good luck."

After breakfast we stood for a few minutes alongside the runway. Frank placed his sunglasses on and stared down at the neglected runway, where a few small chunks of asphalt had been ripped out and grass sprouted. Other places had been repaired.

"You know, the runway is the heart of any airport, but only part of the picture," he said. "Besides the buildings, there's all that land, beautiful land that could be developed. I know I've told you a bunch of times to look over those passengers you fly, but maybe we have our boy right here, someone who'd enjoy real expansion. Most people want to add to what they already have. Build it up, make it better."

"Some people like to just hide out. I think that's what the waitress was trying to tell us."

"I know. She's not a real happy person. Who knows, maybe her husband or her kids don't fall in line." Frank looked across the runway in the direction of the lake. "You just got to take a chance. I bet this fella never heard of our relationship with Sea World."

Years ago Frank had finally talked the Sea World people into enlarging the lake, just beyond the Christmas tree forest. The new lake would allow their skiers to practice in privacy. Frank got a bigger lake but Sea World never used it. I hadn't seen it since the excavating.

Frank swept his gaze up and down the runway. "After we meet the new owner, I'll drive you back there and we'll check it out. We'll park and walk. My car won't make it through those ruts."

As we started toward the maintenance hangar, as we had many times before, I looked over at Frank, his head lowered, swinging his arms in time to his own thoughts, moving his hand in a command motion, making a point that needed emphasis. We walked along the open grass where the Seabee, a Canadian amphibian, sat an entire summer with Frank and Russ climbing all over it, arguing about its mysterious engine problem. In the hallway between the restaurant and office, the Corbis had hung a list of Russ's students who earned their private pilot ticket. It was now gone. Russ Miller's accomplishments were remembered by fewer people. Even though he was retired when the Corbis ran Miller Field, he was there to congratulate me on my emergency landing and to needle Frank about working with him on the exotic Silver Thing project. And when Russ stayed away for long stretches of time, his name came up often, and his many accomplishments were discussed. Under a warm September sun, the memory of Russ Miller glided past us, a light wind drifting slowly over the grass, a few parked cars, old hangars, toward the airport's boundary, making me wonder who else remembered this man's life.

At the hangar entrance, Frank and I examined the ultralights. They resembled insects in various stages of dismemberment. I remembered Alan describing them as a folding chair stuck inside a mosquito net hung from a wing. A short man with thinning hair approached us and asked our business. Frank started explaining his history with the airport, and the man looked around but never directly at Frank.

"I'd like to talk with the new owner," Frank said.

"I'm not sure if he can talk. He's busy with a client," the man said defiantly.

"Well, how about if we look around the hangar, if you don't mind," Frank said diplomatically.

The man walked off without answering.

I grew tense, angry that Frank was being snubbed in a place he had owned and worked in for years. We stopped at the different machines and examined their nylon wings and canvas cockpits, tiny engines and propellers. I grudgingly admitted they appeared somewhat intriguing and made the mistake of saying so.

"You see, you're getting the bug also. Now with your background you never know what opportunities may lie ahead for you."

Frank started saying something about a two-seater when the owner appeared. He towered over us, a chrome pipe in one hand and a rag in the other. His long, reddish-brown hair touched his shoulders.

"Can I help you?" he asked.

"I'm sure glad to meet you, Mr. Hornfischer," Frank said, full of charm. "Your mechanic told us to look around, and I'd have to say, this is some operation. These ultralights represent a new stage in aviation."

"It's my hobby," Hornfischer answered.

"I think you've got a pretty profitable hobby."

"I'm not interested in making my hobby profitable."

"Well, I can understand that," Frank shot back. "But you like nice things. And this airport is one of the nicest in the county."

"Frank used to run the airport," I said, matter of fact.

"You're the guy who ran it before Bob Markey?" Hornfischer asked.

"That's right. For sixteen years. My son and I—he's not here today—but I'd like you to meet him. Well, we had a good run with it. Of course things got a little screwed up at the end, with the investors and all, too many chiefs, but I still have a vision for this place."

"I own this place now," the owner said, wiping the chrome piece with the cloth. "I've got plans."

"That's great," Frank replied. "Look, I came close to developing the land back there with a lake and plans for cabins. And I feel, you know, it's not only the money you can make, it's the fun everyone can have building on a great piece of property."

"Sir, I'm not interested in developing the land except for my family. In a few years I'll build a house on that little lake. I like my privacy."

"We all like our privacy, but you have a lot to work with—a runway with repairs—"

"Look," Hornfischer said, "I'm not interested in the runway. You saw those patches?" Frank nodded. "That's the last time I put a dime into it. I don't need it."

"Well, I've heard some pretty crazy ideas. A runway is the heart of an airport."

"Hey, I need only a hundred feet to take off and land. You see all the grass out there, the grass parallel runway, the grass north-south runway? That asphalt runway can go to hell, crumble right before my eyes. Now I've got things to do."

He turned and gave a nod to the mechanic, who watched us, ready to spring if his master commanded.

"What about the pilots, for God's sake," Frank spoke loudly. "What's going to be here for them?"

"Bingo," the man said, turning and smiling for the first time at Frank and me. "I don't care if another private pilot ever lands here. Don't have any use for them."

Frank started scratching the back of his head vigorously, unable to comprehend such stupidity.

"Let's get out of here, Frank."

We were almost to the restaurant when Frank stopped and said that maybe he should have introduced himself to Hornfischer in the restaurant, anywhere but the hangar.

"I know when I worked, I didn't like to be bothered."

Actually, the opposite was true, but I wasn't going to argue with him. Frank and his son would go out of their way to be gracious to the people that interrupted their work constantly. Hornfischer never once called Frank by his name. Frank's history was unimportant to him. Yet as we got in his car, he was thinking of more angles to impress the new owner with.

"He doesn't need much money to operate this place," I said, watching the owner and his son race across the runway on quads.

"Maybe he's just a big kid," Frank said, smoothing back his hair, relaxing from the encounter.

We drove to the northwest corner of the property. The lake was a half-mile away on foot, and Frank grabbed his camera. We started walking through bursts of sunlight and shadow. Frank smiled as he walked, looking down until I asked him about the rows of large trees.

"Miller's dad planted them over eighty years ago. You see, he was doing something about the future. I guess this fella doesn't care much about the future." Frank sighed loudly. "I feel like a ghost today, a little ghost drifting along, from one place to another. It's not so bad though. Maybe I'm not really here anymore for those folks. But I can appreciate the work they're doing and this pretty walk."

Once again Frank somersaulted through his dreams and landed back on his feet.

He stopped walking and took out his digital camera. After describing its features, he instructed me to stand in front of an old maple and took my picture.

The woods opened to a golden field, a lake and Russ's ancient log cabin.

"Russ was a scout leader, and he got the kids to build this for him. He laid out the plans and taught them how to read the drawings and use the materials."

The roof had caved in, but Frank said that was to be expected with age and neglect. The log walls and floor were solid, like the red brick buildings of Miller Field. With a new roof and cleanup, the cabin would be a fun place again, especially with the lake. You couldn't see the lake from the runway, and its size was impressive. The gentle "S" shape made it even more attractive.

"So, this fella might build his house right on the lake," Frank said rhetorically, walking the bank. "That's a good idea. The lake has the creek and a spring to keep it fresh. It'll always be nice."

Frank turned when he heard the sound of quads approaching. But none appeared. There were many paths cut through the Christmas tree forest. After a few minutes, the quad noise receded like killer bees that had changed direction, finding someone else to torment.

"Alan and I always had too much going on to get out here and fix this log cabin," Frank said. "I bet it's beautiful out here at night. A big fire."

"Cooking a big piece of meat," I added, and Frank laughed.

"That's right. You'd starve out here if you didn't bring the grocery store with you. I'd be happy with some marshmallows. You probably want to eat again when we get back."

Before we left, Frank had me take some pictures of him standing by the lake and then in front of the cabin. We started into the woods, neither one of us saying much. I increased my stride, and Frank kept up until I heard his breathing become labored.

"Let's stop a moment," he said, trying to catch his breath. "You're not trying to kill me, I hope. I'm not leaving much behind."

"Frank, just relax and quit talking. Catch your breath. I'm sorry I got into such a rush."

I had never seen him overexerted and wondered if I needed him to stay put while I got the car. The dried-out ruts weren't that deep. I suggested this to him, and he said to forget it. Just give him a few more minutes. Every time he tried to say something, I started talking.

"You and Alan have a lot to be proud of. Maybe you didn't get around to fixing Russ's cabin or building more hangars or length-ening the runway, but you found the energy for me and a lot of other pilots who had a real ball out here."

"I know," he said, his breathing normal again as I helped him up. "I think everyone did a lot of good for everyone else. That's how it's supposed to be."

Frank didn't need for me to respond, but I did anyway.

"That's exactly how it's supposed to be."

46

CHIPPER AND DUKE

MONTHS BEFORE FRANK became ill, I drove down to Alliance to have breakfast with him. On my previous visit I had found the door unlocked and no Frank. His daughter Cindy wasn't home, so I carefully started moving through the rooms of the house, calling his name. After a few minutes, I started anxiously looking along the side of his bed next to the wall and opened the shower curtain in the bathroom. I went downstairs and looked in Frank's laboratory of video and computer equipment, worried that I'd find him crumpled on the floor. When I reached the top of the basement stairs, Frank walked in. He had forgotten our breakfast date and had gone on an errand with a friend.

This time, Frank greeted me, and then immediately excused himself and walked into the breezeway leading to the backyard. Moments later I heard the deep blast of a shotgun. I ran into the breezeway and saw Frank cradling his .12 gauge, walking back in.

"I must have got five of them this time. These blackbirds are a nuisance."

He had obliterated a group of starlings, those gregarious competitive little pricks that shoved the bluebirds into the shadows of the avian kingdom just one hundred years ago. It pleased Frank that he was five up in his ongoing war.

Driving to his favorite diner, I asked Frank about his battle with starlings.

"I've been hunting them since I was a kid. My dad used to take us into the cornfields in the fall, and we scared up and blasted dozens of them. Then my mom plucked and cleaned them and threw those birds into a pot full of tomato sauce. They were delicious. They only ate corn."

I never told Frank that it was human folly that introduced starlings into the U.S.

Around 1890, starlings were released in Central Park by a Shakespearean club. They wanted to ensure that every bird ever mentioned in Shakespeare's sonnets and plays lived in America. Eventually, the starlings pushed the bluebirds out of their habitat, beating the good-looking birds into submission and perpetual nervousness. I always wondered if it was a matter of the ugly going after the beautiful—the bluebirds, a flash of sky and sun, and the starlings, a bunch of extras from Hitchcock's *The Birds*.

At the diner I met another Alliance aviator, eighty-year-old Duke Holtz. Duke was walking out with a white-haired lady on his arm just as the hostess seated Frank and me. Frank called him over and asked him to sit with us. As they approached, both smiling, Frank said that Chipper, Duke's lady friend, had Alzheimer's. After Duke introduced me to Chipper, she stared at me and said, "My girlfriend had a Fred." She smiled, started to say something else but then went mute for the rest of the visit.

I discovered that Duke did nearly all of his flying during World War II as a basic flight instructor in props and gliders. His brother died flying a P-51 in the European Theatre. Even sixty years later Duke discussed his brother's demise with disgust.

"He was still a student pilot in the Mustang. He was out with a couple other greenhorns when they stumbled across thirty German fighters. They thought they'd take a few kills and call it a day. He never opened his canopy. They killed him in his seat."

Chipper had become more distant as we talked of flying and first solos. After a brief forty-five minute lesson from a local aviator, Duke had soloed in a Jenny, a Curtiss biplane used to train pilots between the wars.

"Duke, you know how to shoot a gun?" the pilot asked. "The end of the barrel is the nose of the plane, and you aim down that sight. Aim the barrel at that fence, then when you get close, gently raise the nose up and land."

Chipper needed to go to the bathroom, so Duke asked her if she remembered how to get there and waved over the waitress to have another pair of eyes on her. When Chipper returned she was not only aloof but agitated as well. She refused to sit down at first and started tightening her fists and cocking her elbows, preparing to throw a punch. Frank and Duke ignored this. After she sat, she turned in her seat and stared at the other people in the restaurant.

Duke asked about the Boeing Business Jet that I flew. He wanted to know its glide ratio—the wing's lift to drag numbers that result in its gliding so many feet forward for every foot dropped.

"I can't remember the exact numbers, but it has a better glide ratio than the Cessna two-seater I instructed in."

When Chipper stood up and started to walk away, Duke followed her, asking if she wanted to leave. She kept walking and said nothing. Frank leaned over and said Chipper was lucky to have a man so dedicated to her. She stopped at a table with two women and a baby in a high chair. Bending down to look at the child, Chipper said something to the baby and then the mother. The mother looked wary, glancing at her baby then at the white-haired lady. Finally, Chipper pulled up a chair and sat with them. She smiled and talked to the infant. Not forgetting the mother, she spoke to her as well. The mother looked relieved and handed a pacifier to Chipper, who placed it in the baby's mouth. In a few minutes the mother smiled brightly as the pleasant lady entertained her child.

Now that Duke was satisfied that his Chipper was in good hands, he returned to our table and mentioned a machine that he had been working on that would cut gears for a clock. Even at eighty, Duke was a busy man, designing machining tools for companies in Canton, Ohio.

Chipper's face was close to the baby's. She was not the same woman who sat at our table only a few minutes ago. Now she appeared whole, a woman brought back from the dead.

Frank and I finished eating and Duke announced that it was time for them to leave. He stopped at the table where Chipper sat with the baby and gently led her out. She turned toward us with only a faint smile, as if the seconds were wearing away her most recent memory. From our booth we watched them walk to his car, where he carefully helped her into the front seat without hurry. Chipper was old again, a lost soul accompanied by a goodhearted man.

Her girlfriend "had a Fred" and now Chipper had a Duke.

47

DNA

WE WERE ALL huddled a few feet from Frank Corbi's bed, talking about Mel Gibson's film *The Passion of the Christ*. Like most movie discussions, the conversation soon jumped to other favorites and Frank's daughter Linda mentioned *Chicago*.

"We made Dad watch it last year. And you know what he said?" She looked about the room, still wary of her father's response. "He said that everything wrong with this country was in that movie. God, I had no idea he'd dislike it so much."

Other family members laughed and said they enjoyed it. I kept quiet. After all, it was only a movie, and I had no intention of putting in my two cents while the Corbi family waited out the final days of their dad's life. But quietly I cheered the old man. That musical, about a couple of money-grubbing whores who murder with impunity, was truly awful.

I looked over at Frank as he struggled for each breath and his heart raced. A week ago, the doctors had given him only hours to live, maybe another day, after a burst abscess had caused a massive heart attack.

Shortly after Frank was admitted to the Cleveland Clinic, I made it up to see him and found him connected to a catheter, IV and a machine that monitored his vital signs. He told me things didn't look so good. "I'm looking for a way out of this mess," he said softly. "I try to think of a direction I need to take. But it's not clear to me. I might exercise." He trailed off, exhausted by his own speech.

Alan walked over to his father's side and asked if he needed water. A week ago Frank could still chew on ice, and I had fed him a spoonful that he chewed forcefully. Now his strength had diminished to the point where he could only sip water through a straw. But that hadn't stopped him from enlisting his son Alan as an exercise coach.

"Last night, he sits up and says, 'I have to fight this.'" Alan started to laugh. "We were pissing off the nurses. They'd come in, and I had the old man propped up so he could do a few sit-ups. Dad knew he might die doing something crazy like that, but he had to try."

Alan's laughter when it erupted was big and genuine, a response not only to his dad's follies and strengths but also to the many people who moved through his life. It was a laugh of acceptance, of complete trust in a world that was beautiful and incomprehensible.

His sister Linda moved closer to her father's bed. "We noticed his heart rate, which was already fast, had jumped to one-eighty. He told us that he was trying a new breathing technique. I said, 'Are you crazy? You're going to blow up your heart.'" She leaned close to him. "You remember how ornery you were last night?"

Frank made an expression like he understood, then continued his struggle with breathing and moved a bit, showing his discomfort at being trapped in a bed for so long.

"Dad, tell Fred about the DNA." Alan looked at me with a warm grin. "Tell him about how you need to change your DNA. That's where the problem is."

Frank looked at me and shook his head. After a lifetime of fixing cars, aircraft and solving the daily problems of survival in a Japanese POW camp, Frank now struggled to get all the pluses and minuses lined up—the necessary alignment, he had told Alan, for his recovery. Over the years, DNA had been in my thoughts too.

* * *

Flying is woven throughout the double helix of every human cell. Desire leaped into birds, and poets distilled the experience into verse and melody. Every dream of flight has struck the planet's base elements until an impression began to form. And like a footpath worn in stone by centuries of prayer, the craft became visible.

The first airplanes were mud pies: the smell of the barn, baling wire, fabric, the spray of oil and gas to lubricate and to power. I heard once of a farmer and his son building their own plane and soloing without instruction.

Not long after the Wright Brothers, a citizen army of pilots and mechanics arose from the American countryside. Fifty years after Kitty Hawk, a young man would purchase a P-51 Mustang on a rainy day in Louisville then fly home, low and fast, to a grass landing strip in northern Ohio.

That pilot flying the P-51 was Frank's brother, Mario, who loved to tell the story about the one that got away. In the mid-fifties, he sold a P-51 Mustang shortly after he purchased it, making a few thousand dollars and losing one of the prizes of aviation that would have been worth hundreds of thousands today.

48

HORSESHOES

I FOUND FRANK alone. His daughter Cindy was outside having a cigarette, and Alan had disappeared after sharing with me a full hour of stories down in the hospital's cafeteria. Frank gave me a half-smile then a wistful "Oh brother, look at the shape I'm in." A few blue toes stuck out from his blanket, and I heard a soft-spoken thanks when I covered them. A doctor walked past, but I didn't recognize him. I wished that my flight doctor, Dr. Hobart, stood with us. He was a gentle man, quick to smile. I once told Frank about him, how I enjoyed the six-month visit and how good I felt afterward. "Well, that's a real doctor," Frank had said. "Anybody can prescribe pills and tests, but a good doctor knows how to keep you in good spirits. And that's worth its weight in gold."

* * *

Dr. Hobart dropped his FAA examiner status after bureaucrats made his job more costly with new regulations. For twenty years I had visited him annually at his Akron office for my flight physicals then, later, every six months to maintain my airline transport rating.

The biannual exam was a positive experience. Since my twenties I had kept up a moderate workout schedule, maintaining a low-normal blood pressure and healthy pulse rate of sixty. Dr. Hobart said I had an athletic heart. Once he asked if I did a lot of repair work at home. I told him not much and mentioned my workouts.

"Do you run?" he asked.

"Sometimes. Mostly I just walk."

"That's good. Running is awful, especially as we get older."

Dr. Hobart was the only GP I ever had as an adult. My entire body was scrutinized at each visit, and I left his office feeling peaceful, unfettered. On the drive home I'd review my diet and exercise program and plan ways to improve on them.

After the shock of learning I'd have to find another doctor for the flight physical, I still expected to keep Dr. Hobart as my GP. But a few months later when I called his office to set up an appointment for an ear infection, I discovered that he was retiring at the end of June. How could he? If someone was going to tell me I had six months left, I wanted it to be Dr. Hobart.

After setting up my last appointment with him in mid-June, I sat on the end of the exam table, observing the simple room: a poster of inspirational sayings, an old spring-and-weight scale, a small table with a few instruments and a glass jar with tongue depressors.

After he greeted me, we went through the customary exam: pulse, eyes, throat and carotid arteries. Dr. Hobart had me lie on the table then pulled down my socks and touched the hair near my ankles, saying the loss of it in this region might point to a circulation problem. On the table he felt my liver for enlargement. When I asked him about retirement, he smiled and said that he looked forward to dividing his time between a house in Ohio and another in Phoenix.

There were a number of questions I wanted to ask Dr. Hobart, but I was unusually tongue-tied. Years had passed, yet I knew no more about him than when I first started coming to his office. But I understood that he was a healer. After each visit I left feeling whole, peaceful, without fanfare. This nondescript man with his incisive kind eyes smiled a lot when he talked. He was smiling as we walked out of the room together. He asked about the new house my wife and I recently bought.

As he spoke, he looked me over one more time then added that I did a good job of staying in shape. "Is it all the housework?" I told him I wasn't handy inside, but I could move dirt, cut up dead trees and mow the grass. "You know," he said, "try horseshoes some time. It's a gentle workout." Dr. Hobart drew his right arm back like he was getting ready to pitch. "It's a great way to stay in shape."

49

XB-45

OUTSIDE THE CLEVELAND Clinic, Alan and I heard the rumble of an airliner buried in the clouds.

"I need to get outside every few hours, even if it's cold," he said, looking at the congestion of traffic and people. He glanced at the low overcast framed by the buildings. "Did Dad see the 737?"

"I never flew into Akron-Canton with it."

Currently I was flying the Boeing Business Jet.

"Well, he got to see the Citation Ten," Alan said.

"Yeah, he took a bunch of pictures and warned me about crashing before he left."

We both laughed at this. Frank had a way of calmly segueing into potential disasters. It usually happened as he was leaving, a last-minute reflection, a biblical utterance of ashes-to-ashes without sermonizing.

"I yelled at him about that," Alan said, still laughing. "I'm in California, and he's talking about this incredible plane you're flying and then he tells me—"

"That if I lose pressurization at altitude, my blood will boil. Down we go. He was amazed we weren't wearing pressure suits."

The Cessna Citation Ten rolled out in the mid-nineties, flying faster and higher than any other corporate jet at that time:

six hundred miles per hour in still air; one hundred miles per hour faster than anything else. It also had a service ceiling of fifty-one thousand feet. Although that was not a practical altitude, it would fly in the mid-forties routinely, placing it a mile or two above the corporate and commercial traffic. Frank saw trouble in the design. After World War II, he was in the Bomber Flight Test Division where high-altitude experiments were part of his job.

"Remember your dad saying that they brought the guys up to high altitudes without pressurization, just sucking oxygen?"

"And guys would get the chokes," Alan added, "with a doc there to help them breathe."

I looked at the gray clouds covering the sky.

"I forgot to tell your dad that a crew flying the Ten had one of the panes crack. They were cruising along, and it sounded like a .22 rifle. They jumped into each other's laps."

"Well, if Dad gets some energy back this week, we should tell him. It'll make him feel good that you guys are getting a taste of reality. But seriously, Dad was real proud that you were flying that plane. What beautiful lines."

The day Frank came out, he just stood a few feet from the nose, admiring its muscular beauty, its fast appearance. The Citation Ten had a prominent belly to slow the airflow and reduce the drag, and a swept-back wing, enabling its high-speed performance. It was like a sumo wrestler with angel wings, especially when one's eye moved from nose to tail. The large engines, out of proportion to the plane's size, were packed with a lot more thrust than any mid-size corporate jet. After takeoff we climbed at speeds that other aircraft cruised.

"You know, I'll miss Dad's reaction to things when he's gone," Alan said. "Not always pleasant, sometimes mean. He just couldn't turn his back on life. He had no choice but to confront problems head on. His mind was always playing out the scenarios, like you getting boiled alive at fifty thousand feet."

"When you have the kind of ride your dad did in the B-45, no wonder he sees disaster around every corner," I said.

On a hot August morning in 1949, Frank took off from Wright-Patterson Air Force Base with test pilot General Boyd at the controls of the XB-45, a four-engine bomber with a crew of three. After takeoff, the right gear started to retract and then stopped.

Frank, sitting in the Plexiglas nosecone of the plane, conversed over the intercom with the general on a possible fix. Climbing to thirteen thousand feet they leveled off and worked on lowering the gear, but to no avail.

The electrical and cooling systems failed, and the number four engine gave up the ghost, leaving the crew with asymmetric power, unable to communicate with anyone on the ground and an interior that became hot as hell. Without ejection seats and having to crawl to the escape hatch in the bomber's nose, the general initially decided against bailing out. Instead, he made an approach and bounced the plane on the runway, hoping to lock the gear in the down position. The maneuver failed and during the climb-out, passing through fifteen hundred feet, he asked Frank and his copilot if they wanted to bail. Both men said no.

When General Boyd turned final at four hundred feet above the ground, setting up for a controlled crash-landing, he slowed to an approach speed of one hundred and fifty miles per hour. As he lowered the flaps, a hinge failed, rotating the right-side flap from down to up, becoming a giant speed brake, killing the lift on the right wing. The plane rolled violently, nearly on its back, until General Boyd added power on the remaining engines, fought with the flight controls and stopped the roll.

Coming over the field, the XB-45 hit the ground then skidded for the next mile across grass and runway, destroying lights along the way. As they gradually slowed, a large ditch appeared in their path. For a few moments the men believed their fate was sealed, but luckily, the plane came to rest just a few feet from the edge.

"Dad always said great things about General Boyd," Alan said. "He's probably the only pilot he respected without question."

I shook my head, thinking of Frank's front row seat as the four-engine bomber screamed across the ground.

"Like your dad, you do well with the unexpected. For better or for worse, you've got a lot of the old man in you."

"Maybe," Alan smiled. "I came out here last night to get some fresh air, and there was a guy sitting on the bench over there." He pointed at the empty bench across the street. "The guy waved at me, I waved back. I forgot about him until I heard him yell something. He's saying something to me in a loud voice. I crossed the street, and he looks like someone, maybe like me, who came outside to ponder things. I'm thinking maybe he has someone dying too. When I'm close enough, he starts asking me for money. I can't believe my ears, so I ask him to say it again. And you know what he says? 'I need some f***ing money.' I stare at him then I let him have it. I tell him he's the one begging, and he won't get up, walk across the street and ask for the dough? He's yelling at *me*—makes me come over to *him*! I called him every name I could think of. If I had told Dad that story, I bet I'd have him up and dressed and on his way home. That's a story that would get anybody's blood boiling."

50

SWORN IN

ALAN HAD TO leave town for a couple of days, but he was reluctant.

"I just need to get over to Chicago for a day and a night, but I'm afraid that he'll die and I won't be here," he said over the phone.

Alan and his sisters' lives had been turned upside down for weeks. Now he needed a quick break to take care of some business.

Sounding distracted, he said, "Dad knows it's time to go, but he really enjoys fighting and making problems. I don't know if I'll ever have his courage."

I asked Alan if his dad knew about the woman copying his Bataan diary. He wasn't sure and wondered if he should mention it.

"He'll try to talk. I'll have more questions," Alan said. "Then he'll have questions, and I won't have answers. Then he'll get pissed off and hang on for another month." He broke into a loud laugh, saying that it was no use asking the old man any more questions. "This is it. It's a shame, but there's things that happened to him we'll never know about. But look at everything he's leaving us."

On the plane that night, he sat next to a young man who wanted to talk. But Alan ignored him, feeling grumpy, not wanting to say anything. When he finally engaged the young man, he discovered that he had been sworn into the Air Force that very day. And what had the young soldier all pumped up? He would be studying to become a jet mechanic. "One leaves and another arrives."

51

ALMOST HEAVEN

SITTING QUIETLY NEAR Frank's bed, I thought of Aggie, who had passed away three years earlier. Even though their marriage had been difficult over the decades, I felt that her presence might have insured more days for Frank, another kind of exercise, the kind made up of affection, kicking and screaming. Another end of life story came to mind as I said a silent prayer for Frank.

* * *

A few years earlier, while still flying the Citation Ten, I was in Aspen, waiting for the passengers. From a bench alongside the FBO, I watched the planes come and go and peacefully stared at the sunlit rocks and green mountainside. When my twenty-something copilot approached, wagging his head with a pained look of bewilderment, I knew one of mankind's sins had gotten hold of him. We occasionally argued politics, but recently I had taken a more passive approach, letting him rant, asking a question or two, before I watched him bite into fresh new material and not let go. Hands on his hips, he started complaining about our dependency on oil as he scanned a full ramp of corporate jets. I reminded him that he flew a plane that guzzled more fuel on a two-hour flight than most people would burn in a year driving. But he was uninterested in facts. He looked at the mountain and told me about his aunt who had recently died of cancer.

"She was in hospice. And at first, when I went to visit her, I didn't know what to say. Our family's not very religious, and it seemed hypocritical to read from the Bible or anything like that. So I started talking about anything—family members, my job and then I felt like sharing some of my ideas with her. Growing up, we visited her in Florida, where she lived. But we just did family stuff. I never told her what I thought about anything. So I started with the environment, saying that it was a shame we still had the gasoline engine, but that a new day was coming when not only cars, but even planes would be powered by the sun. She smiled a lot. She couldn't really talk anymore, too weak."

I kept quiet. I saw his aunt in the next world driving an electric car, passing fields of windmills and solar panels creating good clean energy for heaven's populace.

He crossed his arms and spoke to the mountains. "Too much greed, I told her. And she'd nod her head in agreement. That meant a lot to me."

I thought he was finished when he started again.

"When my aunt was near the end, I read to her from a preventative health book. Sound a little weird?"

I shook my head no. I wanted to hear the rest of the story.

"In this book there're several prayers that you say before dinner. I thought it was appropriate to say a prayer. Nothing Christian, of course."

"Of course," I replied.

"The prayer gives thanks to the earth for all her blessings and asks that the food we consume nourish our bodies and our souls. We've got to give people hope," he finished, satisfied with his good deed.

I didn't respond, watching the windsock alongside the runway shift directions one hundred and eighty degrees, not unusual in a box-canyon airport—one way in, one way out.

"Anything we need to do before the passengers arrive?" my partner asked.

"Yeah, have the line crew put a quart of oil in each engine."

For a moment, he looked troubled.

"Don't forget," I said, "the oil's synthetic."

He laughed good-naturedly. "That's a start."

52

LEAVING

WHILE HE WAS still at the Cleveland Clinic, Frank got the idea one afternoon to video his hospital experience. He talked a family friend from Alliance into bringing Frank's newly purchased digital camera to the hospital. Alan told me they set up some lights, got the camera in position and put a baseball cap on the old man's head. Just as the camera started to roll, Frank told everyone he was too worn out and that they all should leave and come back tomorrow and try again. My wife did record Alan and his dad's last Labor Day visit. Unfortunately, she wasn't close enough to pick up Frank's words. But we have him gesturing and Alan laughing at the escapades of a pilot called Dunkel and his girlfriend, Monkey.

Dunkel flew a Stearman, a large open-cockpit biplane with a radial engine. He often would land at Miller's and leave the plane chocked, engine running while he and Monkey came in for coffee. Frank had warned him of fouled spark plugs from long periods of engine idling. Not heeding the warning, Dunkel arrived alone one summer morning for his coffee break. After the plane sat on the grass, engine chugging at low rpm for twenty minutes, he took off and lost power and crash-landed in a lady's backyard, not far from her kids playing in a small swimming pool. The mother stormed out of her house and proceeded to beat on Dunkel for almost killing her children.

Another loose end in Dunkel's life was his inability to pay his fuel bill on time. Eventually he paid, but it made the Corbis nervous with the amount of fuel they pumped for him over the weeks and months and the large bill he accrued. Alan said that one afternoon, Dunkel surprised them with a check for two thousand dollars. Once again Dunkel had come through, and the Corbis could continue to pay their bills. Dunkel said goodbye, climbed in his car and left. Later that day he died, trying to outrun a train.

* * *

For several weeks I had been devouring the *Lonesome Dove* saga. Starting with *Dead Man's Walk* and then *Comanche Moon*, I finally was reading the big boy—the nearly nine hundred pages of *Lonesome Dove*. For years I kept my reading to history and politics. But Larry McMurtry's books kept me up late, eyes burning, bad posture, not wanting to give up until the wee hours of the morning. One line I easily remembered: "Leaving feels a lot like dying."

One of the older pilots, who once flew for the Strategic Air Command, had told me that I'd either get accustomed to long stretches away from home or I wouldn't. I was in the never-get-accustomed-category, even though I slept and ate well on the road.

I was seven when my parents left for vacation in Florida. The Sheas, our neighbors across the street, took me in and my grandparents had my brothers. This large Irish-Catholic family was a circus with a hovering, beautiful older daughter and the boys who kept me busy with games that moved through the house and out the back door. After dinner the father made jokes about the peanuts he made selling peanuts. It was a fun, oddball family with Mrs. Shea at the center. I saw an old home movie of her walking up our driveway—a sturdy woman with clear features who leaned a little forward as she walked, her powers not diminished after several children.

I don't think Mrs. Shea tucked me into bed that first night. I believe it was Jenny, her daughter. I was on the lower bunk, talking with the Shea boys in low whispers. There was a hall-way night-light, and I told one of the boys that the wood floor glowed. Today I can still see that amber glow. Down the hallway a radio sat on a stand with the volume low yet the music eas-ily heard. I was almost through my first day without my parents when the tune "Around the World in Eighty Days" started to play. The instrumental brought out grief, longing and great distances. Leaving felt like dying.

53

PREPARING TO DIE

"YOU KNOW, DAD'S hanging on not because he's afraid to die, but because he loves life so much," Alan said, hitting the elevator button. "That's what I told the nurse when she caught me helping him exercise. It's in his blood to solve a problem, like he did on the Death March and all that time as a prisoner." We were pushed to the back when a few more people joined us.

Alan lowered his voice and continued, "Hey, I know he could drop over dead anytime, and so does he. But it's still got to be hard to leave your friends and everything you love. Look at his photography and computers." Alan paused, stepping aside for an old couple shuffling off the elevator. "You know, you wish, you say to yourself, why couldn't he just drop dead at home, like Russ Miller did, working on his plane. Why couldn't Dad, working on someone's pictures?"

"Great," I deadpanned, "it'd probably be my pictures. Suzie and I are still waiting for that DVD he produced from our home movies."

We both started laughing then quieted down as we walked off the elevator and headed back to his dad's room.

* * *

While still working with his dad in the early nineties, Alan Corbi traveled to Costa Rica.

"I'm preparing to die," Alan said excitedly. "I can see it clearly. I know what I've done, what I can't do."

"This is your Costa Rican experience? Death in Central America?" I countered.

"Costa Rica is coming," Alan said, looking for the sugar bowl as I poured his coffee.

"I'm not talking about headstones, funeral arrangements. This idea of not being around doesn't scare me anymore. Not too long ago, I feared dying every time I got in my car. You know, I eventually wrecked the truck. I worked myself right into that accident." His laugh made my cat leap over the couch and dart for the bedroom.

"I'm becoming like my old man. In the Philippines he lived with death the way we live with bills. My preparation is knowing what I can do; what I should do, like visiting you—not making excuses."

"When did this vision strike? Before or after the trip?"

"Before, thank God. I couldn't have appreciated it otherwise. We'd just be looking at the pictures right now. Everything would be different." His voice lowered, and I stopped interrupting him.

"I saw poor people, but they weren't begging. They didn't seem scared of anything. Beautiful people down there, so polite. This is going to sound crazy, but the more rude people are, the more scared of death they are. Isn't that what we see on people's faces—their fear? And it turns into daily rudeness." Alan started laughing again.

"On the plane, coming out of Cleveland, I'm having all these thoughts. And then, this fat guy flops down in the seat in front of me, and as soon as we're airborne—boom! He throws his seat back, and it's right in my face. His weight pressed it back even further, and he kept it there the entire trip. This is it, I thought, our rudeness, our belief in our endless right to be obnoxious. Now, I'm in Costa Rica, at dinner, and I'm trying to explain this to my in-laws—God, what a mistake. But that's my old man in me. There's something else that came out of all this. If the guy across the street doesn't interest me, I don't feel obliged to spend my time with him. I can be nice in passing, but no more guilt trying to like everyone. You know what I'm talking about? When my dad and I ran the little airport, there I was always trying to be everyone's friend."

When I returned from the kitchen with a fresh cup of black coffee for him, I turned the living room lamp up a notch.

"Alan, you look fifteen years younger."

He sat back in his chair.

"Last night I went to hear this Russian fighter pilot talk. He defected six years ago. He got shot up during the escape. Maybe you heard about him. Anyway, I'm sitting there listening, and he's talking about what a great country this is and I know that, I believe that, but I'm not impressed with him. Years ago I would have sat there and called this guy a hero. But some part of me is saying, this guy's a traitor, a traitor to his own land, his people, his family, and I know damn well that as a fighter pilot he had it pretty good in Russia. And then, like my old man, I can't keep my mouth shut. Some of us guys go out to eat afterward and I'm talking, telling them I don't really care what this guy did. I'm more impressed with the beautiful nobodies I met in Costa Rica.

"Now, back in San Jose, I'm telling my in-laws over dinner that the people I see here are a sensuous people. They looked at me like I was sick. Boy, it seems every time I'm out to eat I get into trouble. But it was true. Their bodies are beautiful, the men too. The fella that was our guide told me that they walk everywhere. And when he came to the States to teach one summer, no one would let him walk, they kept sticking him in a car.

"This whole preparation for dying makes me see things differently. I can do my work, do a good job for my dad, be on the phone, get in the airplane and go somewhere. But something happens. People become visible, like Uncle Mario's mechanic at the airport. You've met Charlie before. He reminded me one day what a lonely people we can be.

"One day, at lunch, he starts talking. He hardly ever talks. He's telling me about Washington D.C. He lived there fifteen years with people everywhere, yet felt so alone. He had to get out, live in the sticks to shed his loneliness. His wife felt the same. She died not too long ago. Her heart just exploded. I don't know, some kind of heart disease, but they knew it was coming. She at least made it back here to die.

"Now, you know my uncle is a good man, but after Charlie's been off work for a week, he asks his secretary where Charlie is. I'm standing there and have to remind him that the man just lost his wife, and my uncle says that was a week ago.

"Mario appreciates Charlie, but Charlie is the kind of man that can drive him crazy, like my dad does. And like my dad, he works kind of slow, but does a beautiful job of restoring the interior of a plane, or arranging a new panel. So when I'm having lunch with Charlie, and he's talking about his life, he mentions that he's a painter. He loves to paint with watercolors. I never knew this. Then I ask him, 'Do you look at the panel in an airplane the way you look at a canvas?' 'Exactly,' he says, 'that's why I love it so much. I get to imagine what your uncle wants, what's possible, and I begin to move it about, play with it inside my head.' Okay, now I'm excited. I understand something about the man. He's not just quiet and strange. He has this artist inside him. So what do I do? I tell Mario. And he looks at me for a moment, then says, 'You're kidding.' "

* * *

The next day I dressed quickly, stretched and headed out to the cemetery for a run. Passing the headstones, I wondered how many of the spirits had prepared themselves for death. The randomly arranged headstones resembled a boulder field created by a retreating glacier.

The wooded cemetery sloped into a large grassy area free of graves. At a good pace I circled the field several times, roughly a quarter mile, a reminder of the high school track and my father waiting for me at the finish line.

Later, I headed back into the thick of the cemetery, using the narrow asphalt roads to walk and cool down. Not far from my home, a line of cars had entered by the south entrance. I was headed for the congestion, so I left the road.

I walked with my head down, starting to feel the cold. As I stepped onto the road again, a slow procession of cars turned in my direction. I felt spied upon and changed course, accustomed to having the cemetery to myself even when a funeral was taking place. Making a beeline for home, I had one more road to cross before I would have a clear path to my house.

The cars were everywhere, moving slow. Could there be several funerals at once? I broke into a run when another line of cars blocked my path.

Once I reached my house, I stood by the front door for a few minutes, watching the procession. The parade of cars had forced me out of a cool Eden where I believed I had all the time in the world.

54

TOOLS

FRANK STRUGGLED TO sit up in bed, pointing at the opposite wall. I asked him what he needed, and he mentioned his
tools again. Not an unreasonable request for a man who spent
nearly his entire life handling them and thinking about the daily
problems before him. I fantasized about finding that special tool
that could repair Frank's heart. I looked at the wall and tried to
imagine something there he might use to rid his body of the infection and blow energy back into his heart.

When I worked with him in the maintenance hangar at Miller's, I obediently ran about, getting what he needed, listening
to his explanations as I sandblasted spark plugs in a glass case,
blasting away the carbon that formed during the process of combustion. The infection worked under different principles, but that
didn't stop Frank's struggle to find a way out of his predicament
or me fantasizing a way to blast the infection from his body. I
lacked the tools, the skills to change Frank's condition an iota, but
was given a gift: an old memory surfaced.

* * *

Shortly after I started at EJA, I returned home to a slow-motion paradise of friends, raccoons on the porch, fallen branches littering the backyard. A recent spring storm had intruded during my absence—a burglar who shook out the dead, ruptured the earth so that the soil could breathe again. My house bordered the south side of one of the prettiest cemeteries in North America. A few days later, I was flung back into the upper regions of arid jet routes, a demon of speed.

Before leaving town, I decided to visit Frank, who was finishing the annual on an owner's Cardinal, a Cessna similar to the Skyhawk but with a retractable gear. Frank and I would test fly the ship, a sharp contrast to the test flying he once did on the first fighter-bombers miles above the earth's surface. Although he had flown on a number of jet aircraft, he now believed that monkeys could fly jets.

"Look at these tools." Frank unrolled a dark, oily rag. He stood over his workbench, admiring the various wrenches and sockets. "How old do you think these tools are?"

I picked up a wrench. Frank's attention to these tools had already imbued them with the power of gems, though they appeared no different from a set of tools from Sears. His proud gaze made the wrench in my hand feel perfect in balance and weight. I grabbed a socket and rolled it around in my hand.

"I have no idea. You're always buying tools. But this one looks older."

Frank plucked the shiny socket out of my palm. "You're rolling it around like it's a marble. Look closely. Look how this socket has been machined."

"It's not worn much."

"You're damn right. I bought these tools thirty years ago. The White Machine Company made beautiful stuff. Nowadays, unless you get Snap-on, you buy junk that breaks in your hand."

"You buy tools from Kmart."

"Well, I only expect to use them for a few years. It's junk and it's cheap." He looked over at the Cardinal. "Let's button her up and get something done today."

We walked the engine cowling over the spinner and propeller. A slight gust grabbed the metal shroud, almost sending it airborne. Frank handed me a Phillips screwdriver to lock the Dzus fasteners.

The warm wind was from out of the south. The day alternated between periods of overcast and bright sunlight. We climbed in the Cessna, and I primed the engine a couple of times, slightly cracked the throttle and the engine started instantly. Frank reached past me and switched off the alternator, which he had replaced during the inspection. When he saw a discharge on the ammeter, he switched the alternator back on and smiled, watching it charge.

"Look. There's that son of mine." He pointed to a V-tail Bonanza that had just touched down. "That's how it always works with Alan. We're always crossing paths. I'm here, and he's somewhere else. He vanishes when I need him."

"You're right about the disappearing act," I said while checking the magnetos and watching the drop in the rpm. Alan could be talking with you one moment, leave the room then disappear from the airport with his car still in the parking lot and his plane sitting on the ramp. He was almost impossible to track down. He had spent years indulging pilots at the airport with his time, endless hours of coffee, flights where he played babysitter, driving miles to visit some dentist-pilot that had remodeled his office. When it occurred to Alan that he might not ever accomplish much in life due to the enormous energy expended being everyone's friend, he tapped into the Houdini part of his soul and made his escape.

"Should we call him on the radio?" I increased the power and began taxiing.

"I've become a good detective with that son of mine. We've got maybe an hour before he heads back to Akron-Canton. I'll corner him right after we land."

The wind was nearly straight down the runway at ten miles per hour. With just the two of us on board and half-tanks, the Cardinal jumped off the runway. Starting a right turn to the north, Frank leaned against the window to view the forest and small lake adjacent to the airport.

"This land should be put to use. It's beautiful. Maybe one of those rich folks you fly might need a place for their money," Frank said. My attention was given to the plane, overcontrolling with the ailerons in order to get the feel of the slow-moving ship.

"You're not using the rudder," Frank said, confirming my

sloppy turn. Without sufficient rudder pressure, the airplane
yawed, preventing the nose from moving in the direction of the
turn. Since jet aircraft had an electric yaw damper that offset this
tendency, I had become lazy, forgetting the basics.

I fought with the controls as I leveled off at three thousand
feet. I was a stiff ballroom dancer, pushing my partner through
the steps. Frank told me to fly north while he manipulated the
throttle and mixture controls.

The sky had become overcast. The fields below were plowed
and bordered by faint patches of green. The turbulence knocked
us around, and I fought with a plane I had flown for hundreds of
hours. Frank continued his adjustments and methodically tapped
the glass face of each engine instrument, a spring wake-up call.

"I've got to get going on this airport project. I don't want to
end up like my wife's brother." I didn't respond, instead I rolled
the plane into a steep bank. He continued his brother-in-law
story, then shifted to his fly-in-resort scheme for the airport. He
talked of the potential success for everyone connected with the
airport, but I couldn't answer him. I was determined to get back
the feel of this plane.

"You're not even listening to me."

"Sorry, Frank, I thought this would be fun. I didn't think I'd
be working so hard."

"You're flying jets now. Why even bother doing steep turns
with these silly little airplanes?"

"Do monkeys fly these too?"

"Well, the machine interests me more than the pilots who fly
them." His relaxed smile made it impossible for me to be angry.
"It's the airplane that does all the work. Years ago, a pilot had to
be a mechanic if he flew all the time. You know what a beautiful
flying ship Cessna made with that little jet of theirs. And those
engines! They keep running like the sun. Our engines used to quit
all the time when I was learning to fly."

I enjoyed this. Anyone else, I would have gone for the throat.

On the downwind leg I saw the thin runway as a sentimental
line drawn in the earth, an idea mixed with asphalt.

My landing made Frank laugh out loud. I carried too much
speed, so that when I pulled back on the yoke to slow the rate of
descent, the wing produced enough lift to stay airborne, skim-

ming the runway. I landed hard on the main gear. We taxied past the restaurant, spotting Alan and a couple of people standing outside.

"Why is it that I always make my worst landing when someone is watching? If no one had been there, I would have greased it on."

Frank shrugged.

We parked the Cardinal in front of the maintenance hangar. Over our slow-turning prop we could hear the engine of the Bonanza fire up.

"Well, he got us both today. You on your landing, and me, the deserted father once again." Frank rapidly scratched the back of his head, his face tightening into a frown, a sign of his frustration.

"You mentioned your brother-in-law. Is he in the hospital?" I pulled out the mixture control and the fuel-starved engine died with a final vibration.

"Yes, he's dying of cancer. But what puzzles me is that damn toy he found in his barn. He talked about it every time I went to see him. Then he decides to give it to me."

We pushed the plane into the hangar. "Can I see it?" I asked.

"Hell, there's not much to see. It's in the back seat of my car. I don't know what to do with it."

I went over to Frank's Cadillac, parked alongside the hangar, and grabbed the heavy, foot-long object. It was a ceramic wagon and horse. Reddish and gold paint that had decorated the horse and wheels was practically worn away from the bone-white finish.

"Before he went into the hospital, he found this," Frank said. "It had been in his barn since the Amish built it over forty years ago."

"He never knew it was there?"

"He said he didn't. Why he was clearing out the barn when he was so sick is a good question. At his place, I'm standing on the porch, and he comes walking out of the barn holding this thing like it was the most precious thing in the world. He carried it like it was some treasure. He called it a toy. Hell, the wheels don't even move." Frank scratched the back of his head more slowly, a thoughtful rhythm that told me he was more philosophical than angry now.

"The Amish just left it there?"

"Who knows? They're good people, just a little strange at times. Probably one of their children left it. My brother-in-law said the Amish children were allowed to play with it once all their chores were finished. Could you imagine my grandchildren playing with a toy and the wheels don't even move?"

We watched his son take off, and then Frank asked me to place the toy back in his car. He said he had a call to make, and if I had time, he'd buy me a piece of pie.

55

FORK-TAIL DEVIL

ONE EVENING WHEN I couldn't get to the hospital, I called Alan on his cell. He said he was starting to go batty and asked about people we both knew for any gossip. Then he asked if I knew of any good books he could look forward to reading. I brought up Saint Exupéry, mentioning that his P-38 had been recently fished out of the Mediterranean. There was a theory that maybe the Frenchmen intentionally drove his own plane into the water.

"I can't believe he'd end his life like that," Alan said.

"I can't either. He was on a reconnaissance flight. A brave guy, but his poor skills probably did him in. I know the allies were tired of him destroying aircraft. Some reports show him going in vertical, or possibly shot down. Maybe he just drove it in, unaware, scribbling out some new story idea."

"Maybe. I guess it's more glamorous to imagine he ended it all like some Kamikaze guy."

"Alan, your dad ever read St. Ex?"

"Don't know. But I like the book you gave me."

"*Wind, Sand and Stars*—great title, great book," I said. "This year I read his fable, *The Little Prince*."

"I heard of it. How is it?"

"Terrible."

"Why?"

"It's about this self-absorbed alien kid who's bored and comes to earth to piss on us."

A sonic laugh erupted from Alan, and I imagined the nurses at their station looking up in unison.

"It should be called *The Little Prick*. The bad guys are the adults, businessmen, on and on about all the dumb, stupid things grown-ups do. I suffered from the same delusions too when I was young. It's a shame. For years I thought St. Ex's unique voice would apply to any topic he wrote about. But this book brings out his arrogance, his disdain for us losers who can't see what's really important in life."

"Now I'll never be able to read it without laughing."

"Yeah, the book's mopey, the little prince is mopey, the kind of baby-boomer mopiness—you know, 'Why has the world made things so difficult for a great prick like myself; why can't they see my greatness?' "

Alan continued to laugh and said the nurses were watching him.

Finding the writer's P-38 reminded me of Uncle Cletus, Bernie Reymann's brother who flew the *fork-tail devil* in the Pacific. Not long ago at a post-funeral dinner for his missionary brother, Father Al, Uncle Clete sat with me and described his missions in the P-38. Based less than two hours from the Philippines, he made bombing runs against the Japanese still holding the island. Uncle Clete said many of the accidents were pilot errors: missing the small island on the pilot's return, crashing on takeoff due to the heavy load of armament or forgetting the proper sequence for switching fuel tanks. He praised the Aussie coastal watchers that signaled the airmen to their targets, and the pilot's worry of bombing their own prisoners of war. An Air Force reservist, Uncle Clete still put on his uniform to lecture junior and high school students in the Akron area. Recently he was warned by the teachers at one school not to put the seventh and eighth graders together for fear of chaos. He scoffed at this and started his talk by telling the kids he had given up a lot to be there.

"I yell at them quite a bit, but they settle down. They hear things they'll never hear from nobody else. I tell them I'm giving up my time. I could be out golfing. So they're going to listen. When I'm gone, all this information goes with me, I tell them."

The teachers were amazed that he could get the kids to listen and ask questions. Clete looked directly at me as he spoke, his clear blue eyes drilled me with a fighter jock's determination, still possessing the fire that pulled him through hell sixty years ago.

Uncle Clete gave these students a dash of patriotism and discipline they had longed for, making them shut up and listen. The girls especially reacted warmly toward him. When those kids were reminded of their remarkable heritage, they became quiet, respectful. According to Uncle Clete, history was no longer taught, except to point out all our sins.

56

FAITH

"I HAD FAITH in America," Frank told the reporter. I read that line in a fifteen-year-old newspaper article I had found in my desk. My wife and I had just returned from the Alliance hospital where Frank had been moved, putting him only ten minutes from his home. I read through the story, with a photo of a seventy-year-old Corbi holding a jet fighter's helmet in his lap.

In his eighties Frank began talking more about his years as a prisoner of war. His earlier reluctance was perhaps due to his sense that what happened long ago wasn't as important as the job at hand. And staying alive didn't equate to hero status, Frank believed. But he knew he had a story that needed to be told. Understandably, Alan wanted to know what his father had lived through and couldn't accept that decades must pass before his dad would say anything.

Shortly after his eighty-first birthday, I took Frank out to lunch. Before we ordered, I asked him how he got his knack for survival.

"Well, at the time, probably my age, if you were too young or too old, you died more easily. The older guys had wives and children, and the youngest had left home for the first time—a terrible fix to be in. Myself, I was old enough to be away from my family without dying of heartache, but not old enough to have a family. Then, I had some luck too," Frank said, referring to his ring.

"You didn't want to hide anything from them, so I took my ring off and strung it with my dog tags, keeping it outside my shirt," Frank said, holding his hand up, showing it. This ring from his parents bore their first-name initials on the inside of the rose-gold band. The engraved letters overlapped.

In the strip searches following the Americans' surrender, the Japanese eagerly punished those who had taken articles off dead Japanese soldiers and seized the usual valuables: jewelry and money. In Donald Knox's *Death March*, an American struggled to get his wedding ring off his finger while his impatient captor reached for his sword. The man took a swipe of blood from a bleeding companion, lubricated his finger and wiggled the ring free.

Frank stood in line while a Japanese sergeant grabbed watches, rings and money. Waiting his turn, Frank saw a Japanese officer approach the sergeant. A rough command from the officer stopped the soldier from plucking his ring. Frank believed the officer saw something in him. "I didn't want to lose that ring, and he must have seen that in my face." Throughout his imprisonment, no one ever tried to snatch it from him again.

* * *

After I dropped off Frank, I had a message from a good friend living in California.

Steve Buck and I had been friends since 1968 at Kent State, where the two of us had passed out leaflets the day before the May 4th shootings, advertising the noon antiwar rally. Thankfully we both had changed; had slowly grown up over the years, knowing that the beauty of the sixties was short-lived and, our protesting, unfortunately, enduring—a sweeping tide against all things traditional. He knew of Frank's condition and was checking in. He also had a memory he wanted to share.

On the phone he reminded me that he and his new bride had gone to the Smoky Mountains in the summer of '70 for their honeymoon. They were coming down from a mountain trail when Steve spotted an enormous American flag over an open pavilion. The flag, slightly suspended in the blue haze, caught him by surprise. Its sudden appearance, its beauty moved him to tears. Later, he discovered that Bataan and Corregidor survivors had picked the Smoky Mountains retreat for their reunion that year.

I never found out if Frank was in attendance that weekend with men who laughed, talked and cried in the arms of America's oldest mountain range. But I'm sure the quiet glory of our flag brought comfort not only to those survivors who walked beneath it at the reunion, but to those faraway that passed it every day on the way to work or raised it in their front yards.

57

PUMPKIN PIE

"A FEW DAYS ago you could get him to talk; now he's not interested," Mario said. Frank wasn't talking unless you stood over him and waited for the moments when he was conscious and had the energy to speak. I sat next to Mario, who shook his head at his brother's condition.

"You know, everyone thinks that he survived the war years just with luck and being in good shape. Well, those things are true, but my brother survived because he could focus so much on a project that he could forget about eating. Sometimes in business, he'd focus so hard he forgot to make money, and I wanted to kill him. When we were kids, Frank would be out in a cold garage working on a car, and lunch and dinner would come and go. My mom never bugged him, and he'd just pass up one meal after another. Me, I'd never pass up a meal."

* * *

The next day I walked into Frank's room just as his relatives from his wife's side of the family filed out. After they left, Linda approached my wife and me.

"Did Alan tell you what we found in Dad's car?" Linda said, looking at me, resting a hand on her dad's shoulder. "Remember I kept yapping about the trunk. So Alan goes to Dad's house and pops the trunk. Every square inch is filled with stuff from Sam's Club! A lot of it was still in the package. It never made it to the house."

Frank moved his mouth, trying to say something in his defense, and I leaned closer, unable to make out what he struggled to say. I wasn't even sure if he understood what Linda had just said.

His shopping sprees were a necessary balance against life's uncertainties. When they found the trunk of his car overflowing, it appeared more indulgent than practical. But Frank could always muster a good rationale: The sale might not return, and if one thing was really good, why not two of the same thing, or maybe one of his kids or friends needed to share in his good fortune.

My wife started to take the foil off the pumpkin pie and pulled plastic plates and forks from a large handbag. Alan and his sisters agreed that it was time for hospital food to take a backseat. Frank hadn't been eating much for the last few days, and the dessert got his attention. Seeing the pie as his next goal, Frank managed, with our help, to sit up on the side of the bed, and Alan pushed the tray closer. On the bed, I sat behind Frank and gently propped him up so he could concentrate on the pie. He struggled with the fork then stabbed a piece and lifted it to his mouth. Nothing that the hospital had sent up in days made Frank so determined. With my back supporting his, I glanced over my shoulder and watched him repeatedly stab at the pie topped with whipped cream until it was gone.

A few minutes later Alan and I gently held his dad under the arms and maneuvered him back into bed, sitting up, so he could breathe more easily. As he fell asleep I saw a tear roll down his cheek. His face relaxed after releasing this tear of exertion, and the inevitable hour approached. In this expansive, defining hour, death would walk in like the tall, dignified doctor we met a few days ago. "You know, my profession requires me not to get attached to the people that come through here, but your father's different. I know something of his history. He's an exceptional man," he had said, shaking Alan's hand. "It's a privilege attending him."

I wasn't at the hospital when Frank died, but I sensed that his last hour was monumental, a final mark, indivisible, without minutes and seconds, the magic hour when a tall presence entered solemnly, sweeping away time and struggle.

58

LIKE CHRISTMAS

ALAN INTRODUCED ME to Mr. Louis during calling hours, a man who had been a prisoner of war with Frank in the Philippines. We moved to a couch and a couple of chairs at the back of the room.

Short, his face deep-lined, the flesh sagging, Mr. Louis carefully lowered himself into his chair, using the arm to steady himself. He said, "I don't want to make this into some big deal. I know Frank. He'll haunt me if I do, but I got to lay out the story. You see, what we did, what we had to do, every day, just to stay alive, meant there wasn't a lot of room for the hero stuff. None of us thought that what happened from day to day was brave or unusual."

For all the ruined flesh, the man's eyes had grown brighter with age, even as time was running out.

"But listen, we got through one day in particular because of your dad," he said, drilling Alan with his gaze. "Let me be perfectly clear—Frank Corbi saved my ass and another fella a long time ago."

Alan mouthed a few words, shook his head, trying not to laugh or cry. His dad had decided, once again, not to share another story we all needed to hear.

"You know about the Hell Ships?" he asked. We both nodded. "They needed us in Japan for slave labor, but we got attacked on the second day out by American aircraft. Our ship, the *Oryoku Maru*, had no Red Cross insignia. We were traveling with a convoy, hugging the west coast of Luzon and ran aground after being strafed and bombed. The Japs spent the next twenty-four hours removing their first-class passengers and servicemen. They grabbed the few lifeboats and left us to swim to shore, about a quarter mile. Frank, me and another fella somehow made it off the ship into the water.

"I got to say, as frightening as it was to be hit, we were pleased as punch that the Japs got attacked. And what a relief from that madhouse in the cargo hold—horrible things went on down there. We knew it was safe to climb the ladder when no one was screaming at us not to. I don't remember how we got in the water—jumped, climbed down a rope, but we got in, and then the Japs started yelling at us, from shore, to stay together, not to stray or they'd machine gun us.

"Can you imagine, these idiots warning us not to run away? Run away to where?" the man interjected to the delight of a young woman who walked past us, quietly signaling Alan with a smile that she'd catch up with him later.

"When the three of us made it to shore, we collapsed. We were starving, cold, practically naked. After a few minutes, Frank raised himself up and said what all of us knew: Without food and clothes, we wouldn't make it another night. The Japs were too busy taking care of their own, and Frank said he was going back to the ship. Now sure, we were family, the buddy system and all that, that's how we survived the camps. But we didn't want him to go. We said we'd stop him, but we couldn't, we were too weak. So, Frank swims out to the ship. It's listing, explosions going off every few minutes. We never expected to see him again. We just stared at the water, the ship, our hearts broke.

"Both of us just stood there, it seemed for a long time. Then I spotted these sticks in the water. It took a few moments for my brain to make sense of what I was looking at—your dad," he pointed a finger at Alan's chest, "was steering a wooden table through the water—*dog-paddling*. We helped him onto the beach and saw all this stuff piled on the table—food, blankets, clothes. We were kissing him, crying and then we both started yelling at Frank."

Here, Alan let go a big laugh. "Dad's car!"

I saw both Frank's backseat filled after a shopping spree and the recent discovery of a full trunk. Now I envisioned a distant shore and three men celebrating over a miracle.

"Looks like Frank established a tradition," I said.

The man squinted then shrugged as if he understood.

"Well, you know how friends are. Good friends are family, and we were grateful but still wanted to know why it took him so long, why he worried us so. I'm a practical man. I thought he should have done the trip in half the time."

This time, all of us laughed. But the man's eyes shone brightly. There was more.

"Frank tells us he got aboard and began collecting everything we needed to survive. He found the table, threw it overboard and then filled the center of the table with all these wonderful things. He said it was like Christmas. Then he paddled back to shore.

" 'Too damn long,' I yelled. 'Corbi, what happened?' Now, he gets embarrassed. He says he stumbled upon a tub of vanilla ice cream in the commissary, and there was no way that ice cream was going to make it to shore. So, he sat down and ate every bit of it. We hugged him again, laughed, kissed each other and yelled some more. I said, 'Corbi, you actually took out time for dessert on a crippled ship, working it off with a little swim, where you could have drowned or been shot?' "

59

FIRST DAY OF SPRING

OUTSIDE OUR BEDROOM window, the swamp is dark and alive, a thick gruel of dead vegetation, mud, cattails; above, the birds are noisy, darting about. The storm's intensity increases as I write. Frank is close. This is his day, the first day of spring—cloudy and fifty degrees. The field beyond our pond is partially snow covered; the dark clouds touch the forest in the distance. As the rain intensifies, I think of Frank saying how spring is a bigger killer than other seasons, with its floods, high winds and storms—a wet, cold, muddy world at our feet.

Frank often said I could call him anytime; that he didn't need much notice; that he'd work me into his schedule. We got together a few times a year, but I never made the time for him that I could have. Sometimes a volatile phone conversation where he announced the stock market's demise and our way of life going to hell satisfied my need for a visit. I always believed I had other obligations, more *important* things to do.

Today is March 20, 2004, the vernal equinox, an appropriate time to say goodbye to a man who balanced terror and joy throughout his life.

In the last few years of Frank's life, he had an urgency to get more things done, especially related to his time as a POW. It ran from reparations for the men to photography and computer work while a few of us wrote about his accomplishments.

I just enjoyed being in his presence, watching life flit about or old memories surface, hearing heated discussions on the culture, witnessing random encounters with friends and the occasional epiphany at breakfast. Those big, radiant moments had happened with others, but with Frank it was ramped up. You needed always to carry a tape recorder, have pen and paper ready or simply possess a good memory. From Frank Corbi I learned a kind of bird-watching, training my sight on the stream of life, recording its turbulence and unexpected stillness.

A GOOD TAKEOFF

FRANK ALAN CORBI
OCTOBER 22, 1951—APRIL 12, 2013

TWO MONTHS BEFORE my friend Alan Corbi passed away, he and I were having breakfast with a mutual friend at a local restaurant. Finishing up, reaching for our wallets, I asked my buddies what plans they had for the rest of the day. Alan listened as we ran through the day's goals, big and small, and a few errands. He replied:

"That's over for me. Those aren't my goals anymore." He laid a few bills on the table next to his plate. "We always think we have more time. I did."

There wasn't sadness in his voice, only certainty. He slowly stood up. His shrunken frame and narrow shoulders of a once tall, vibrant man in full, affirmed his every word. He flashed a handsome smile, saying, "My goal today is to find one person to be kind to. If I can do that, then I'm successful."

People often startle us with their brilliance, their far-reaching epiphanies, but Alan would startle you with his goodness—a virtue that his wife, Dabney, knew well. She told me that in the last week of his life, one of the nurses that came to check on him usually arrived sullen, mad about her job or offended by one of her coworkers. One night she made an offhand comment about another RN, and Alan asked her to have a seat on the bed. He told her he had been watching her go about her work angry, easily frustrated with her duties. He added that she did a fine job but that eventually she would end up missing something important and paying the price. He said she had to figure out how to bring patience into her life.

"He was being himself right to the end," Dabney concluded.

In the last months of his life, during one of our many talks, Alan had said that kindness grew out of patience and that without kindness everything falls apart, and we can never truly be happy.

Alan and I knew there's great satisfaction in a good landing: a moment of happiness born of patience. Too much or too little power or leveling off too soon can ruin the last few seconds of a wonderful flight. We talked often—like all pilots do—of greasing it on, rolling it on, a final squeak of the tires that pops like a trumpet, velvety, accomplished. Alan accrued a lot of good landings during his life and made some great takeoffs as well. But we shouldn't be fooled. His April departure wasn't his last, but the first leg of a long and fabulous journey.

ACKNOWLEDGMENTS

Frank Corbi and his son Alan are no longer here to preflight the Skyhawk with us or accompany us on long trips, but their love of flying will be remembered by many, both in and outside the aviation community.

I've been fortunate to have several fine editors including Joe Coccaro of Koehler Books, writer and editor Diane de Avalle-Arce, my lovely wife, Sue, and my good friend Steve Buck, who understood the spirit of this book from the beginning. Also, I'd like to give a shout-out to my longtime friend Alan Czarnecki for supplying the history of his dad's heroics aboard the USS Wren.

I especially want to send my love and appreciation to my parents, Fred and Rose Tribuzzo, for their years of support. To current Netjets Captain Glenn Laird and former employees Flight Attendant Lisa Hyatt, Captain Rod Kramer and Executive Vice President Richard G. Smith III—a special nod to each of you for your encouragement and advice throughout our careers together. And to all the pilots, flight attendants and employees at Netjets Aviation, who daily practice the art of the pro, I send my heartfelt thanks, wishing you safe travels.

CPSIA information can be obtained at www.ICGtesting.com
Printed in the USA
LVOW13s1036220414

382719LV00004B/280/P